Library Programming for Adults with Developmental Disabilities

ALA Editions purchases fund advocacy, awareness, and accreditation programs for library professionals worldwide.

LIBRARY PROGRAMMING
FOR ADULTS WITH DEVELOPMENTAL DISABILITIES

Barbara Klipper and Carrie Scott Banks

ALA
Editions
CHICAGO 2021

BARBARA KLIPPER, a retired librarian, has championed library access for people with disabilities since 2002 when she worked at the Ferguson Library in Stamford, Connecticut. Her 2014 book, *Programming for Children and Teens with Autism Spectrum Disorder* (ALA), was recently updated by Dr. Amelia Anderson. With Ronda Shapiro-Rieser, Barbara published *The Secret Rules of Social Networking* (AAPC) in 2015. Barbara is also the creator and funder of the Autism Welcome Here grant.

CARRIE BANKS has been in charge of Brooklyn Public Library's Inclusive Services since 1997 and taught Including Youth with Disabilities at Pratt Institute from 2013 to 2015. In 2012 she was named a Library Journal Mover and Shaker. Active in ASGCLA and ALSC since 2000, she was the 2020 President of ASGCLA. In 2014, she substantially revised *Including Families of Children with Special Needs: A How-to-Do-It Manual for Librarians* (ALA). *Libraries and Gardens: Growing Together* (ALA), written with Cynthia Mediavilla, was published in spring 2019.

© 2021 by Barbara Klipper and Carrie Scott Banks

Extensive effort has gone into ensuring the reliability of the information in this book; however, the publisher makes no warranty, express or implied, with respect to the material contained herein.

ISBN: 978-0-8389-4866-8 (paper)

Library of Congress Cataloging-in-Publication Data
Names: Klipper, Barbara, author. | Banks, Carrie Scott, author.
Title: Library programming for adults with developmental disabilities / Barbara Klipper and Carrie Banks.
Description: Chicago : ALA Editions, 2021. | Includes bibliographical references and index. | Summary: "This book provides a contextualized guide to programming for adults with disabilities and offers a wide variety of implementable program ideas"—Provided by publisher.
Identifiers: LCCN 2021004725 | ISBN 9780838948668 (paperback)
Subjects: LCSH: Libraries and the developmentally disabled—United States. | Libraries—Activity programs—United States.
Classification: LCC Z711.92.D48 K57 2021 | DDC 027.6/630973—dc23
LC record available at https://lccn.loc.gov/2021004725

Book design by Alejandra Diaz in the Gibson typeface.

♾ This paper meets the requirements of ANSI/NISO Z39.48-1992 (Permanence of Paper).

Printed in the United States of America
25 24 23 22 21   5 4 3 2 1

For Sanford Lazar, my uncle,
who survived Polk State School to live with his friends
and loved the Pittsburgh Pirates.
—CARRIE BANKS

For all of the people with developmental disabilities
whom I knew when they were children,
in the hope that they as adults
are able to use and enjoy their local libraries.
—BARBARA KLIPPER

Contents

Contents

Acknowledgments

We want to express our thanks for the adults with developmental disabilities who speak, write, and share their experiences and hopes with the world. We've quoted their written statements throughout the book, and we acknowledge that without them, we who are trying to be allies would have much less of a chance of getting it right. We also want to thank the following people who generously shared their expertise and experience with us for this book. To anyone whom we've inadvertently left off this list, we offer our sincere apologies.

Jan Angliss, Glen Cove Public Library; Mary Barnes, Tuckahoe Area Library; Mark Bartlet, Able Gamers Charity; Valerie Bell and Theresa Rice, Athens Regional Library System; Natalie Bota, Westlake Porter Public Library; Julia Boxler, NEO Adaptive Librarians; Bryan Boyce, Cow Tipping Press; Karen Bradley, Kimberli Buckley, and Addie Spanbock, Concord Library; Janine Brooks, Autism Society of Nebraska Silent Book Club; Deborah Bussinger, Leesburg Public Library; Elena Cabodevilla and Kelsey McLane, Arapahoe Library District; Michael John Carley; Pam Carswell, Minot Public Library; Candice Casey, Hart Memorial Library; Ruth Chiego, Grapevine Public Library; Susan Cooper, Hennepin County Library; Edith Craig, St. Charles Public Library; Nataya Culler, Brooklyn Public Library; Kristin DeMay, Columbus Public Library; Jeff Edelstein, University of Massachusetts; Tom Fish, Next Chapter Book Club; Ellen Fitzgerald and Caity Reitzen, Free Library of Philadelphia; Meg Godbey, Nashville Public Library; Marti Goddard, San Francisco Public Library; Erna Golden, Brooklyn Public Library; Renee Grassi, Dakota County Library; Lisa Hagen, Germantown Community Library; Katie Hench, Infiniteach; Helen Hokanson, Johnson County Library; Cynthia Hosang, West Hempstead Public Library; John Huth, Brooklyn Public Library; Vicki Karlovsky, Deerfield Public Library; Younshin Kim, Queens Public Library; Alice Knapp and Sophia-Maria Michalatos, The Ferguson Library; Kayla Kuni, New Port Richey Public Library; Bernadette A. Lear, Penn State Harrisburg Library; Amy Little and Kathy Middleton, Sacramento Public Library; Susan McBride, Hinsdale Public Library; Mary

Acknowledgments

Medjo Me Zengue, Addison Public Library; Lori Merriam, Homeward Bound; Jeny Wasilewski Mills, Evanston Public Library; Kate Monsour, Port Washington Public Library; Kate Niehoff, Schaumburg Township Public Library; Ed Niemchak and Jen Taggart, Bloomfield Township Public Library; Sharon Noble, Ridgedale Library; Maggie Nygren, American Association on Intellectual and Developmental Disabilities (AAIDD); Noreen O'Gara, Bedford Free Public Library; Josh O'Shea, Glen Ellyn Public Library; Kristi Olabode, Grand Prairie Public Library; Morénike Giwa Onaiwu, Autistic Women and Non-Binary Network; Clare Papay, Think College; Tracey Phillips, Louisville Public Library; Angela Pilkington, Iowa City Public Library; J. J. Pionke, Urbana Undergraduate Library, University of Illinois; Andrew Plait, Medicine Hat Public Library; Jen Ripka, Naperville Public Library; Jill Rothstein and Andrew Heiskell, Braille and Talking Book Library; Susan Rozmiarek, UT Austin board game class; Vivian Rutherford, Waco-McLennan County Library; Jay Sellers, University of Delaware; Erin Silva, Liberty City Public Library; Patrick Timony, D.C. Public Library; Grace Walker, Pickerington Public Library; Lisa Powell Williams, Moline Public Library; Suzanne Williams, College of Adaptive Arts; Jessie Witherall, Iowa City Autism Community; Rebecca Wolfe, Allen County Library; and Weiqi (Vicki) Zhang, Brooklyn Public Library.

Our thanks also go to our editor Jamie Santoro for having faith in us and saying yes when we approached her with the idea for this book during ALA Annual Conference 2019 and to each other for the challenges, corrections, and questions that made this a better book than it would have been if either of us had written it alone.

—BARBARA KLIPPER and CARRIE BANKS

Introduction

This book's contents grew out of our combined experiences and work on this topic over many years. We supplemented that with extensive reading as well as interviews with librarians and other professionals who we feel are ahead of the curve in terms of what they offer for the adults with developmental disabilities (DD) who live in their communities. Our goal is to provide a context for serving adults with DD, offer a wide variety of program ideas you can implement, and support you in creating a culture of inclusion in your library. Our hope is that all adults who walk through the door of a library, regardless of their cognition, communication style, behavior, or appearance, will be treated respectfully and will find themselves welcomed and valued by a knowledgeable staff.

Some of what we discuss affects everyone in the library and community; however, our focus is on adults with DD and their needs. So, what are developmental disabilities? There are as many answers to that question as there are people to answer it. Congress uses a legalistic view, the Centers for Disease Control and Prevention (CDC) a medical one, and self-advocates a third, strengths-based definition. In the Developmental Disabilities Assistance and Bill of Rights Act of 2000 (DD Act), which is the main source of government funding for DD services, Congress defines DD as

> a severe, chronic disability . . . attributable to a mental [and/]or physical impairment . . . [that] manifest[s] before . . . age 22; is likely to continue indefinitely; results in substantial functional limitations in three or more . . . areas of major life activity . . . ; and reflects the individual's need for . . . services, individualized supports, or other forms of assistance that are of lifelong or extended duration.[1]

The CDC emphasizes the conditions that fall under the DD umbrella, although no two groups who list specific disabilities include all of the same ones.

In sharp contrast to these definitions is that of the Autistic Self Advocacy Network (ASAN): "Autistic people have a unique set of characteristics, which can manifest as difference, disability, or gifts/skills, from person to person and within the same person."[2] Unlike the medical and government-generated definitions, the ASAN one focuses on attributes not deficits and is embraced by many self-advocates.

DEFINING DEVELOPMENTAL DISABILITIES

Common elements in DD definitions:

- The disability starts in childhood, before age twenty-two.
- It is a lifelong disability.
- Intellectual disabilities and autism are included.

Developmental disabilities impact:

- communication
- behavior
- cognition
- day-to-day living

Because they are always included in definitions of DD, we focus primarily, but not exclusively, on autism, officially called autism spectrum disorder (ASD), and intellectual disabilities (ID).

We made some other choices as we developed the book that you should understand before you read further:

- The term *self-advocate* appears throughout. It comes from the self-advocacy civil rights movement begun in the 1960s, which is based on "the idea that people with disabilities have the right to speak up for themselves. People with disabilities also have the right to choose the services they want."[3] We consulted and quote self-advocates when possible because they are the true experts on their experience and needs.
- We frequently mention those adults with DD who come to the library in groups escorted by agency personnel. We do this because these groups use many public libraries, and a number of the programs we present were designed for them or include them as participants. However, people in congregate housing or those who attend day programs are not the only

adults with DD. In fact, those in residential programs represent only about 13 percent of people with DD.[4] Many others use our libraries independently or are accompanied by a parent or other caregiver, and still others are not library users. There are library staff with DD, including librarians. Libraries need to serve all of these individuals as well as the groups.

- The book contains an extensive discussion of current terminology. With this in mind, we use *people with developmental disabilities*, which is an example of person-first language, but we also use *autistic people*, which is an example of identity-first language. These choices reflect the preference of self-advocates.
- We use the term *developmental disabilities* (DD) throughout, although some quotes use *intellectual and developmental disabilities* (IDD). Both are in current use, but ID is technically a subset of DD.
- The word *focused* is used to denote programs designed specifically for people with disabilities. *Inclusive* programs are those for people with disabilities and the nondisabled, participating together. Not all programs will work well for every patron, so we introduce both types to help you serve the widest variety of adults with DD.
- As used in this book, a social story is a linear narrative, usually with visuals, that describes a situation or experience in order to make it more comprehensible and predictable for autistic people. This is a widespread, though imprecise, use of the term as developed and defined by Carol Gray.
- As we wrote this book, libraries experienced a seismic change in how they operate because of the COVID-19 pandemic. Most of the in-person programs we were writing about were suspended. Some went virtual. We don't know how any of these will be impacted when their libraries return to full service; however, they still represent good, replicable ideas, so we share them. We hope the new postpandemic programming model has inclusion at its core and retains the best of in-person and virtual programming.
- Because it is new to so many of us, we include guidance on virtual programming, both in a dedicated chapter and throughout the volume.
- We intend this book to be both inspirational and aspirational. We realize that many libraries will not be able to implement anywhere near all of the things that we suggest in the near term. However, we want to present what we believe is the ideal, allowing readers to decide on the best starting point for their own institutions and communities while understanding what they can aspire to and move toward over time.

Underlying the premise of the book is the understanding that people with DD have the right, as codified by several laws, to full access to our libraries. The DD Act and the better-known Americans with Disabilities Act (ADA), which prohibits disability-based discrimination, are the primary civil rights laws covering people with DD. The Individuals with Disabilities Education Act (IDEA), which covers students with disabilities between the ages of eighteen and twenty-two, and the Higher Education Opportunity Act (HEOA) are also important. IDEA funds services such as employment and daily living skills training and provides opportunities for community involvement for transitioning high school students. Many transition groups use our libraries, and in the pages that follow, we introduce some programs done with and for these groups. HEOA provides access to student loans and prohibits discrimination by institutions of higher education, enabling many more students with DD to attend colleges and universities. Because of this law, academic libraries work with increasing numbers of students with DD. There are also state and local laws that may confer additional rights. It is a good idea to know about those as well.

What these laws have in common is the understanding that people with DD are full members of society and should be treated as such. As the DD Act states:

> [D]isability is a natural part of the human experience that does not diminish the right of individuals with developmental disabilities to live independently, to exert control and choice over their own lives, and to fully participate in and contribute to their communities through full integration and inclusion in the economic, political, social, cultural, and educational mainstream of United States society.[5]

Our professional standards also mandate full inclusion. The American Library Association (ALA)

> recognizes that people with disabilities are a large and vibrant part of society. Libraries should be fully inclusive of all members of their community and strive to break down barriers to access. The library can play a transformational role in helping facilitate more complete participation in society by providing fully accessible resources and services.[6]

Our aim is to help you break down barriers and achieve full inclusion in your libraries, in part through programming. To do that, we start with general concepts and issues that are important to understand, then move to specific programs you can replicate and resources you can use. Part I discusses institutional ableism and the ideas and biases that impact the lives of people with developmental disabilities. It also explains how to create a library-wide culture of inclusion. Part II describes how libraries can prepare for programming and presents a variety of elements to put in place to ensure programming success. Part III introduces a large assortment of programs, organized by topic. Because some programs are multifaceted and others don't easily fit into these somewhat arbitrary groupings, we suggest you consider all of the chapters in this section as you look for program ideas for your library. You might find some that would be perfect for your community in a chapter that didn't initially appeal to you. In the final section, we talk about what to do after reading the book and provide a number of resources to help you stay up-to-date on this ever-changing topic. Finally, we leave you with a list of best practices to follow as you begin to program.

Now that you know some basics and what we will cover, you're ready to get into the meat of the book. We hope you don't read it through once and shelve it. Rather, we hope you refer to this volume often, dog-ear your favorite pages, write in the margins, share favorite ideas and programs with colleagues, and even spill your coffee on it, if unavoidable. We'd like to see you make this book your own, and then apply what you find here in your library. Learning this material is not an academic exercise. There will be no grades. Rather, the work you do to create a culture of inclusion in your library and programming that truly serves adults with DD will affect the lives of real people in your community. It also has the potential to have a meaningful and positive impact on your institution, and on you.

NOTES

1. Developmental Disabilities Assistance and Bill of Rights Act of 2000 (DD Act), Pub. L. No. 106-42, 114 Stat. 1684 § 102(8)(A) (October 30, 2000), https://acl.gov/sites/default/files/about-acl/2016-12/dd_act_2000.pdf.
2. ASAN, "About Autism," https://autisticadvocacy.org/about-asan/about-autism/.
3. Self Advocates Becoming Empowered (SABE), *Self Advocacy Start-Up Toolkit* (Self Advocacy Resource and Technical Assistance Center [SARTAC], 2018), 11, https://selfadvocacyinfo.org/wp-content/uploads/2018/07/Self-Advocacy-Start-up-Toolkit-more-power-more-control-over-our-lives-2018.pdf.
4. Katelyn Li, "A Crisis Decades in the Making: Disability Housing Policy and COVID-19," *Harvard Political Review*, October 11, 2020, https://harvardpolitics.com/congregate-care-covid/.
5. DD Act, tit. 1A § 101 (Findings, Purposes, and Policy).
6. ALA, "Services to People with Disabilities: An Interpretation of the Library Bill of Rights," www.ala.org/advocacy/intfreedom/librarybill/interpretations/servicespeopledisabilities.

PART I

Developmental Disabilities, Inclusion, and Support

CHAPTER 1

Perception and Self-Perception

The ways in which individuals and society perceive people with developmental disabilities have a profound effect on our ability to program inclusively, so we start with an examination of these issues. The first thing to know is that despite the existence of laws and policies that call for inclusion, people with DD experience rampant discrimination called ableism.

BIAS AND INSTITUTIONAL ABLEISM

Ableism is the parallel to racism and sexism. Institutional ableism is the set of laws, policies, regulations, practices, and cultural norms that prevent the full participation of people with disabilities in society. Institutional ableism has dominated the lives of people with DD for generations, creating and maintaining discrimination in every area of life, including education, employment, health care, benefits, housing, and the criminal justice system. One example of this is the fact that Medicaid pays higher reimbursement rates for services provided in nursing homes than it does for services offered at home. This pushes people who need services into congregate care facilities. In libraries institutional ableism manifests in such practices as having fixed loan periods that do not account for varied reading and comprehension speeds, requiring a noninstitutional address to get a library card, building high desks at points of service, and writing job descriptions that require librarians be able to lift fifty pounds of books.

Challenging the Dominant Narrative

The dominant narrative about people with disabilities is simultaneously created by and supportive of institutional ableism. We are told, tell ourselves, and share with others stories comprised predominantly of negative myths and stereotypes. To explain this, let's go back to the Medicaid example. The dominant narrative asserts that many adults with DD are not capable of making decisions for themselves and living independently. This stereotype justifies the belief that adults with some conditions like ID get better care in institutions than they do at home in the community. Medicaid policy then pushes these people into congregate care. We accept the fact that they are institutionalized because we accept the narrative. It is a circular trap, and it hurts everyone.

The truth about individuals with DD is quite different from the dominant narrative. It is certainly more nuanced. Did you know that there are people with DD who

- live independently and have numerous responsibilities?
- are musicians, artists, doctors, teachers, actors, writers, carpenters, or athletes?
- go to community colleges or universities or have PhDs?
- have hobbies they enjoy and a myriad of interests and tastes?
- like to read many genres in a variety of formats?
- work in service, manufacturing, information, finance, child care, education, retail, farming, and every other sector?
- had autism as children and continue to have autism as adults?
- are strong advocates for themselves and others and accomplished public speakers?
- communicate in many ways: verbally, with augmentative and alternative communication (AAC), i.e., sign language, pictograms, or electronic devices?
- are single, married, birth parents, adoptive parents, transgender, gender queer, gay, heteronormative, or bisexual?
- speak every language and sometimes more than one?
- come from every culture in the world?

We mentioned that many common stereotypes are negative; some are also infantilizing. As autistic mental health advocate Emily Burke posted on Twitter:

> I may have interests which you judge to be "childlike," get excited over small things which you also judge to be "childlike" and my autistic joy may come across to you as me acting "childlike," but none of these judgements you have mean you can treat me like a child.[1]

Not all stereotypes are negative, however, at least not on the surface. For example, people with Down syndrome are commonly thought to be sweet and friendly; people with the type of autism we used to call Aspergers syndrome are expected to be smart and excel in technical fields. Despite their seeming positivity, these stereotypes are also harmful because they are othering and one-dimensional.

The bottom line is that there isn't a typical person with a developmental disability. There are adults with DD who have high support needs and others who do not. Some adults with DD have notable achievements in one area and need supports in another. Some don't need supports at all. They are all unique individuals with strengths and talents in addition to things they don't do well, just like everyone else. Our patrons will be better served if we ignore the stereotypes, dismantle institutional ableism, and focus on the work of including everyone.

How Libraries Can Counter the Narrative

Institutional ableism is perpetuated through the placement of people with DD in special, segregated schools or classes as well as in institutions. Isolating them from the community in these ways allows misperceptions to continue and hinders us all from moving beyond the dominant narrative. One way to counter this is to get to know individuals with DD. Librarians who do this report very positive experiences. For example, Nataya Culler from Brooklyn Public Library acknowledges that she was anxious and had misconceptions before she started programming for adults with DD, but with time and familiarity her feelings changed. She concludes, "There needs to be more . . . exposure. Because I feel like a lot of people have a nervousness and stigma . . . I'm not going to lie, I had the same nervousness, but after a couple of months it went away."[2] Renee Grassi of the Dakota (MN) County Library goes even further, saying of that library's staff, "We are becoming champions for accessibility as we become more aware."[3]

MODELS OF DISABILITY

It is also useful to know a bit about the four basic models through which society views disability. Traditionally, the most widely accepted of these have been the predominantly negative medical and charity models. The medical model views disability as a disease to be cured. It focuses on medication and assistive devices to "fix" disability. The charity model, based on the ableist assumption that people with disabilities are inferior to the nondisabled, leads to pity, not empathy, and the belief that people with DD need to be taken care of, whether they want that or not.

Since the 1970s, disability activists, self-advocates, and allies have argued for and adopted new stigma-free models of disability, including the social model, which sees the problem as lying not with individuals with disabilities but with the barriers imposed by a society that fails to meet their needs. Lisa Rutledge, a woman with cerebral palsy, explains:

> [The social] model makes a distinction between disability and impairment. . . . The model suggests that if biases are overcome and access barriers are removed, a person with impairments will have less of an experience of being disabled. Having impairments is a condition, while having a disability is an experience—one that can change, even if the person's condition does not change.[4]

Another model considers discrimination against people with disabilities a human rights issue given that disability is a natural aspect of the human condition. The latter two models align with the concept of institutional racism; in both, the emphasis is on a society that prevents access. So, with this in mind, as library workers, will we expect people with disabilities to change things in themselves that they cannot change or act to take down the barriers that exist in our institutions? This book offers many suggestions on how to go about removing barriers if we are willing to take action.

UNDERSTANDING BEHAVIOR

Some library staff avoid interacting with or programming for people with developmental disabilities out of concern about behaviors they don't understand and fear they can't control. They worry that patrons with DD might be disruptive, destroy materials or library property, be loud, have a meltdown, or violate societal norms of personal distance.

While we tend to associate disruptive behavior with patrons with disabilities, library patrons without disabilities are capable of destructive or disruptive behavior, and in almost all cases, the unexpected behaviors manifested by people with DD are no different. The fear of possible behaviors may even be more destructive than the behaviors themselves if it causes librarians to steer clear of these people or treat them differently from other library users.

Librarians who program for adults with DD report that potentially upsetting behaviors are rare and easily handled. For example, the Arapahoe Libraries staff who run the New Day Storytime for adults note:

> As fun as storytime can be, there are occasional jarring incidents. At one
> time . . . a staff member had her hair pulled by a client. . . . While this
> doesn't frequently happen, such experiences teach us to pay special
> attention to the clients involved that day. When so and so is here, you
> learn to put your hair up into a ponytail.[5]

Understanding what behavior really is can ease concerns. Seen from the outside, unexpected behavior can seem random, but there is generally a reason for it. Behavior is a brain-based response to stimuli. It can be a form of communication, a way of self-regulating, a result of confusion, or a response to pain. Whatever else it is, unexpected behavior is not meaningless. One way of thinking about it is the ABC method. Every action has an antecedent, *A*, something that sets it in motion or triggers it. *B* is the behavior itself, and *C* is the consequence of the behavior. If the behavior gets us what we want, it is successful, and we will use it again. If not, most people will try a different strategy. In the case of the hair puller, the patron might have just wondered what the librarian's long hair felt like and not had the ability to understand that it is not socially acceptable to touch other people in this way.

A type of behavior that is often misunderstood by others is the stim or self-stimulatory behavior. Stims are repetitive behaviors, and many people do them, although they are most commonly associated with autistic people. Autistic stims include hand flapping, spinning or rocking the body, and spinning or lining up objects. However, if you twirl your hair while you read, click a pen over and over, or doodle, you too are stimming.

Some who work with autistic people feel that stims are bad, that they kept autistic people from focusing, are disruptive, and will cause other people to reject them. Their goal is to control stims through treatment, an application of the medical model that seeks to fix something that is inherently part of a disability. But autistic self-advocates have pushed back against the notion that stims are bad, and some experts have come to acknowledge that they have a positive function. For sensory seekers, stims can be arousing and stimulate endorphins; for sensory avoiders, they can be soothing and calming. They can help autistic people regulate their sensory systems and prevent meltdowns. Beyond asserting that stims are natural to them, autistic individuals describe stims as pleasurable. For example, Cynthia Kim reports:

> Last night . . . I found myself twirling in the kitchen and instead of stopping, I let myself enjoy it. I kicked out my foot and made a full spin to
> the right, then kicked out my other foot and twirled to the left. I did it
> again and again and soon I found myself laughing out loud. Twirling
> around in the kitchen feels good. It feels right.[6]

Other common autistic behaviors are equally misunderstood, and in a series of tweets, Steve Asbell, who is autistic, explains what some of these mean: "What LOOKS like 'stubbornness' in an autistic is really 'an innate need to understand the request and its reason' before unnecessarily expending precious mental resources, wasting time and possibly subjecting ourselves to sensory and emotional overload."[7] He goes on to say that what others see as "unusual and restricted interests" is really a manifestation of passion about a topic. What appears as aloofness is really an inability to understand and to please others. Perceived laziness is really a mix of anxiety, overwhelm, executive functioning disorder, and a lack of coping mechanisms and supports. And so on. As we said, behavior always has a meaning.

Once we understand what behaviors really are, it becomes easier to lose our concern about them and to provide for them as we program. If a behavior is loud but not harmful in any way, we can cheerfully provide a safe space where the person with a disability can practice it. We can be welcoming and understanding instead of fearful and dismissive.

TIPS FOR WELCOMING ADULTS WITH DD
- Set clear behavior policies but be flexible.
- Manage expectations.
- Communicate effectively.
- Utilize natural supports like family members or caregivers.
- Provide a supportive physical and sensory environment.
- Ask people with DD what they need.

CHOOSING WORDS CAREFULLY

Terminology that describes the disability experience is another thing, like disability models, that evolves over time. For instance, *mentally retarded* was actually coined as a less offensive replacement for earlier terms like *moron* and *idiot* that were used to describe people with cognitive impairments. Now, *mentally retarded* and its derivative *retard* are considered dehumanizing and offensive and the accepted term is the name of the condition, *intellectual disability*.

Dated and Offensive Language

It is interesting to note that many of the outmoded terms are routinely used as insults against people without a disability or to describe ourselves if we make a mistake or forget something. How many of us call ourselves an idiot or say we are stupid under those circumstances, without thinking twice about what those words actually mean? Using these labels in this casual way is a microaggression, in the same way that using racist terminology would be. Imagine being a person with an intellectual disability overhearing someone use offensive words that describe your life experience as a casual insult. In language, as in other areas, institutional ableism runs deep. Author and editor Eric Michael Garcia described how he had to work at breaking this pattern in his own speech:

> I've tried to stop using the words "moron" and "idiot." Hell, I've even tried to stop using the word "crazy" and what surprises me is how common these terms are and how often I am at a loss for an alternative because they are so ingrained in our language.[8]

It may be hard to find alternative words, but it is important to try.

At the other extreme are words that people might intend to be positive but are essentially condescending and insulting. *Inspirational* and *special* fall in this category. Harilyn Russo, a disability rights activist and psychologist with cerebral palsy describes how she feels when told she is an inspiration:

> Well, frankly, I'm not an inspiration. I'm damn boring, if you ask me, which you rarely do. I worry about paying the rent, eating too much chocolate, and finding telltale wrinkles—sound inspirational yet? . . . I know, I know, if you were me, you'd never leave your house and maybe even kill yourself. So, I am inspirational because I haven't committed suicide—yet.[9]

A video created for World Down Syndrome Day in 2017 makes the case against the widely used term *special needs*.[10] A woman with Down syndrome narrates as actors demonstrate a series of truly special needs like having to eat dinosaur eggs, wear a suit of armor, or be massaged by a cat. The video points out that education, jobs, opportunities, friends, and love, the things that people with Down syndrome or other disabilities really need, are not special; they are what everyone needs.

Terminology can be confusing and even a bit hard to keep up with. However, an effort to understand what the terms mean and to use the ones that are currently

---

BEST PRACTICES FOR TERMINOLOGY
Stick with person-first or identity-first language and avoid these offensive terms:

- afflicted with
- defective or birth defect
- differently abled
- exceptional
- handicapped
- high functioning/low functioning

- mentally retarded or retard
- spastic or spaz
- special needs
- has Down's
- crippled
- inspirational

---

accepted is an indication of our willingness to value the humanity and dignity of people with DD.

Person-First or Identity-First Language

Another source of linguistic confusion in relation to people with disabilities is the choice between person- and identity-first language. Since the 1970s person-first language (PFL) has been the standard, based on the understanding that a person is made up of more than their disability. For example, someone is a *person with a disability*, not a *disabled person*.

For some self-advocates, however, disability is a matter of identity and pride and they see PFL as a negation of a basic fact of their existence. These people refer to themselves as *disabled* or as *autistic*, if their diagnosis is autism, and they may not like it when people tell them they need to use person-first language. In a series of tweets, self-advocate Emily Paige Ballou scolds professionals who call out people for using identity-first language:

> I know you were taught that person-first language . . . is always cor-
> rect. . . . I KNOW you mean well when you . . . snap at someone to use
> person-first language. But the problem is you've been taught out of
> date information, and as a result you're often just snapping at disabled
> people who are using language natural to our communities.[11]

A preference for person-first or identity-first language can vary from person to person and group to group. Parents of children with disabilities and the intellectual disability community often prefer person-first language; persons who are d/Deaf or hard of hearing and autistic people often prefer identity-first language. Like we said, this matter of terminology can be confusing, but it is important to use the terminology the individual with the disability prefers, as Ballou suggests. When you don't know, starting with person-first language will convey respect and your willingness to get it right.

THE NEURODIVERSITY MOVEMENT

The neurodiversity movement posits another way of looking at people with DD. It is based on the idea that peoples' brains are all wired differently, and a wide variety of neurological conditions are naturally occurring. The goal of neurodiversity advocates is to provide systems of support that allow people who are neurodiverse to be who they are and to live their best lives as themselves without a need to fit someone else's idea of normal.

Autistic people who are part of this movement embrace the social model of disability and use the neurodiversity spectrum-colored infinity symbol. They find the puzzle piece, historically used to identify organizations and products for people with autism, outmoded and offensive with its implication that people with autism are either impossible to figure out or deficient in some way. Using blue during April, as promoted by a controversial autism organization, also does not represent the feelings of many autistic people. Jess Benham, an autistic teaching fellow at the University of Pittsburgh and director of development for the Pittsburgh Center for Autistic Advocacy (PCAA), says this about what people with autism prefer:

> I'm tired of politicians "lighting it up for blue" for a day or for the month, then not listening when I'm in their offices advocating for the issues that impact our lives. Autistic people need seats at the table where decisions are being made about us, not a month in which public figures and Autism organizations highlight negative stereotypes.[12]

Journalist Jessica Semler elaborates

> A common theme when talking to actual autistic folks about this month is that they'd much prefer "Autism Acceptance" or "Appreciation Month." "Awareness" is a word we use to talk about negative things like sexual assault, domestic violence, cancer and other diseases. We shouldn't be talking about neurodivergent people like this.[13]

So, reconsider the color blue and the puzzle pieces on prominent display in April for Autism Awareness Month. Instead, highlight acceptance all year and include self-advocates. Take a page from the Charleston (SC) County Public Library, which hosts panels of autistic people they call "Ask an Aspie," as part of their Human Library program series. Started by author and consultant Tori Boucher in 2017, "Ask an Aspie" has continued because of strong positive community response.[14] Or follow the lead of Jennifer Murphy of the Palms–Rancho Park Branch Library, part of the Los Angeles Public Library (LAPL) system, and host an Autism Awareness Workshop. Theirs was sponsored by two local agencies and led by a panel of autistic teens and young adults. The session consisted of interactive presentations and time for discussion, and the event flier described it in this way: "You will hear insights about autism and get tips on how you can help individuals with Autism feel more a part of your local community."[15] This is a worthy goal for any library program.

NOTES
1. Emily Burke (@emburke), Twitter, August 8, 2020, 5:41 p.m.
2. Nataya Culler, personal communication, September 27, 2019.
3. Renee Grassi, personal communication, January 20, 2020.
4. Lisa Rutledge, "Why the Social Model of Disability Doesn't Fully Reflect My Experience," The Mighty (digital health community), posted November 11, 2019, https://themighty.com/2019/11/medical-social-models-disability/?utm_source=engagement_bar&utm_medium=email&utm_campaign=story_page.engagement_bar/.
5. Arapahoe Libraries, "Community Impact Outside the Library(ish): Library for All and New Day Storytime," staff handout provided by Elena Cabodevilla, December 16, 2019; quoted with permission.
6. Cynthia Kim, "Unlearning to Accept," *Musings of An Aspie: One Woman's Thoughts about Life on the Spectrum* (blog), posted January 24, 2013, https://musingsofanaspie.com/2013/01/24/unlearning-to-accept/.
7. Steve Asbell (@SteveAsbell), Twitter, May 28, 2020, 1:19 p.m.
8. Eric Michael Garcia (@EricMGarcia), Twitter, September 8, 2019, 10:55 a.m.
9. Harilyn Ross, *Don't Call Me Inspirational: A Disabled Feminist Talks Back*. Philadelphia: Temple University Press, 2013, 25.
10. SUDPRESS, "Not Special Needs," YouTube, March 21, 2017, www.youtube.com/watch?v=tZ7I-IFJpRO.
11. Emily Paige Ballou (@epballou), Twitter, August 19, 2019, 3:45 p.m.
12. Jessica Semler, "Puzzling Motives: Rethinking Autism Awareness," *Pittsburgh Current,* April 16, 2019, www.pittsburghcurrent.com/puzzling-motives-rethinking-autism-awareness/.
13. Ibid.
14. Charleston County Public Library, "Human Library Series: Get to Know Someone with Aspergers," www.ccpl.org/events/human-library-series-get-know-someone-aspergers.
15. Palms–Rancho Park Branch Library, LAPL, Autism Awareness Workshop event flier provided by Librarian Jennifer Murphy, February 10, 2020.

CHAPTER 2

Creating a Culture of Inclusion

What is inclusion in a library? We want people with developmental disabilities to be able to access our facilities, programs, and services, but inclusion is not just accessibility. Think of it this way: "Accessibility is being able to get into the party. Diversity is being invited. Inclusion is being asked to dance."[1] If our programming for people with DD is to be successful, our libraries need to be places where everyone can participate fully and feel welcome. To achieve this goal, we must move from thinking about access to embracing inclusion.

Inclusion means that everyone can use the library as they are. It does not mean that everyone always does everything together. It is about opportunity and choice. Teens are unlikely to attend a travel program for seniors, nor will seniors want to be part of the library's teen advisory board. But teens and seniors may opt to attend music, movie, or speaker programs together. This same degree of choice should be available to patrons with DD. Providing choice involves offering both focused and inclusive programs. As Alice Knapp, president of the Ferguson Library in Stamford, Connecticut notes:

> General adult programs, such as concerts, movies, and lectures offer
> an opportunity for adults with developmental disabilities to participate
> and belong in the library community. I have noticed over the years that
> a percentage of our users with developmental disabilities are active
> program attenders, and they are warmly accepted by staff and other
> attendees. I believe it is also important to provide specialized program-
> ming for adults with DD."[2]

We discuss both types of programs throughout the book.

INSTITUTIONAL BUY-IN FOR INCLUSION

The impetus for inclusion is often bottom-up, coming from public service staff with a personal connection to people with DD, a need to respond to a patron request, or a desire to intervene when witnessing users with DD struggle to access what the library offers. Their efforts to better serve these patrons sometimes alerts them to ways in which their libraries effectively discriminate. They may search for and identify things they want to change. They may start a new program or service. This approach can be problematic, in part because it can result in one-off programs with no relationship to the library's mission or other programs. If the program is tied to a specific staff member, the risk is that the program may end if the staff member changes positions or institutions. This happened among staff at a library we tried to interview for this book. A 2015 article featured a program they were doing, and we reached out for more information. Although it was only a few years since the article had appeared, library staff knew nothing of the program, where written records might be, or how to contact the programmer, who had since left the library. Finally, waiting for a complaint or request invites bad feelings and possibly bad publicity.

It helps if public service managers are supportive and work to communicate the benefit of these initiatives and practices up the line to the administration and board, but it may take persistence, persuasive data, and cogent arguments in these cases to convince those in leadership positions to buy in. Community support in the form of grants, positive media mentions, and other outside accolades can facilitate the process and move the administration and board toward institution-wide inclusion, but this can often be a slow and possibly painstaking process.

In other situations, which in our experience are rarer, the decision to develop more inclusive practices comes from someone at the top. The benefit of the top-down approach is that it provides a unique opportunity to look at ableism institutionally with an eye to implementing more systemic changes. The downside is the possibility that inclusion could be mandated without line staff understanding why or how this is now part of their jobs.

In both scenarios, communication and training are needed to help get everyone on board. In both cases, creating a culture of inclusion means confronting institutional ableism. It is only once public service staff, management, and the board all understand the need and the benefits of inclusion that meaningful and sustained institutional change will be possible and the adoption of the basic principles and practices that constitute a culture of inclusion can take place library- or system-wide. But you don't have to wait until then to start. Integrating the concepts in this chapter into your programs and services can begin the process or help it along.

UNIVERSAL DESIGN AND UNIVERSAL DESIGN FOR LEARNING

Implementing universal design (UD) and Universal Design for Learning (UDL) is foundational to erasing institutional ableism and promoting inclusion. Without them, you may be left scrambling to adapt a program or service at the last minute when someone with a disability asks to be included. This approach can be traumatizing for the patron and embarrassing for library staff. Without UD and UDL, the onus for ensuring inclusion falls on people with DD or their advocates. Autistic journalist Sara Leuterman tells us that "asking . . . is difficult and often humiliating. People who are totally unqualified feel like they get to decide if you 'deserve' it. Universal design is important because it means not having to ask to do the same things everyone else does."[3] We simply provide better and more seamless service when we integrate these principles into all aspects of how the library does business.

Universal design is "the design of products and environments to be usable by all people, to the greatest extent possible, without the need for adaptation or specialized design."[4] There are seven UD principles:

1. *Equitable use:* No user group is placed at a disadvantage.
2. *Flexibility in use:* Many personal capabilities and preferences can be accommodated.
3. *Simple, intuitive use:* Most people can easily figure out how to use the design.
4. *Perceptible information:* Information about the design's use is built into the design itself.
5. *Tolerance for error:* The design is safe even if used incorrectly.
6. *Low physical effort:* It is comfortable to use the item, and minimal effort is required.
7. *Size and space for approach and use:* People of a wide range of sizes, postures, and abilities can use the design.[5]

These principles apply to how we design all aspects of a library's physical space, not just the entrances. UD shows up in easy-to-use doorknobs, varied heights on checkout desks and tables, options for moving between floors, and the availability of seating choices.

Through UDL, UD also applies to the materials we collect, the tools we provide, and the programs we design. UDL has three principles, which are based on neuroscience research:

1. *Multiple means of representation:* Provide a variety of ways learners can acquire information.
2. *Multiple means of action and expression:* Offer options in how learners can demonstrate their knowledge.
3. *Multiple means of engagement:* Engage learners by tying activities to their interests and abilities.[6]

If libraries base program design on these principles, a wider variety of patrons, including those with DD, will be able to participate.

Some of the programs described in this book model the application of these principles. For example, a crafts program that offers a range of activity choices with different degrees of difficulty demonstrates the UDL principle *multiple means of engagement*. A book club that allows members to select their own reading materials and formats and to share about them in their own ways applies all of the UDL principles.

MULTIPLE INTELLIGENCES THEORY

Multiple intelligences is another theory that can be applied to help a library become inclusive. The theory grew out of Howard Gardner's recognition that IQ tests were too limiting because they measure only linguistic and mathematical abilities. While some of us are strong linguistic and logical-mathematical learners, many people learn and excel in other ways. The theory posits eight different types of intelligence:

- *linguistic intelligence:* word smart
- *logical-mathematical intelligence:* number/reasoning smart
- *spatial intelligence:* picture smart
- *bodily-kinesthetic intelligence:* body smart
- *musical intelligence:* music smart
- *interpersonal intelligence:* people smart
- *intrapersonal intelligence:* self smart
- *naturalist intelligence:* nature smart[7]

Programs can be designed to be more inclusive by adding elements that address the different intelligences. For instance, a program can incorporate music and movement, nature, visuals, and interpersonal interaction so that everyone has a chance to shine. You can easily find charts online that show all of the intelligences. We suggest you keep one handy as a sort of checklist as you design programs.

You don't have to address every intelligence in every program, but mix it up and remember that although as librarians our strong suit is most likely linguistic intelligence, this is not going to be true for all of the people who attend our programs.

TRAUMA-INFORMED LIBRARY PRACTICES

Many people have experienced trauma and a library with a culture of inclusion is cognizant of how this can impact patrons' library use. People with DD experience the same adverse childhood experiences as others as well as additional traumas specific to their disabilities. These include the use of restraints, seclusion, social isolation, and out-of-home placements in institutions and residential schools. Many autistic adults have been traumatized by applied behavioral analysis (ABA), a common autism therapy. Even the goals of therapeutic interventions, such as extinguishing stimming behaviors, can be traumatizing. It is estimated that adults with DD are three to four times more likely to have experienced childhood trauma than are adults without DD.[8] Further compounding the harm, adults with DD may be less able to communicate their trauma and have less access to mental health services. As a group, people who have experienced trauma have increased health and mental health concerns, including post-traumatic stress disorder, over the course of their lives.

A fundamental aspect of trauma-informed practice is knowing that peoples' histories affect how they respond to situations. Understanding the role that trauma can play in people's lives allows us to shift our perspective from *what's wrong with them* to *what happened to them*. This perspective is less judgmental and more conducive to creating a welcoming library. It broadens our ability to be patient without hesitancy and flexible in the face of unexpected behavior because we come to understand that it may not be personal or even intentional.

A trauma-informed framework operates on the principles of safety; trustworthiness; peer support; collaboration and mutuality; empowerment, voice, and choice; and cultural, historical, and gender issues.[9] Applying these can involve the following practices:

- scanning for microaggressions and actively preventing bullying
- being honest, respectful, and consistent with individuals with DD
- allowing supportive peer networks to meet in the library
- involving patrons with DD in the planning of programs, materials, and services

- acknowledging and addressing the complexities of intersectionality
- offering sensory tools in the library

We discuss sensory tools at length in the next chapter.

This is just the barest introduction to trauma-informed practices in libraries. If you are interested in learning more, look to Rebecca Tolley's book *A Trauma-Informed Approach to Library Services.*[10]

CULTURALLY INCLUSIVE LIBRARIES (CILs)

Another important concept, culturally inclusive libraries (CILs), derives from culturally relevant education (CRE). Both acknowledge the vast diversity of humanity, and CILs reflect and incorporate the cultures of their communities. They are comfortable and welcoming for all users no matter their life experiences. Teens with cerebral palsy (CP) may feel alienated from the library because they cannot easily access the top row of books or because they do not see themselves reflected in book displays. CILs address both types of barriers.

Culturally inclusive libraries should have these qualities:

- socially . . . empowering . . .
- multidimensional . . .
- validating of everyone's culture
- socially, emotionally and politically comprehensive . . .
- transformative . . .
- emancipatory . . .[11]

CILs reject the idea of a single cultural norm and understand that insisting on only one alienates a significant number of potential patrons.

To understand what a CIL looks like, consider these suggestions from the Alaska Library Association's *Culturally Responsive Guidelines for Alaska Public Libraries*:

- "[B]e open and inviting to all members of the community."
- Utilize "local expertise."
- Sponsor "ongoing activities and events that observe cultural traditions."
- Involve "local . . . representatives in deliberations and decision making."
- Have programming based on the "expressed needs of the community."
- "[R]each out and adapt delivery to meet local needs."[12]

In CILs, librarians do not assume they know what people want. Services and programs are developed, planned, and led in partnership with local stakeholders, including adults with DD. For example, Inclusive Services at Brooklyn Public Library (BPL) reached out to self-advocates, community organizations, educators, and faith-based organizations to plan a conference on autism. Those invested in the planning provided speakers, resource tables, and discussion facilitators and helped with publicizing the event. It was a community partner who suggested the break-out section Sex, Sexuality, and Gender Identity that attracted an overflow crowd. A capacity crowd attended the whole event, demonstrating the effectiveness of addressing the needs of community members in partnership with them.

Materials selection is also a crucial part of creating a CIL. Purchasing books in a variety of languages and in several formats, including audio, braille, and graphic editions helps ensure inclusion. Bernadette Lear, behavioral sciences and education librarian and coordinator of library instruction at Penn State's Harrisburg campus realized this when she was approached by the director of Career Studies, an on-campus certificate program for students with DD. Unsure of what to do to serve these students, her first concern was with collections. She mused, "[T]hese are adults. What sort of books should I be purchasing for these folks? They aren't children. They have adult interests." She concluded, "Things that are adult, aligned with the program's curriculum."[13] She ended up purchasing materials intended for English language learners and new adult readers, graphic fiction and nonfiction, some audiobooks, and some downloadable books, and when she realized students needed help accessing these materials, she created a LibGuide for them.

In addition to accessible formats, CILs select materials whose content represents the experiences of everyone in the community and highlights them throughout the year, not just during commemorative periods, such as Disability History, Black History, or Autism Awareness/Acceptance Month. Being a CIL means that we purchase books whose characters have varied backgrounds and ones by authors writing from their lived experiences. We select the biographies of presidents JFK and FDR that discuss their disabilities and the books about Greta Thunberg that introduce her autism. We display and showcase those books so that everybody sees themselves represented in the library.

INTERSECTIONALITY

To be effective, CILs must also acknowledge that people have multiple identities. Audre Lorde once said, "There is no such thing as a single-issue struggle because we do not live single-issue lives,"[14] yet we tend to think of people with disabilities as a monolithic group. For example, the predominant image of a person with autism is a white, elementary school–age boy. There are autistic women and autistic people of color, but a 2021 Google image search for the term *autism* yielded images that were 74 percent white and 64 percent male. This misrepresentation is mirrored in the media; most autistic characters in television and movies are white males, yet the actual incidence rates, as collected by the CDC, tell a different story.[15]

This lack of representation can be further alienating to those who are excluded:

> We—the autistics of color—are seldom acknowledged. Our faces, bodies, and voices are conspicuously absent from not only literature and media, but also from much of the discourse surrounding race *and* that of autism as well. And when we do appear, we are rarely depicted favorably. We are painted as defective, flawed, undesirable, different. To be pitied. Not only are we non-white, but we are also disabled too? Uh oh (or wahala–o!).[16]

Stereotyping and the lack of representation in popular culture and the media are just one part of the picture. Children with multiple identities get fewer and poorer special education services and have worse outcomes, receiving traditional diplomas at a much lower rate than their white peers.[17] Barriers and uncertainties make it hard for intersectional people to be deemed competent and to get the help that they need for themselves or for a family member. One autistic multiracial mother had to switch doctors three times before she

> found a private psychologist, who respected me and my son enough to listen, test and confirm my suspicions. . . . At times I do wonder— did I not get adequate help/treatment because I am a POC [person of color]? Did I end up getting help because my son is not technically a POC? Did I not express the seriousness of my concerns properly at the time because of my disability (Autism)?[18]

The lack of representation can also contribute to feelings of isolation and despair. In a graphic essay, Mercedes "Cibby" Acosta describes her experience as a "Monster Girl":

> I'm told I'm just "un poco differente" by my parents. I'm told by everyone else I'm a freak. . . . I know one thing for sure. I'm not the only "monster" out there. We just have to find each other. Then we can be scared together. And maybe one day, not at all.[19]

While her isolation is clear, so is her hope to find others and connect to them. Our libraries can play a role here.

Many, many people do not fit the accepted stereotypes of disability, including those who are gender queer. According to pediatric neuropsychologist John Strang, one study found that a higher percentage of autistic people compared to the controls wish to be "of the opposite sex." Strang quotes a person with these various identities, who says:

> I'm Kristy. I'm a Black, genderqueer autistic. . . . I've tried to fit in with all of the so-called "cool kids" when I was in school. . . . Act your age. Be straight. Don't stim. . . . If I had a time machine . . . I wouldn't try so hard to mold myself into a person whom I was not meant to be. . . . [N]ow I don't care what people think of me. I stim freely. I wear what I feel comfortable in. I am an out and proud queer non-binary person. And I love kids' TV shows and movies like *The Lego Movie*. If people can't accept those things, that's their problem, not mine.[20]

BEST PRACTICES FOR ADDRESSING INTERSECTIONALITY

Morénike Giwa Onaiwu suggests the following:

- Listen to and welcome the stories and insights that autistic people of color have to share with us.
- Provide a safe space and platform for autistic people of color and make it a point to hear their voices with sincerity.
- Be the change. It only takes one person, and then another, and another . . . to clear away old thought patterns and ignorance and to provide fertile grounds for new approaches. . . .
- Monitor assumptions and realize that an approach that works for one person might not work for another.
- Invite autistic people of color to speak at . . . [events] that bring the very people together who can enact significant changes.
- Brainstorm your own creative ideas and then run them by autistic people of color.

Source: Morénike Giwa Onaiwu, "Preface: Autistics of Color: We Exist . . . We Matter," in *All the Weight of Our Dreams: On Living Racialized Autism,* ed. Lydia X. Z. Brown, E. Ashkenazy, and Morénike Giwa Onaiwu (Lincoln, NE: DragonBee, 2017), xiv.

Sexual orientation is another aspect of identity that is often overlooked in people with DD. At a library-sponsored conference on bullying at Brooklyn Public Library, one self-advocate with an intellectual disability talked about his experiences in school. He told everyone that he had been bullied, not because of his disability, but because he was gay, a part of his identity he had not previously revealed. It was a narrative no one expected, and people were shocked. But why? The answer lies, at least in part, in the commonly held myth that people with DD are not sexual beings like everyone else.

We need to listen to people with DD and other marginalized identities and make sure they have a seat at the table. We also need intersectional materials in our collections and programs, because as library staff we understand the importance of offering people the right book at the right time. Onaiwu points out the impact the right book can have:

> I was a minority group within a minority group within a minority group within a minority group! . . . Even those who accepted me, cared for me, loved me still did not understand me. Having something of my very own, like the anthology [*All the Weight of Our Dreams*] by people and for people who were like me . . . just as different . . . would have been inexplicably meaningful.[21]

Libraries are the place where everyone belongs, the place where you see yourself, the place where you find that perfect book. To accomplish this, we must commit to libraries that are CILs and that operate more broadly from a culture of inclusion.

NOTES

1. Michael Heron, "Board Games with Great Lessons for Accessible Design," Meeple Like Us (website), July 15, 2019, https://meeplelikeus.co.uk/games-with-great-design-lessons -for-accessibility/2/.
2. Alice Knapp, personal communication, October 29, 2019.
3. Sara Leuterman (@slooterman), Twitter, September 4, 2019.
4. Institute for Human Centered Design (IHCU), "Inclusive Design: History," www.human centereddesign.org/inclusive-design/history.
5. IHCU, "Inclusive Design: Principles," www.humancentereddesign.org/inclusive-design/ principles.
6. CAST, "About Universal Design for Learning," www.cast.org/impact/universal-design -for-learning-udl.
7. Project Zero, Harvard Graduate School of Education, "Multiple Intelligences," www.pz .harvard.edu/projects/multiple-intelligences.

8. Steve Marcal and Shawn Trifoso, *A Trauma-Informed Toolkit for Providers in the Field of Intellectual and Developmental Disabilities* (Philadelphia: Center of Disabilities Services, 2017).

9. Center for Preparedness and Response, "Infographic: 6 Guiding Principles to a Trauma-Informed Approach," Centers for Disease Control and Prevention, last reviewed September 17, 2020, www.cdc.gov/cpr/infographics/6_principles_trauma_info.htm.

10. Rebecca Tolley, *A Trauma-Informed Approach to Library Services* (Chicago: ALA Editions, 2020).

11. Brittany Aronson and Judson Laughter, "The Theory and Practice of Culturally Relevant Education: A Synthesis of Research across Content Areas," *Review of Educational Research* 86, no. 1 (March, 2016), 165.

12. Alaska Library Association, *Culturally Responsive Guidelines for Alaska Public Libraries*, (Alaska Native Issues Roundtable, last revised 2018), https://akla.org/publications/culturally-responsive-guidelines/.

13. Bernadette Lear, personal communication, October 19, 2019.

14. BlackPast, "(1982) Audre Lorde, Learning from the 60s," BlackPast.org (online reference center), August 12, 2012, www.blackpast.org/african-american-history/1982-audre-lorde-learning-60s/.

15. National Institute of Mental Health (NIMH), "Prevalence of Autism Spectrum Disorder (ASD) in 8-year-olds (2014)," www.nimh.nih.gov/health/statistics/files/autism-table_155274.pdf.

16. Morénike Giwa Onaiwu, "Preface: Autistics of Color: We Exist, We Matter," in *All the Weight of Our Dreams: On Living Racialized Autism,* ed. Lydia X. Z. Brown, E. Ashkenazy, and Morénike Giwa Onaiwu (Lincoln, NE: DragonBee, 2017), xi.

17. Emmanuel Felton, "Special Education's Hidden Racial Gap," *The Hechinger Report,* November 25, 2017, https://hechingerreport.org/special-educations-hidden-racial-gap/.

18. Kelly Johnson, "On Race, Diagnosis and Privilege," in Brown, Ashkenazy, and Onaiwu, *All the Weight of Our Dreams,* 129–30.

19. Mercedes "Cibby" Acosta, quoted in Helene Fischer, "Monster Girl," in Brown, Ashkenazy, and Onaiwu, *All the Weight of Our Dreams,* 255–58.

20. John Strang, "Why We Need to Respect Sexual Orientation, Gender Diversity in Autism," *Spectrum,* November 27, 2018, www.spectrumnews.org/opinion/viewpoint/need-respect-sexual-orientation-gender-diversity-autism/.

21. E. Ashkenazy, "Foreword: On Autism and Race," in Brown, Ashkenazy, and Onaiwu, *All the Weight of Our Dreams,* xxxviii.

CHAPTER 3

Accessibility Tools and the Library Environment

In their efforts to comply with the law and welcome people with disabilities, libraries often focus on providing ramps and other physical accommodations. But not all barriers are physical. Barriers stem from the ways in which ableism is embedded in all of our practices. As wheelchair user Eddie Ndopu notes, "What makes a space accessible is the empathy, connection, freedom and possibility it engenders for people of all abilities and identities to come together."[1] Libraries must also pay attention to the sensory environment if they want to create the type of welcoming space Ndopu describes.

For some people, the beep or thunk of the self-checkout machine, the whir of a vent fan, the vibrations from suspended floors, the sounds of children talking, or the feel of paper may be overwhelming. For others, the hushed tones of the library, the need to sit still, or the dullness of gray carpets can result in a craving for sensory input. The visual environment is also important. Is it distracting? Does it facilitate or impede what we are trying to do? Creating a welcoming environment also means understanding and supporting the use of tools that assist patrons to self-regulate and communicate.

FIDGETS

Fidgets, probably the most widely known and accepted sensory tool, help people self-regulate. They are most often associated with autistic people, but they are used by many others. Stress balls and the fidget spinners that were all the rage a few years ago are examples, although almost anything that can be manipulated by hand can work as a fidget. Carrie has many favorites, including bubble wrap, and Barbara likes to introduce people to chenille sticks, also known as pipe cleaners.

Fidgets provide tactile input, and they can be calming as well as help with focus and attention, serving the same function that knitting during meetings does for some people. They are frequently available in libraries, often as one of the items in a sensory kit, and they are readily found in stores and online.

SENSORY KITS

Many library sensory kits primarily address the two main types of sensory needs: increased input for sensory seekers and less input for sensory avoiders. For example, the Tranquility Kits at the Undergraduate Library at the University of Illinois at Urbana–Champaign contain therapy bands for sensory input and noise-canceling headphones to block input. The kits at San Francisco Public Library (SFPL) address even more needs. SFPL's Inclusion Tool Kits include not only fidget items like stress balls, finger gel fidgets, tangles, and a squishy ball bracelet but also items like a bumpy gel cushion and a massager to support large muscle (gross motor) activities and a visual timer to help people manage their time in the library. The "Inclusion Tool Kits" web page (https://sfpl.org/services/accessibility-services/accessible -technology/inclusion-tool-kits) describes the contents in detail. Deerfield (IL) Public Library's separate sensory kits for children and adults include emotion sheets in addition to sensory items. When the staff looked to buy pictures of adult faces with varied emotions for these kits, all they could find were ones with children's faces. Their solution was to make their own! Since launching the kits, use of the Deerfield library by autistic patrons has increased. "I don't know if it's the kits or a big push on the part of the library overall," says Vicki Karlovsky, but she believes that the kits play a role in this increase in use.[2]

Some library's kits are for in-house use. These are kept at service points such as reference, children's, and adult services desks. Signs posted at the Deerfield desks read "Sensory Kits . . . No need to ask—take what you need! Please return item when you are done." Although checkout is not required, the staff there try to keep track of what is used, and they discovered that the kits are popular with all patrons, not just those with DD. For example, during finals season they are used by students as they study in the library. In contrast to Deerfield's informal use policy, the Tranquility Kits at the University of Illinois need to be checked out even though they are for in-library use.

Sensory kits make libraries and library programs more accessible in two ways. They send a clear message that people with sensory issues are welcome, and the items in the kits can help patrons stay calm while in the library and focused during programs. Sensory tools can block noise during loud programs and energize

COMMON SENSORY TOOLS

Items that help sensory avoiders:

- noise-canceling headphones
- smooth finger gel fidgets
- sunglasses or ball caps to block lights
- weighted blankets, lap pads, or plush toys

Items for sensory seekers:

- a mini massager
- stress balls and other fidgets like tangles
- a vibrating pen like the Squiggle Wiggle Writer
- items with lots of textures
- resistance bands to stretch or tie around chair legs and kick
- gum or mints, if your library allows them

people during quiet ones. At Deerfield, they are available to help people participate in both focused and general programming.

Other libraries circulate sensory kits, allowing patrons to try tools at home before purchasing. Since some items are expensive and everyone isn't comfortable with the same sensory tools, these kits help users avoid making wasteful purchases. They also provide temporary access for patrons who cannot afford them. These patrons can then be referred to the local Assistive Technology Act Technical Assistance and Training (AT3) Center for further assistance. You can find your center at www.at3center.net/stateprogram.

Public libraries in Nova Scotia worked with Autism Nova Scotia to develop a variety of circulating kits that each focus on a different need. Their Sensory Kit has many of the standard sensory kit tools, including items for both sensory seekers and sensory avoiders. The Fidget Tools Kit has items that can help people stay focused during programs. Neighboring province Prince Edward Island (PEI) also developed its own set of circulating kits, which are seen as valuable resources for people with Alzheimer's, attention deficit hyperactivity disorder (ADHD), and dementia. The Arapahoe Libraries in Colorado circulate their kits in backpacks. Whether or not your kits circulate, it is a good idea to disinfect the items after each use.

SENSORY ROOMS AND SPACES

While sensory kits provide portable tools for any environment, sensory rooms are immersive, site-specific experiences. Known alternatively as sensory, meditation, quiet, or reflection rooms, these spaces allow people to center themselves and focus. As seen by their various names and in the best traditions of universal design, sensory-friendly spaces in libraries serve multiple audiences and can be used in a variety of ways. The Reflection Room in the Health Sciences Library at the University of Arizona, created in response to student requests for a place to pray other than between shelves, was designed to facilitate quiet reflection and meditation. The Comfort Room at the Ramsey County Library in Shoreview, Illinois, advertises that it is a sensory-friendly space for anyone, including nursing mothers, in need of a calm space. Whatever they are called, these types of spaces meet a variety of patron needs.

Like sensory kits, sensory rooms can cater to both sensory seekers and sensory avoiders. The Undergraduate Library at the University of Illinois at Urbana–Champaign has two Reflection Rooms developed by health science librarian J. J. Pionke. The first is a calming space, equipped with a white noise machine, a yoga mat, and a cushion, which encourage mediation and prayer. The second allows for sensory input when people need it, with a rocking chair and a fixture that can provide lighting across the visual spectrum. The rooms can be booked by students using an internal reservation system and Tranquility Kits can be used to enhance the Reflection Room experience.

Public libraries also have sensory-friendly spaces. The Louisville (OH) Public Library's Sensory Strategy Spaces, funded through a Library Services and Technology (LSTA) grant, are spaces "whose visual and auditory environment is controlled and designed for children and adults on the [autism] spectrum."[3] One side addresses the needs of patrons who are feeling overstimulated with a soothing wall color, dim lights, and yoga mats. The other focuses on the needs of people who seek stimulation. That side includes a balance beam, musical vibration bench, and touch wall. When these spaces opened, they were an instant success, attracting the annual goal of 1,000 people in the first week.[4]

The Grapevine (TX) Public Library Sensory Zone is a circular space that connects the three main areas of the library: the children's room, adult room, and circulation area. The Sensory Zone has components for both sensory avoiders and sensory seekers. Gel tiles, low lighting levels, a weaving wall, and a cozy canoe are all popular calming items in the Sensory Zone. For people looking for sensory input, touch-activated light activities, sandpaper-textured blocks, and LEGOs are also available. One patron with Tourette's syndrome approached a staff member asking, "Sometime I want to read out in the open. Is it OK if I use the sensory room?" Director Ruth Chiego commented, "We are giving somebody a place that they previously never had."[5]

Although they often are, sensory spaces do not have to be rooms. Three of the branches of the Essex Libraries in Great Britain have sensory walls. According to the libraries' website, the walls have an activity panel, an infinity tunnel, an interactive LED light panel, mirrors, and an interactive video floor. Designed to support people with a variety of needs, the wall area is flexible, and it can be enclosed to make a sensory room. Other libraries fill a small area like a tent or section of a room with sensory tools, creating an inexpensive sensory retreat space. Even just having space in the room for those who need to pace or stim can create a sensory-friendly environment.

Programming in Sensory Rooms

Some libraries do programming in their sensory rooms. The staff at the Louisville (KY) Public Library host sensory storytimes, teen sensory relaxation sessions, and sensory chair yoga for adults in theirs. Yoga programs are commonly held in academic library sensory rooms. At the Grapevine library, the Champions program, done in collaboration with a day habilitation program, takes place in the Sensory Zone. Champions starts with an activity, such as a drumming circle or puppet show, and then the group disperses to activity stations so people can explore their own interests. Participants plan the next program before leaving. According to Chiego, "We suggest ideas and they suggest ideas and we . . . end up morphing the things together."[6]

Sensory-Friendly Browsing

The Northwest Library in Columbus, Ohio, goes one step further, making the entire library sensory friendly for a program developed and marketed in partnership with the Autism Society of Central Ohio (ASCO). Once a quarter the library opens only to people with autism. Before the program, staff are offered training so they are able to meet the needs of those who come. Registered patrons receive a social story to help them prepare for the program. Other changes made within the library include the following:

- turning the lights down and relying on natural lighting
- shutting off the hand dryers in the restrooms
- not permitting loud carts on the floor
- offering visual aids

ITEMS FOR SENSORY SPACES

For calming spaces:
- adjustable lights
- noise-canceling headphone
- white noise machines
- weighted blankets or lap pads
- yoga mats
- fidgets
- carpets
- pillows or cushions
- nature pictures
- plants

For stimulating spaces:
- adjustable lights
- therapy or resistance bands
- medicine balls
- balance beams
- rocking chairs
- bright therapy lights
- vibrating seats
- balancing cushions
- musical touch walls
- balance pads
- bright colors

During the event patrons can browse, check out books, use the computers, or do whatever else they want to do at the library. In part because of outreach done by ASCO, "They come from all over Columbus. We want them to know that we understand who you are . . . and we want you to come," explains Kristin DeMay, adult services library associate, adding, "We have regulars who come . . . [and] we have people who started coming to the browsing hours and now come during normal hours."[7]

VISUAL SUPPORTS

People with DD are often visual learners, and librarians who work with these patrons have learned that providing visual supports is helpful in programming. According to the Rutgers Cooperative Extension website, visual supports "enhance learning by helping visual learners understand activities, tasks, directions, and discussions . . . [they] facilitate attention-getting; make ideas and concepts more concrete; aid in recall of verbal information; serve as effective prompts; cue appropriate behavior; and ultimately facilitate independence."[8] Overall, they reinforce communication and can reduce frustration and anxiety.

Visual schedules are one useful type of visual support. An agenda can list program elements that are checked off as they are completed. Providing a written or, even better, a pictorial guide to the steps in a craft or maker session can also be supportive to everyone in a program, including English language learners and new adult readers. Instructions should be in easy-to-understand plain language and the steps should be simple. Use large print, fourteen point or bigger, with lots of white space. When you create these types of visual supports, think of a cookbook and how the steps of a recipe are laid out and often illustrated to guide you. You can use commercially available products, such as Boardmaker, or create your own visuals with clip art, photographs, or simple drawings.

Visual supports can be found in the Nova Scotia Libraries Visual Tools kit, which, among other items, includes sand timers and visual clocks, sequencing cards, and a daily schedule template. Nova Scotia's kits circulate, but the tools in them can also be useful in programming. First/Then cards, which indicate the sequence of activities, and the schedule template can be used to create visual schedules for programs, and the timers can help participants keep track of time allotted for activities like crafts. Both tools can help people with executive functioning issues and those with some mental health issues attend to the content of programs with less anxiety.

Another aspect of visual support during programs is minimizing distractions. Eliminate items like colorful posters and extraneous objects in program rooms, even if this requires covering them. Have a focal point for the program. Help attendees with joint attention (focusing on a presenter) by presenting from the front of the room and orienting seating to face you.

COMMUNICATION AIDS

People with DD may have communication barriers and use augmentative and alternative communication instead of or to supplement verbal communication. When they do, they will usually bring their own communication devices or aids to the library. The role of library staff is to have enough familiarity with common ones to be able to communicate effectively with these patrons. This is important because communicating directly is always preferable to communicating through someone else.

It is also useful for libraries to offer some AAC devices for in-library use and to make these items available at public service desks and during programs. The tools to keep on hand can be low-tech or high-tech. The simplest low-tech tools are pen and paper or whiteboard and marker. If someone has difficulty getting words out verbally, is nonspeaking, or does not speak English, having simple writing tools available can make all the difference. Picture Exchange Communication System (PECS) cards are also useful to have on hand to assist with communication. Ready-made ones can be purchased online, or you can create your own using common library words or phrases and ones that convey your library's behavioral expectations.

A free, downloadable communication guide that you can use can be found on the Libraries and Autism: We're Connected website (http://librariesandautism .org/newresources.htm). The guide includes common library phrases in pictograms, English, Spanish, and the manual alphabet.

The simplest high-tech solution to have on offer is the iPad or other tablet. There are a number of AAC apps that you can load onto these devices to turn them into communication tools. Some, like Proloquo2Go, can be pricey, but others are less expensive, and there are even free options on the market that you can find easily through an online search. The system your local school district uses is the one that adults with DD in your area are most likely to know, so reach out to the district to find out what that is before purchasing anything. When Barbara lived in Connecticut, she relied on the New England Adaptive Technology Center (NEAT) at Oak Hill in Hartford for guidance on these types of tools, and Carrie relies on the TechWorks Center in Brooklyn. NEAT and TechWorks are part of the federally funded Assistive Technology Centers available in each state. You can find your local AT3 Center online at www.at3center.net/stateprogram.

The success of your library's programming for people with DD will in part depend on the environment you create and the tools you provide. By addressing the whole library, from the architecture and sensory features to how you communicate and present material, you can truly eliminate barriers for adults with DD and for others. When you do so, your programs are likely to run more smoothly and your patrons will find it easier to participate in and enjoy what you offer them.

NOTES

1. Eddie Ndopu, "It's Time to Rethink the Language of Accessibility—And to Imagine a More Equitable World," *Time,* May 21, 2020, https://time.com/5839846/rethink-the-language -accessibility-more-equal/.
2. Vicki Karlovsky, personal communication, May 16, 2020.
3. Michael Damron, "A Sensory Wonderland: A Programming Space for the Special Needs Community," *American Libraries,* June 3, 2019, https://americanlibrariesmagazine.org/ 2019/06/03/a-sensory-wonderland/.
4. Damron, "A Sensory Wonderland."
5. Ruth Chiego, personal communication, March 31, 2020.
6. Chiego, pers. comm.
7. Kristin DeMay, personal communication, April 8, 2020.
8. Jeannette Rea-Keywood and Michelle F. Brill, "Developmental Disabilities Series: Visual Supports," Cooperative Extension Fact Sheet FS1287, New Jersey Agricultural Experiment Station, Rutgers University, https://njaes.rutgers.edu/fs1287/.

PART II

Preparing for Programming

CHAPTER 4

Determining Programming Needs

As we mentioned earlier, programing for adults with DD is often haphazard and rarely planned. It behooves us to plan our programs to ensure that what we offer fits our libraries and meets the needs and interests of our communities. A robust planning and evaluation process will also ensure that our programs continue beyond the tenure of the staff member who started them.

INTERNAL CAPACITY ASSESSMENT

In a book about programming for adults, library director Brett W. Lear defines programming as "a process by which the informational, educational, and recreational needs of your patrons are met by bringing patrons into contact with the human resources best able to meet those needs."[1] Programming goes beyond what is offered; it also includes the support mechanisms for bringing patrons and human resources together. All of these elements are examined in an internal assessment.

Strategic Plan and Policies

Lear explains why and how to create programming that aligns with a library's mission and priorities. Because programming for adults with DD should not be an add-on, this is a good place to start an assessment. Does your strategic plan and mission statement include language that supports full inclusion for people with disabilities? If your library has a written programming policy, does it mention diversity and inclusion, specifically the inclusion of people with disabilities? Do other policies and services also reflect this commitment?

Some libraries do a good job with this. Arapahoe Libraries embedded their commitment to equitable service in their 2019 strategic plan, listing *inclusivity* as one of four areas of focus, the first on the list. Their plan also talked about, in a review of accomplishments from the previous year, the new diversity and inclusion outreach specialist staff position, work on inclusion with consultants from Equity Project, and the Library for All program for patrons with DD. Librarian Grace Walker says of Pickerington Public Library in Ohio:

> [I]nclusion is a priority . . . [and] the library . . . strives to be as inclusive as possible in all efforts. That includes updating our policies when appropriate, supporting staff training or awareness when possible, offering a variety of accessible materials within our collection for checkout, events and programming, and making the library a safe, accessible public place for all customers and community members.[2]

What she is describing is a culture of inclusion that manifests in many areas of the library's operations and policies.

Existing Adult Programs

Another thing to consider is the types of programs your library already offers adult patrons. Do you have speakers, panel discussions, workshops, demonstrations, hands-on classes, live performances, exhibits, technology and maker programs, book clubs and discussions, film showings, or wellness programs? Which are most popular? Look back at what the library has offered over the past year or two to see where you can make existing programs more inclusive. Are there any programs that adults with DD already attend? If so, what is their appeal? Then think about where you might introduce parallel programs for adults with DD. This review can help you begin to ensure that programming for adults with DD is an integral part of your overall programming.

Available Materials and Services

The internal capacity assessment should also ascertain what services and materials your library already has for adults with DD and what is missing. Consider questions like these:

- Are individuals or groups of adults with DD regular library users? What materials and services do they use during visits?

- Does your website welcome people with disabilities in an accessible way?
- Are sensory tools like fidgets and noise-canceling headphones and low-tech assistive technology available at public service desks and at programs?
- Are all program fliers accessible and do they encourage people with disabilities to participate?
- Does the library have collections that are especially suitable for adults with DD, such as large-print books, book and audio pairs, or hi-lo material?
- Do staff teach patrons how to slow the speed of downloadable audiobooks or use accessibility features on library technology?

Programming Space and Resources

Assess the degree to which the library's physical space and resources allow for inclusion:

- Can the program room be configured to accommodate people who need wheelchairs and walkers or people who need to pace or stim?
- Does the library have adaptive supplies such as easy-to-grip scissors, pencil grips, and highlighter strips for reading?
- Is Boardmaker software or other means of producing visual supports available?
- What type of lighting is available in program rooms? Is there an alternative to fluorescent lighting? Is it easy to dim lights if needed?
- Are quiet or sensory spaces or rooms available? Are there places where a patron can make noise if needed?

Personnel Resources

Determine what staff support is available for programming:

- Are staff trained in inclusion? Do staff and volunteers feel comfortable and prepared to work respectfully with adults with DD?
- Does the library have an accessibility, outreach, or programming specialist who can help with planning and participant recruitment?
- Is there a working staff accessibility or inclusion committee?
- Is there a regular pool of volunteer helpers to draw on or will they need to be recruited?

It is best to get answers to these questions from more than one staff member.

As librarian Lisa G. Kropp advises:

> [A]sk staff members to answer the same questions so you can compare the results. You should also ask your supervisor and/or another building administrator to look at the questions. Others often see the larger picture beyond one specific library department and offer a different perspective.[3]

The answers to these questions should help you develop a plan that is realistic for your unique institution.

EXTERNAL NEEDS ASSESSMENT

Go into the Community

After evaluating what your library already has in place, look at what is available in your community. This will help you avoid duplication of effort and ensure that community members have a range of options available to them. The external assessment offers a secondary benefit; it is a good excuse for reaching out to service providers, helping you start to develop relationships that can lead to productive programming partnerships. Most libraries that offer programming for adults with DD have such partnerships and find them a vital element in programming success. Before you reach out into the community though, Kropp suggests you do some exploring in the University of Kansas's Community Tool Box, found online at https://ctb.ku.edu/en/toolkits.[4] It has hundreds of free resources in both Spanish and English that can help guide you in developing surveys, focus groups, and other assessments.

Start your outreach with an online search for places where people with DD hang out in your community. Contact your local Recreation Department to ascertain if they offer programming for people with DD. Reach out to community organizations like YMCAs and community centers. Contact some local speech or occupational therapists to see if they know of any local programs. See what the Special Education Department of your local school district offers for transitioning students aged eighteen to twenty-one. Talk to local residential and day programs that serve adults with DD. All of this research should let you know if you live in a community that is rich with offerings or in a programming desert—useful information as you move forward in your planning.

Naperville (IL) Public Library reached out to local community groups and school transition programs after a strategic planning process ascertained that people with disabilities were underserved by the library. That outreach led to, among other things, the development and successful launch in 2019 of the Sensory NPL app. In addition to items like event listings, found on most library websites, the app has specialized information, including a map of each branch and notes about busy times and available assistive technology. This app was developed by an outside vendor, InfiniTeach, and cost $5,000 per year, and the strategic plan made it possible. If that price is prohibitive, consider using an in-house expert or academic intern to develop your own app.

Nothing about Us without Us

Feedback from adults with DD is at the core of this process. Make sure to talk to advocates/allies, parents, and service providers as well. Use instruments you find in the aforementioned Community Tool Box or elsewhere to help elicit the social, recreational, and informational needs and interests that might be addressed by library programming. Just make sure to keep language clear, concrete, and simple and any research instrument you use short, to make it easy for adults with DD to respond. Paul T. Jaeger, library science professor from the University of Maryland, says, "[A]ll library activities related to disability can be enhanced by interviewing disabled people and incorporating those . . . perspectives directly into development and refinement of such activities."[5] In fact, these perspectives are not just useful—they are essential.

TIPS FOR INVOLVING THE DD COMMUNITY
- Talk with patrons and caregivers who already use the library.
- Design pen-and-paper or digital surveys and make them available at public service desks.
- Send surveys to community agencies for completion by staff and the people they serve.
- Conduct formal in-person, online, or telephone interviews with adults with DD, caregivers/parents, and agency staff.
- Facilitate focus groups or community conversations.
- Create an advisory board that includes people with DD.

Focus groups, community conversations, and advisory boards promise to yield the most detail and the richest information. Bringing self-advocates, parents, caregivers, and service providers together to discuss their needs and wishes can leave you with some great ideas. Even better, hold separate sessions for each group. Self-advocates may feel they can express themselves more freely with their peers, and the same may be true for agency representatives or parents. For example, agencies that bring groups of adults to the library sometimes tell librarians that they are interested in educational and therapeutic programs, but librarians report that the adults with DD who come to their programs often just want to have fun. If they disagree with the desires of parents and agency personnel, adults with DD may have difficulty expressing their preferences in a mixed group. Another caution: if you hold a focus group for parents and caregivers, be sure to have volunteers available in another room and appropriate activities to engage their adult children during the session. Otherwise, many of these parents will not be able to attend.

Sacramento (CA) Public Library provides an example of what can happen as a result of talking with and listening to people with disabilities and their families. The library hosted community conversations using the model designed for ALA by the Harwood Institute for Public Innovation.[6]

During the sessions, people with disabilities said:

- People don't see me as a person with ideas to share.
- I feel alone and isolated.
- We need to create an environment where it is ok to be different.
- I fear being judged.[7]

Several themes emerged:

- We want to be accepted and included in our community.
- We need a central, trusted hub of information and resources.
- We need more opportunities to become involved in community activities and programs.[8]

Based on this information, the library made a series of changes to improve service to adults with DD. They created a staff AccessABILITY Team and seven regional AccessABILITY "Hub" libraries to serve as models of inclusion and offer a variety of focused programs, resources, and services for people with disabilities. Staff Ambassadors at the Hubs are prepared to mentor and train others, creating a mechanism for spreading AccessABILITY programming to other branches in the system. For this initiative, among others, in 2019 the Sacramento Public Library was awarded the inaugural Jerry Kline Community Impact Prize.

Once you complete both an internal and external assessment, you should have a much clearer picture of your library and community and what stakeholders want to see at the library. The next step is to develop partnerships that can help you transform the good ideas you identified into reality.

NOTES

1. Brett W. Lear, *Adult Programs in the Library,* 2nd ed. (Chicago: ALA Editions, 2013), xv.
2. Grace Walker, personal communication, January 12, 2020.
3. Lisa G. Kropp, "Know Your Neighborhood: A Community Needs Assessment Primer," *School Library Journal,* June 21, 2014, www.slj.com/?detailStory=know-your-neighbor hood-a-community-needs-assessment-primer.
4. Kropp, "Know Your Neighborhood."
5. Paul T. Jaeger, "Designing for Diversity and Designing for Disability: New Opportunities for Libraries to Expand Their Support and Advocacy for People with Disabilities," *International Journal of Information, Diversity, and Inclusion* 2, no. 1–2 (2018): 59. https://jps.library.utoronto.ca/index.php/ijidi/article/view/32211/24620.
6. American Library Association and Harwood Institute for Public Innovation, *Libraries Trans-forming Communities: Community Conversation Workbook,* www.ala.org/tools/sites/ ala.org.tools/files/content/LTC_ConvoGuide_updated_final2.pdf.
7. Sacramento Public Library, "AccessABILITY Awareness: *Focus on People First,*" training mate-rials provided by Amy Little; quoted with permission.
8. Sacramento Public Library, "AccessABILITY Awareness."

CHAPTER 5

Working with Stakeholders

Programming for adults with developmental disabilities will probably entail meeting and working with an array of people. While it is vitally important to know how to communicate directly with the adults with DD whom you encounter, by itself that will not be sufficient to guarantee success. Your programming efforts are much more likely to be successful if you also understand and know how to work with the many others who support adults with DD, including those who accompany them to the library.

ENGAGING COMMUNITY SELF-ADVOCATES

"Nothing about us without us!" is one of the seminal demands of the disability rights movement, and libraries that take up this rallying cry can both build better programs and broaden their audiences. Inclusive Services at Brooklyn Public Library (IS/BPL) embraces this idea, and the IS/BPL advisory board includes self-advocates, people with disabilities who speak up for themselves and others. IS/BPL also sponsors a monthly program for a local self-advocacy group called Voices of Power. Participants come from schools, from day habilitation programs (also known as day habs), or on their own. The program is cofacilitated by an Inclusive Services staff member and Trina Hazell, a disability rights self-advocate and former Miss Wheelchair for New York State. The group plans its own monthly programs. A couple of times a year, one of the facilitators asks the group what they would like to cover and who they would like to invite to the program. In case no ideas are generated by the group, the facilitators have some suggestions ready. Many topics have come out of these discussions, including voter registration, sexual health, transition planning, money management, and the U.S. Census. A couple of parties and board game programs have also resulted from these sessions.

When BPL went online in spring 2020, Voices of Power took a short break and then resumed its program using Zoom. This was problematic because many of the regulars do not have reliable Internet access. In fact, many of them use the library to access technology. Therefore, it was critical to use a platform with good phone-in access. It was also difficult to get invitations for virtual programs into the hands of the intended audience, so IS/BPL talked to as many individuals with DD, agencies, and family members as they could reach. In the end you may discover that attendance comes primarily from word of mouth, and reaching out to these groups is a great way to generate it.

To build word of mouth, try to identify and connect with your local gatekeeper, that key self-advocate who has access to other people with DD in your area. In Brooklyn that person is Christopher D. Grief, an adult with an intellectual disability and one-time cochair of Brooklyn Family Support Service Advisory Council. He has a vast network of contacts in the DD community that he uses to spread the word about library programs. He also distributes Inclusive Services' leaflets at events that the library staff are not able to attend. If you have trouble identifying your local gatekeeper, try reaching out to some of the resources for staff training that we discuss in the Finding Presenters section in chapter 7.

Focus on interacting with people with DD, not their parents, caregivers, or support workers. Once you identify individuals who want to know more, do some trust building with them so you develop equitable relationships. This may take patience and effort because, as Tom Ott points out, "People with disabilities have been 'taught' and have 'learned' . . . to look toward 'others' (non-disabled and well-intentioned people like parents, family members, teachers, social workers, etc.) for confirmation or directions."[1] Ott says that to create more respectful and equitable relationships, you need to take the following approaches:

1. Be Present . . . focus. . . . Make a time that works for both of you.
2. Listen and reflect, rather than go into "solution" mode. . . .
3. Emphasize and use any natural opportunity to demonstrate that we all make mistakes and that learning from our mistakes is sometimes very powerful.
4. Apologize for your mistakes, especially when you may have overstepped your bounds. . . .
5. Emphasize the importance of "trying something." . . .[2]

COMMUNICATING IN PUBLIC LIBRARIES

It is always preferable to communicate directly with adults with DD, and it is not difficult to engage these adults if we apply some basic strategies. Using these strategies can also help educate caregivers about the capabilities of their companion adults with DD.

If an adult patron with DD is accompanied by a caregiver:

- Get to know both the patron and caregiver. Developing relationships of trust is key.
- Use the communication device or other method of nonverbal communication preferred by the patron. Avoid having a caregiver interpret.
- If you are seeking information about the adult with DD, speak to that person directly.
- Try to make eye contact, but do not insist on it.
- Keep your language direct and simple. Speak slowly. Avoid idioms, complex ideas, and multipart directions. Make sure you are understood before continuing. Repeat if necessary.
- Don't allow the caregiver to hijack the conversation. If this happens, gently redirect your attention to the adult with DD.
- Offer choices, but in a limited way. Those who have a history of not being asked for their opinions and preferences may not be able to identify easily what they want. It may take a number of conversations and the introduction of some simple choices to tease out the interests of your patrons with DD.

These conversations are not all that different from conversations you might have with other patrons. Talk to adults with disabilities about the same things you would discuss with anyone else: why they come to the library, what materials they like, their programming interests, and so forth.

COMMUNICATING IN ACADEMIC LIBRARIES

Unlike in public libraries where people with DD often have aides, family members, friends, or staff with them, in academic settings students go to the library on their own and service is more one-on-one. Public libraries have the opportunity to craft positive experiences from the start, but student users of academic libraries often come in for the first time having had earlier negative experiences in libraries. Bernadette Lear from the Penn State Harrisburg library describes this situation in her institution:

> It was really poignant, pretty much down to each person the students
> had a fear of the library . . . that just really struck me. . . . Quite a few had
> had an adverse experience in their public or school library[;] they were
> told[,] "[O]h, just get a book. . . ." No one was really guiding them. . . .
> So there are a lot of challenges to overcome here.[3]

Lear started to overcome the students' mistrust by communicating with them in the ways that were comfortable for them. She said that the students "have their own devices and I have to learn them."[4] She also developed LibGuides on popular topics to assist them in finding resources.

Suzanne Williams was able to create a library from scratch for the College of Adaptive Arts, an unaccredited institution specifically for students with disabilities. She describes how she involved students with DD in the process with great results:

> When I got to a certain point in creating the library I talked to the student
> council and asked if they had any questions. All these hands went up.
> One young man wanted a book about Gordon McGregor. I didn't know
> who he was and had to look him up. . . . When [the student] came to
> the library . . . I was so proud and excited that I could take him right to
> the shelf and pointed to [the book I bought]. . . . Now every time I see

---

BEST PRACTICES FOR MEETING WITH SELF-ADVOCATES
- Make sure everyone knows about the meeting.
- Create all written materials in plain English and alternate formats.
- Anticipate and provide needed accommodations.
- Offer a variety of communication options.
- Have fidgets available.
- Treat everyone with respect.
- Listen; don't talk.
- Be open to new ideas.
- Guide; don't lead.
- Give advice only when asked.
- Facilitate decision making.
- Enable everyone's involvement.
- Take notes.
- Summarize and ask if correct.

him, he asks me[,] "[W]here are the new books." It's . . . about making the space accessible.[5]

PARTNERING WITH COMMUNITY AGENCIES

With very few exceptions, the libraries we contacted for this book program in partnership with, or with input from, local direct-service or advocacy organizations, and they find these collaborations indispensable. As Lisa Powell Williams, adult and young adult services coordinator at Moline (IL) Public Library says, "Our partnerships are why our programs work! Without them, providing these opportunities for community connection would not be possible."[6] Vicki Karlovsky from Deerfield (IL) Public Library points out that these relationships benefit both parties: "They are resources for the library and the library is a resource for them."[7]

Residential and day habilitation programs are constantly looking for opportunities for community engagement, socializing, lifelong learning, and entertainment for the people they serve. Since their budgets are usually small or nonexistent, the local library with its free materials and programming is a wonderful partner for these organizations. In return, these partners can offer the library valuable assistance. Agency staff can

- inform library staff of the needs, abilities, and communication styles of people they serve
- identify activities that might appeal to the people they serve, and which will reinforce activities they are doing at the day or residential program
- let library staff know about gaps in agency programming that the library can fill
- help with recruiting participants and marketing programs
- provide transportation to the library for regular visits or programs
- assist with crafts, room setup, and other aspects of programs that could use additional sets of hands

Sometimes the library initiates the relationship, sometimes the agency. Ideally, the partnership grows and morphs over time. In Deerfield a negative Yelp review written by a person served by the Center for Enriched Living led to a productive partnership between that agency and the public library. Karlovsky saw the negative review and shared it with the library's director who reached out to the center to see what could be done to improve the situation. That contact led to outreach programming, library tours for those served by the agency, a group of volunteers coming from the agency to the library twice a week to dust, a quarterly in-house library program, and regular interactions. In 2016, just a few years after the negative review, the Center for Enriched Living gave the library its Community Partner of the Year award!

The key to success in these partnership-building efforts is ongoing communication and flexibility, and the communication should go beyond contact with the representatives who bring groups or individuals to the library. They are often not the ones with decision-making authority, so it is more effective to reach out to the correct person at the organization with whom you can cultivate an ongoing collaboration. Be aware, though, that staff turnover is common in some of these organizations, and these staff changes could make it difficult to have consistency, in both whom you communicate with and the agency's ability to bring people to the library.

Once you identify a point person, see if you can meet with them at their own facility. Use this meeting to explain what the library has to offer and see if you can establish a mechanism for planning library visits. Explore what they might want from the library. Determine if agency policy is to do everything as a group or if their approach is more person centered. Ascertain if there is flexibility in transportation or scheduling so individuals can come to preferred library activities. Let this discussion inform your program planning. This initial approach will show them that the library wants to work with and support them, and it can form the basis of a productive partnership.

PARTNERING WITH SCHOOL TRANSITION PROGRAMS

Students with disabilities have an individualized education plan (IEP), and they are legally entitled to stay in school until they either graduate from high school or reach age twenty-two. Although planning for transition from school formally begins at age fourteen for these students, many school systems don't actively begin transition programming until students turn eighteen. Transition programs help prepare these students for the adult world they will encounter after they leave school, and they tend to focus more on independent living skills and vocational training than on academics.

Libraries can and do partner with these school transition programs in a number of ways. Some libraries offer in-house and outreach programming for these students, and some teach them job skills through library volunteer work. You will

TIPS FOR WORKING WITH PARTNER ORGANIZATIONS

1. Be aware that patrons with DD often have to be back at their agencies by a set time for medications, planned activities, or shift changes.
2. Plan programs that are worth the agency's effort to organize and transport people, either because they are fun and appealing or because they meet a stated need.
3. Don't duplicate programs that the agencies are already doing.
4. If you don't require registration, be ready for an audience of anywhere from zero to fifty.
5. Don't give up if program attendance is sometimes low. Inclement weather, a shortage of staff or volunteer chaperones, and other barriers may impact these agencies' ability to bring people to your programs on any given day.
6. Be flexible. Groups could arrive very early or very late for programs because of transportation difficulties.
7. Visit the agencies to get a sense of the environment where your patrons spend their time and to do outreach programming.
8. Send regular monthly e-mails to agency staff, offering details about upcoming programs so they can plan for staffing levels, guidelines for dress, and so on.

Source: The first six tips are adapted from "Inclusive Activities for Adults," a handout developed by Candice Casey for Hart (FL) Memorial Library. The final two ideas come from Kayla Kuni, formerly of New Port Richey (FL) Public Library.

find descriptions of a number of these initiatives throughout part III of this book. In addition to more focused efforts, follow Brooklyn Public Library's lead and make a point of inviting students with disabilities to your standard programs and to use your library's services. For example, the BPL's Business and Career Center offers résumé writing, entrepreneurship, and career assistance, and these are marketed to school transition programs. If your local high school transition program staff have not reached out to you, it is worth contacting them to see how to get their students into the library and to find out what you can do to assist the students in preparing for the adult world.

You can also explore whether your partners are interested in virtual library programming for the adults with DD whom they serve. Virtual programs can bypass transportation barriers and allow participation by those adults with DD who might not be able to attend programs at the library. Determine what your partners' connectivity is like and if they have devices that can be used to bring virtual programs to their locations. Ascertain whether you can bring program materials or sensory tools to their facilities for use during programs. Find out if there is room for people to move around or even dance in the room where virtual programs will be accessed. Once you determine that virtual programming is viable for an agency, look to chapter 9 for details about how to do accessible virtual programming and throughout part III for programs that could translate well to a virtual environment.

WORKING WITH PARENTS OR OTHER CAREGIVERS

Parents and other caregivers often have extensive and even legally mandated involvement in the lives of some adults with DD, so library personnel must learn how to interact with them as well. To do so effectively, it is useful to know a bit about traditional relationships between individuals with DD and their caregivers.

Understanding Caregiver Overinvolvement

It is not uncommon for parents, family members, and other caregivers to treat people with DD like children well into adulthood, and some adults with DD who have been deemed incapable of making medical or financial decisions for themselves by courts are assigned legal guardians or conservators. The result is that often the people closest to them underestimate the abilities of these adults and fail to offer them opportunities based on their interests, dreams, and true potential.

Agencies that serve people with DD have been "historically system-driven and focused on what was best for an organization or state agency. . . . As a result, people were given little or no choice about their life and were seen as passive recipients of service."[8] Happily, in some organizations there is a move toward practices that are more person centered, but some encounter barriers when attempting to move in that direction because of pushback from parents, guardians, and even some professionals who try to step in and seek to control outcomes for adults with DD. This is usually done out of concern and love, but such efforts fail to take into account that "there are risks [in any self-directed life]—to take risks is to be human. Denying people with IDD the opportunity to take some risks can, in effect, strip them of a crucial aspect of their humanity."[9]

Maria Town, president and CEO of the American Association of People with Disabilities (AAPD), agrees; she believes that the right to take risks should extend even to those nonhealthy behaviors that most adults indulge in. She explains, "The DD Community talks about the 'dignity of risk'—the idea that taking self-determined reasonable risks [is] essential to personhood." She goes on to say, in reference to streaming movies and eating pizza, "I think we should have a 'dignity of binge' concept."[10]

You may encounter family members, personal care assistants (PCAs), or agency staff members with this overly protective attitude. Agencies with this point of view will most likely expect everyone in their groups to do the same thing regardless of personal interests or abilities. Caregivers may request programming, initiate library visits, or decide where to go in the library on behalf of the adults with DD they accompany, even if those adults are capable of speaking for themselves and have different preferences. Caregivers may insist on materials or programs they are familiar with or that feel safe to them, regardless of what the adults with DD might think. Libraries can respond to these well-meaning but sometimes unnecessary controls by adopting and introducing a more per-son-centered and empowering approach. If the groundwork is laid carefully through open communication and trust building, library staff will be better able to offer more options and opportunities that are likely to appeal to the patrons with DD and to reassure caregivers that these choices pose no threat.

Supporting Positive Caregiver Involvement

Some types of caregiver involvement can be very positive and helpful. Caregiv-ers can serve as allies and advocates and can help adults with DD convey their communication preferences, challenges, strengths, and needs. They can provide transportation to the library for adults who don't drive and can't negotiate public transportation, if it is even available. They can provide extra pairs of hands in programs that require multiple assistants for success.

But, as we pointed out earlier, at other times caregiver involvement can be unnecessarily intrusive and limiting. Two of Carrie's experiences at BPL illustrate this point. First, she dealt with a parent whose young adult daughter started as a volunteer and later became a library staff member. The mother wanted to receive updates about her daughter's work, asked for more hours for her daughter, and tried to be overly involved in the volunteer job. Carrie patiently and repeatedly discussed human resources privacy policies and laws with this parent, always emphasizing the daughter's need to move toward independence. As the years went by, although she still intruded from time to time, the mother was able to step back and be less involved. The second example comes from an arts program where a staff member Carrie was mentoring encountered an accompanying agency staff person who was overly involved in an adult's art project, suggesting the colors that should be used in a painting. In cases like this, when faced with an intrusive or a pushy caregiver, library staff are often at a loss for what to do because they may be concerned that doing something will offend the caregiver. They may be fearful that the caregiver will lodge a complaint with the administration or the media. Because they are not sure what to do, they do nothing. But it is often simple to redirect a caregiver. In this case, the librarian was able to intervene without conflict by suggesting that the aide work on an art project of her own.

It is a fact of life that serving adults with DD will necessitate interaction with parents and caregivers, whether they are helpful and supportive or demanding and controlling, so it behooves library staff to understand how to communicate with them as well as with the patrons with DD.

TIPS FOR COMMUNICATING WITH CAREGIVERS
- It is fine to try to engage with caregivers as well as the adult patrons with DD. Ask them to give their own perspective but not to speak for the adult patrons with DD.
- If you talk to a caregiver in the presence of the accompanying patron with DD, be sure to also involve the patron in the conversation.
- State your expectations of caregivers up front. If you need them to stay in the room and assist with setup, supervision, or cleanup during a program, say so in promotional material and at the beginning of the program.
- Model confidence in the ability of adults with DD to participate and make choices within the structure of your program. Let caregivers know that you can handle the situation and they can relax and let go a bit.
- If a caregiver micromanages the accompanying patron's participation, follow the example from BPL and offer the caregiver an alternative role.

Some caregivers prefer to use areas of the library intended for youth with their adult charges. If your library has a policy limiting access to those areas to adults who are with children, it may be necessary for you to introduce that policy to the caregiver. This is one reason to have such policies in writing and readily available to patrons. Expect some pushback from caregivers, who may argue that the adults they are escorting are childlike, children trapped in adult bodies, not comfortable with other adults, or able to feel safe only in a long-familiar area of the library. There is little to be gained from arguing about such demeaning stereotypes. A more productive approach is to emphasize the benefits of the other areas of the library, including the adult-sized chairs.

Some caregivers may insist that they and their charges be allowed to continue staying in the children's room even if that violates policy, or they may claim that the library is no longer welcoming to them if you introduce the idea of a transition to adult services or neutral spaces, however gently. Each library must deal with these situations on a case-by-case basis, applying library policy, flexibility where possible, and compassion. But infantilizing adults with DD ultimately doesn't serve them, so don't give up before you even try to transition these patrons to age-appropriate programs, services, and spaces.

If you have worked to establish relationships of trust with these patrons and caregivers, facilitating a transition to age-appropriate spaces may prove easier to accomplish than you think. The same can be said of all of your efforts to provide great customer service and to offer fun and engaging programs for adults with DD. If you take the time to get to know and work with the stakeholders, everything else you do for adults with DD is bound to go more smoothly.

NOTES

1. Tom Ott, "How to Best Support Self Advocates," *YAI: News and Stories* (blog), August 30, 2018, www.yai.org/news-stories/blog/how-best-support-self-advocates.
2. Ott, "How to Best Support Self Advocates."
3. Bernadette Lear, personal communication, October 17, 2019.
4. Lear, pers. comm.
5. Suzanne Williams, personal communication, October 14, 2019.
6. Lisa Powell Williams, personal communication, August 6, 2020.
7. Vicki Karlovsky, personal communication, November 6, 2019.
8. Jody Van Ness, Kelly M. Nye-Lengerman, Rachel Freeman, Erin Flicker, and Claire Benway, "One Person at a Time: Using Person-Centered and Positive Support Practices," in *Community Living and Participation for People with Intellectual and Developmental Disabilities*, ed. Amy S. Hewitt and Kelly M. Nye-Lengerman (Silver Springs, MD: AAIDD, 2019), 27.
9. Van Ness et al., "One Person at a Time," 33.
10. Maria Town (@maria_m_town), Twitter, October 24, 2019, 5:29 p.m.

CHAPTER 6

Collaborating across Departments

Successful library programming for adults with developmental disabilities may require partnering with stakeholders within your institution as well as those in the community.

ADULTS IN THE CHILDREN'S ROOM

In some public libraries, some adults with DD are automatically sent to the children's room. This derives in part from the pervasive stereotype that adults with DD are like children. There are other reasons for this practice as well: children's materials may be easiest for some patrons with DD to understand and what they are most familiar with, children's programs may have appeal, and the physical space may be most familiar and comfortable for patrons who have used it for many years. Parents or caregivers may also feel better bringing the adults they accompany to the library to this space.

This choice, however, is not always what is best for these patrons or for the children who also use these areas of the library. While it is fine to provide adults with DD access to the children's materials they like, we should also introduce them to other possibilities because materials for children fail to address many of the interests or needs of adults with DD, which are often the same as those for the rest of their age cohort. For example, relationships and jobs are common concerns for all adults, and the materials we share and the programs we offer adults with DD need to reflect this. These adults should also be offered the opportunity to experience being in spaces meant for adults.

CHILDREN'S PROGRAMS FOR ADULTS

Sometimes, adults with DD are interested in attending performances, storytimes, and other programs designed and marketed for children. If they enjoy children's programs, they shouldn't be denied access to the content, but it can be beneficial to give them the opportunity to experience these programs in an adult-friendly way. The libraries that do this, like the Waco–McLennan County Library in Texas, have found it to be a real improvement on their former practice. According to children's librarian Vivian Rutherford, for many years adults with DD were included in her library's children's programming, but by 2018 "[w]e had such [a] large group we decided to have one just for them designed around their needs and capabilities."[1] The decision was made to create an adults-only program for these patrons, and the change worked out well for everyone. The adult program was full from the beginning. With very little advertising it can attract more than forty people. Rutherford elaborates:

> I am so thankful to be able to share a one-on-one opportunity with them. When they came as a group to my pre-k story times . . . I could not focus solely on them. But that is one of the advantages of us having a program entirely inclusive for them! . . . The best part is when they all leave, I get hugs and waves, . . . they are always leaving with big smiles on their faces.[2]

HOW TO OFFER CHILDREN'S PROGRAMMING

Here's how to respectfully meet the needs of adults with DD:
- Hire presenters to do a second session of a children's program, but for adults. Provide an orientation, following the guidelines in chapter 7.
- Schedule some inclusive programs for all ages and abilities, like concerts.
- Use adult-respectful materials and themes to create adult programs modeled on your children's offerings.

ADULT/YOUTH SERVICES PARTNERSHIPS

One way to bring programs to adults that are similar to ones for youth is through an adult/youth services collaboration. At Glen Ellyn Public Library in Illinois, librarian Josh O'Shea found this easy to do because the culture of that library already involved frequent interaction between the two departments.[3] In some libraries, staff rotate between departments so everyone is already familiar with all roles. In both of these types of libraries, it will be easy to arrange to display fliers and brochures for adult programs in youth services areas or for carts of children's books to be loaned as needed to adult services for programs or library visits. Children's, teen, and adult services library staff could conduct tours together, helping patrons feel comfortable throughout the library. Adult services librarians could get help in booking presenters who typically do children's programs so they can be available to adults with DD. They could also get support as they design storytimes or storytelling programs, staples for children's librarians but not for adult services staff.

It is also possible to work across departments successfully in a library with more fixed roles. If the presence of groups of adults with disabilities in the children's area or in children's programs is at all problematic or the children's librarians want to offer them other options, youth services librarians can approach their counterparts in adult services to suggest ways they can work together. If library policy dictates that adults without children should not be in the children's areas, youth services librarians can approach colleagues in adult services as well as the library administration to strategize solutions.

Why Collaborate

Adult programming supported by youth services can be a solution to the concerns felt by library managers like Rebecca Wolfe, branch manager at Allen County Public Library in Indiana. She recognized the need for programs for the adults with DD who use her library and started some, saying, "[I]t's great that agencies bring adults with IDD to the library, but sad when they aren't fully utilizing the library in ways we know they can with some simple programming help from us."[4] But she questions who is best suited to organize and present these programs, given that children's librarians are trained and comfortable with storytelling, storytime, literacy learning, music, and singing and adult services librarians are not necessarily. Because these are some of the programs that many adults with DD enjoy, she wonders if youth services staff should be doing these programs for adults. The solution to her concerns could be a collaboration between youth services and adult services.

Successful Collaborations

Bloomfield Township Public Library is one that created a successful programming partnership between children's and adult services staff. Assistant department head of youth services Jen Taggart noticed that group homes were always looking for opportunities for the people they serve and frequently bringing them to the library. After witnessing how much these groups enjoyed a 2015 StoryWalk program and gathering feedback from some groups, Taggart worked with adult services librarian Ed Niemchak to adapt her children's sensory storytime for adults and offer it through adult services.[5] Their program, Sensory Story Time for Teens and Adults, is described in chapter 10. When asked about his experience, Niemchak said:

> As an adult services librarian, if I had been told in graduate school that I would be conducting a story time, let alone a story time for adults and teens with intellectual and/or developmental disabilities, I wouldn't have believed it. That being said, it is honestly now the best part of my month and the one I most look forward to when I come to work.[6]

Deerfield Public Library in Illinois also models an effective way that staff from these two departments can work together. Julia Frederick, a member of the youth services staff, and Vicki Karlovsky, from adult services, have teamed up on a number of initiatives to help make their library a model of inclusion.[7] Together with a third staff member, they conceived and designed the library's excellent "Accessibility" web page (https://deerfieldlibrary.org/accessibility/). They also created sensory kits that are available at public service desks and during programs. The two are an ad hoc working group with lots of informal interchange between them. Their goal is to meet the needs of patrons of all ages and abilities, and they accomplish this both separately and collaboratively.

TRANSITIONING TO ADULT SERVICES

If patrons with DD and caregivers have traditionally used the children's room and attended children's programs, it is not a good idea to force a transition to adult services. However, keep the goal of moving them to more developmentally appropriate spaces and services in mind as you develop relationships with them. Focus on the individual and keep it positive. Tout the strengths of the adult collections and physical spaces. Many patrons do not know that libraries often have comic books and graphic fiction and nonfiction in the adult section, or that there may be more areas in adult departments for quiet reading. Magazines and adult books that are highly visual may also be of interest to adults with DD. Showcase adult programs that might interest them. Keep fliers for these programs on display in both youth services and adult services areas. Offer a social story that highlights what adult services has to offer these patrons using plain language and lots of visuals, like the one created by Deerfield library, which is available on the library's website at https://deerfieldlibrary.org/adult-social-story/. Give patrons with DD and their caregivers a one-on-one introduction to the library's adult areas or, even better, host a periodic tour of the entire library for adults with disabilities and their escorts and caregivers so that staff can address questions and concerns in a leisurely atmosphere. Refer to chapter 10 for more information on library tours. The adult areas of the library may be scary to these patrons because they are unfamiliar, so do what you can over time to make them familiar and welcoming to both adults with DD and their caregivers.

CREATING A NEUTRAL ZONE

In some libraries, the separation between departments is fixed; in others it is more fluid. This is true for staffing, programs, and services and also in terms of a library's physical space. In some libraries, youth and adult departments may be located on different floors or in different wings of the building, making informal interaction less likely. This type of physical arrangement hampers the movement of materials between departments as well as the flow of patrons, and it can also make for a more abrupt transition of patrons from youth services to adult services. It can also serve as a barrier to families or intergenerational groups wishing to enjoy the library together. Youth services librarians are all too familiar with the parents who sit patiently watching their children use a computer in youth services while wishing they could duck into adult services to get a book for themselves. Families who want to play games together at the library or get materials for everyone have to make several stops in the building or end up all together in youth services.

One solution to this is an open area located between fixed library departments, a wonderful example of universal design. Such areas are available to patrons of all ages and are ideal for groups using the library together. Bloomfield Township Public Library created an area of this type in 2019 that they call the Commons. According to Jen Taggart, the Commons was designed to accommodate tutors, student groups, and intergenerational family groups as well as adult visitors from residential and day habilitation programs.[8] The variety of seating makes it a flexible space with less of a need for quiet than in other public areas. Because there are sight lines to both youth services and adult services, it can also serve as the ideal neutral zone for adults with DD to use as they begin to transition from youth services to adult services.

COORDINATING OUTREACH

Adults with DD can be found throughout our communities, and they are part of every immigrant, ethnic, and faith-based group. The ones who come to our libraries in groups are a small percentage of the adults with disabilities overall and only a subset of those with DD. In some ways they are more privileged than others because they receive services from agencies that bring them out into the communities. Many other people with DD also need supports and services but do not get them. Others live in very large congregate care facilities or at agencies that do not prioritize community involvement. Still others are unhoused. Like every other segment of the population, some people with DD are in institutions like hospitals, nursing homes, jails, prisons, and shelters. Reaching those who do not or cannot come to our libraries because of these situations can be challenging.

If these adults with DD cannot come to the library, the library can go to them. One way to facilitate this is to involve the people in the library who do outreach. Offer to work with them to make sure that they are reaching adults with DD when they are out in the community. Approach them to ascertain if they are asking about needed accommodations. Find out if the carceral agencies and shelters are giving them access to people with disabilities. Offer to provide the staff who visit jails and prisons with the materials they need to serve people with ID who are incarcerated. Explain about the potential sensory needs of people with autism or those with Down syndrome who have dementia. Offer to find materials for them in the languages spoken in your communities.

Library outreach experts can provide valuable tips on how to develop and nurture relationships with potential or existing community partner organizations. They can be helpful if you want to take the show on the road and bring your programs directly to these organizations in addition to programming for them at library locations. This may be the best way to reach individuals served by agencies with tight travel budgets and individuals who cannot travel to you because of physical restrictions. There are also adults with DD who live independently and need minimal supports and others who live with family and don't use outside services. These adults may or may not be library users, and if they are not, they may be more difficult than others with DD to locate and serve. Offering and promoting inclusive programs might bring them into the library, but if you need other ideas, your library's outreach specialist may be able to help.

STAFF ACCESSIBILITY OR INCLUSION COMMITTEES

One way to make sure that the entire library welcomes adults with DD respectfully and keeps inclusion front of mind is to create an inclusion or accessibility staff task force or committee. This committee can be made up of assigned representatives from various library departments or branches and/or staff volunteers who have an interest in the subject. However you structure it, make sure that staff members who have disabilities are invited to participate if they wish to, but don't insist if they are not interested. Barbara participated in one at the Ferguson Library in Stamford, Connnecticut, called the Universal Access Taskforce or U Act. Other groups include Community Awareness and Engagement Committee (Allen County Public Library, IN), Inclusion Staff Group (Glen Ellyn Public Library, IL), Accessibility Team (Dakota County Public Library, MN), the Accessible Libraries Team (Hennepin County Library, MN), and AccessABILITY Team (Sacramento Public Library, CA). According to Amy Little, chair of the AccessABILITY Team, the group meets monthly and sets goals that are shared with the entire library. A grant-funded staff training resulted from the work of this team, a good example of what these groups can accomplish.

The Hennepin County Library (HCL) team also meets monthly

> to identify ways to increase access to HCL's buildings, programs and services by prioritizing and advocating for diverse access needs, including the needs of people with larger bodies, those experiencing disabilities, and/or Deaf community [sic] members. The workgroup develops strategies for building awareness and supporting staff in providing inclusive, welcoming, and physically and emotionally safe services and spaces for patrons and staff.[9]

Susan Cooper, one of the team leaders, points out that the team's mandate includes anyone with access needs, whether or not they identify as or would be considered someone living with a disability.[10] The mandate talks about the team being concerned with needs assessment, the use of universal design, the involvement of people with various access needs in planning, and the identification of models and expertise that eliminate barriers. All of these topics are discussed in this book.

Membership in the HCL team is open to all staff, but the group aims to include those with direct experience in disability and access needs. This is a worthwhile and important goal because one in four people in our country will develop a disability over the course of their lives. Every library probably has personnel who have a disability themselves or know someone who does. These staff members bring this background to work with them, and tapping into these lived experiences can make us all better at what we do.

NOTES

1. Vivian Rutherford, personal communication, October 19, 2019.
2. Rutherford, pers. comm.
3. Josh O'Shea, personal communication, October 31, 2019.
4. Rebecca Wolfe, personal communication, November 2019.
5. Jen Taggart and Ed Niemchak, personal communication, October 29, 2019.
6. Taggart and Niemchak, pers. comm.
7. Vicki Karlovsky, personal communication, November 6, 2019.
8. Taggart and Niemchak, pers. comm.
9. Susan Cooper, personal communication, January 7, 2020; quoted with permission.
10. Cooper, pers. comm.

CHAPTER 7

Training for Inclusion

In the fall of 2019, a furor erupted among the library and disability communities when a long-awaited $41 million library building project was completed, resulting in a beautiful building that, although ADA-compliant, was partially inaccessible to patrons with mobility impairments and parents with strollers. Commenting on what happened, *New York Magazine* writer and architecture critic Justin Davidson pointed out that "meeting legal requirements is a false standard; . . . buildings can and should always be designed so that they offer the same *quality* of experience to everyone."[1] He went on to say that he was initially blind to this flaw in the design, as was the large team that included architects, engineers, library staff, and others who spent years bringing this project to fruition. "Maybe there's a workaround," he concluded, "but the design flaw makes it tougher for the building to succeed, a problem that people with mobility issues face every day."[2]

The process that created this building manifested institutional ableism at every point. The building was conceived of by the library, designed by an architecture firm, approved by city planners, signed off on by city inspectors, and touted as a model new library by the system, with everyone agreeing that it did not matter that the most popular books were in a section inaccessible to people with disabilities. Had these planners been more cognizant of the relevant laws, the needs of people with disabilities, and their responsibilities to the entire community, this fiasco could have been avoided.

Staff training might have helped. Regular staff training on inclusion issues can not only help staff understand the needs of people with disabilities but also lead to changed attitudes, better customer service, and significant improvements in how patrons with and without developmental disabilities experience the library.

CHOOSING CONTENT

Researchers Michelle H. Brannen, Steven Milewski, and Thura Mack stress four areas of focus for training based on their work at the University of Tennessee: facilities, attitudes, legal issues, and services. They conclude that training must be relevant to organizational practices, provide reference sources for public services staff, and concentrate on frontline personnel, including custodial and safety staff. All of these elements lead to improved interactions with people with disabilities.[3] Within these content areas, training should shine a light on how ableism is woven into our buildings, collections, systems, and services, and it should offer strategies for remediation. Doing this will allow the library to move toward eliminating institutional ableism and developing a culture of inclusion.

Once you have a framework for training, decide on the topics to cover. There are many to consider, so start by finding out what your library's staff want to know. The library staff we canvassed suggested the following areas of focus:

- defining DD and ID
- sensitivity and awareness training
- making programs inclusive
- communicating effectively, including with PECS
- dealing with intrusive caregivers
- including American sign language (ASL)
- supporting people as they develop skills
- recognizing frustration and agitation
- dealing with meltdowns

It can also be useful to poll patrons to get their suggestions about staff training needs.

DECIDING HOW TO CONDUCT TRAINING

Once you have established the content, the next step is to look at how training will be done. This can take a number of forms, including scheduling in-house speakers or workshops, accessing online trainings and webinars, conducting hybrid trainings, disseminating written materials or other resources to staff, and encouraging attendance at conferences or local networking groups. Some training methods cover only one topic; others may touch on multiple issues.

WHAT TO COVER IN STAFF TRAINING

- basic disability awareness and demographics
- relevant laws
- institutional ableism and microaggressions
- UD and UDL principles
- intersectionality
- assistive technology, both high and low tech
- web and technology accessibility
- communication disability etiquette
- correct terminology
- AAC devices
- unexpected behavior
- program design
- an introduction to resources
- outreach and creating partnerships

In-Person Training

In-person training is the gold standard. It is particularly suited for topics such as basic disability awareness, communication, and unexpected behaviors. In-person training allows time for "directed reflection on personal biases and feelings" about disabilities, an important aspect of addressing these topics, and feedback indicates that the ability "to discuss issues and concerns" contributes to staff satisfaction with this type of training.[4]

If you choose to start with a single speaker or a panel presentation, allow time for questions and facilitated small-group discussions. In addition to assigning a facilitator for each group, recruit a note taker and have that person report insights from the small discussions back to the larger group. In the discussion groups, be careful to share insights but avoid putting people on the spot or shaming them. We all make mistakes, and the point of these sessions is to move beyond them. To this end, it can help to have discussion ground rules that stress active listening, allowing everyone to speak, and limiting criticism to ideas, not people.

Online Training

Online training can bridge the physical distance between experts and audiences. It comes in two forms: live virtual presentations, which allow for interaction with presenters, and asynchronous training, either developed that way or using a saved version of a live presentation, which allows for self-pacing. Conference platforms such as Zoom, Google Meet, Microsoft Teams, and RingCentral offer interaction analogous to in-person meetings, addressing the basic deficit of earlier iterations of remote learning. With these platforms there is also the possibility for facilitated group discussions in breakout rooms. Several platforms, such as Zoom, allow participants to be off camera and change their user names. This can provide some privacy for people during what can prove to be difficult discussions.

Traditional library channels can be sources for some terrific online training content, ranging from one-off workshops to semester-long courses. Modules on accessibility and libraries from WebJunction (www.webjunction.org/home.html) include the 2018 "Literacy and Community-Building with Adults with Developmental Disabilities." ALA and its divisions and offices also offer courses and stand-alone workshops on disability. Look to the Programming Librarian website (https://programminglibrarian.org) for articles and occasional webinars like "You Belong @ Your Library: Programming for Adults with Intellectual Disabilities." Some state library associations also offer trainings and resources. Syracuse University's Project ENABLE (https://projectenable.syr.edu) is devoted to educating library staff about disability issues, and its online self-paced training modules and videos are free.

Information on useful topics is frequently shared not only in the *Programming Librarian* blog but in other blogs like *Targeting Autism for Libraries* (https://targetingautismlibs.com) and librarian Jen Taggart's *Adaptive Umbrella* (https://adaptiveumbrella.blogspot.com). Also look to library websites, wikis, and slack channels as well as Instagram and other social media for training resources. Whatever the modality and format, make sure your online training is accessible.

Using Print Resources

Don't neglect print resources such as articles or books like this one. Others to consider include *Differing Abilities and the Library: Fostering Equity for Patrons and Staff with Disabilities*, edited by C. A. Copeland (Libraries Unlimited, forthcoming), and *Creating Inclusive Library Environments: A Planning Guide for Serving Patrons with Disabilities* by Michelle Kowalsky and John Woodruff (ALA Editions, 2017). Also make sure that staff are familiar with materials written by people with disabilities. If you have these materials in your collection, it should be easy to share them with staff and to use insights from them in your trainings.

Hybrid Training

You can develop hybrid training by utilizing remote resources or fully developed content and combining it with personal interaction. Hybrid training is a good model to use for training on institutional ableism and implicit bias, because as emotionally fraught topics, they require privacy as well a sensitive discussion to fully address them. Start by asking staff to self-administer the disability Implicit Association Test, available at https://implicit.harvard.edu/implicit/. This assessment is best done in private, allowing some time for people to process their results. Next consider referring staff to one or both of these online resources:

- Association of College and Research Libraries, "Keeping Up with Implicit Bias," www.ala.org/acrl/publications/keeping_up_with/bias/, which focuses on academic libraries and racial bias and is easily applicable to disability and other types of libraries
- American Bar Association Commission on Disability Rights, "Implicit Bias Guide: Implicit Biases and People with Disabilities," www.americanbar .org/groups/diversity/disabilityrights/resources/implicit_bias/

Finally, wrap up the topic with a live or virtual in-person session. Try featuring a self-advocate who can answer questions and discuss how bias and ableism has affected their life and how the library can become part of the solution rather than part of the problem. Allow for discussion. Look to the "Understanding and Challenging Ableism" lesson plan, available on the Anti-Defamation League website for other ideas.[5] Your trainings are more likely to be powerful and transformative for your staff if you combine good online resources and in-person discussion.

Assistive technology (AT) is another area that lends itself to hybrid training. Combine online resources and webinars to introduce the technologies with a technology petting zoo, where visitors can try a number of them at one event and have a hands-on experience. Your state federally funded AT3 Center is a good resource to use for consultation and training on all types of assistive technology and your state center may be able to arrange access to the technology you are interested in so that staff can try it out. New York's AT3 Center TechWorks, Brooklyn Public Library's go-to resource for trainings and referrals on AT, has hosted staff trainings at its demonstration library.

FINDING PRESENTERS

Care should be taken when choosing presenters for staff trainings. For example, while popular in larger library systems, the train-the-trainer model can be particularly ill-suited for training around inclusion issues because of the potential effects of institutional ableism. Instead, look for trainers who are confronting their own ableism and are aware of the biases they bring and attitudes they communicate during training. Because "[u]nspoken perceptions of bias or stereotype can be communicated even through postures, gestures, or facial expressions[,] . . . [c]hoose workshop facilitators carefully . . . after observing them in action with other groups."[6]

Getting nearby librarians who do programming to come in to train staff on specific programs can be a good idea so long as you make sure that the programs you are introducing follow best practices and are good models to replicate in your community. One successful example of a replicated program comes from Arapahoe Libraries in Colorado, which used nearby Jefferson County's Library for all programs as the basis for their own programming for adults with DD.

Libraries may consider bringing in local professionals to teach about disability, but a better choice is to use self-advocates alone or in combination with those professionals who subscribe to the social model and understand disability as a diversity issue. Including self-advocates as presenters on ableism, the experience of disability, and community needs will make training more authentic and credible. As autistic self-advocate Sharmin Faruque says, "I find it so strange when non-autistic people are used to train others on autism. It makes no sense to me and just proves how deep ableism runs. If a non-Asian person tried to teach me about my culture I would walk out."[7]

Finding self-advocates in your community to conduct trainings can be as simple as reaching out to your patrons with disabilities or looking for local self-advocates. The Autistic Self-Advocacy Network has local chapters throughout the United States and operates a speakers bureau. Self Advocates Becoming Empowered (SABE), a national network of organizations whose mission includes educating "people—all people—about disability issues that are important in their lives,"[8] is another source for trainers. You can find your local SABE organization through the main website (www.sabeusa.org). Also look to your state's Development Disabilities Council or your community's Center for Independent Living. To find the DD Council and Centers for Independent Living for your state, go to the Administration for Community Living (ACL) website (https://acl.gov) and scroll down. Another resource to check out is the Self-Advocacy Online website (www.selfadvocacy online.org), where you can search for groups by state or zip code. Finally, look to service agencies with local affiliates, such as the Arc. Some sponsor self-advocacy groups that may be able to help identify someone from your community to train your staff.

Workshops offered by community-based organizations can also be a gold mine for professional development. For example, Brooklyn Public Library's staff is routinely invited to both in-person and online sessions hosted by Shema Kolainu–Hear Our Voices, a New York educational and therapeutic center for children with autism. The center's October 2020 webinar workshop "Supporting Autistic People in Uncertain Times" featured well-known self-advocate Stephen Shore. Organizations that support people with disabilities and their families can be useful training resources as well. Library staff may be able to attend these organizations' own workshops, or they can often provide presenters for library-developed sessions. These arrangements can be on a quid pro quo basis, with the organization providing training on a disability-related topic for library staff and library staff providing training on library and literacy topics for group members or agency staff. Local colleges and universities can also be good sources for speakers and more in-depth educational opportunities.

Sacramento Public Library's staff AccessABILITY team developed their own training based on team members' experience, extensive reading, and study of primary source material. Initially their training was presented at an all-staff meeting, and then it was repeated at seven of the system's Hubs, library locations that offer special programs and services for people with disabilities. The training was so well received that the library got a grant to bring a modified version of it to twelve other library systems in California. After the training at Sacramento library, participants offered these comments:

"[I learned to] view all as 'people first' and allow this to shape how we interact. Knowing that many disabilities are invisible, so practice challenging our assumptions and biases."

"[T]he general message of 'don't treat a person like they're a category' is super important."

"[I learned] that people are on a continuum of learning and to forgive mistakes but to also learn from them."[9]

USING TRAINING TO EXPAND AND ENHANCE PROGRAMMING

The result of training is often the development of new programs as staff become more aware of needs and possibilities. New York City provides us with an example. The three metropolitan public library systems, Brooklyn, New York, and Queens Borough, held a half-day Tri-Li Accessibility Summit during which individuals with disabilities talked about their needs, librarians presented what they were doing, and agencies provided resources and contacts for future partnerships. The goal was to increase accessibility in the participating library systems. It was achieved when, following the summit, a branch library in Queens booked a self-advocate to conduct two workshops, the first time a self-advocate had been invited to present a program! A year later the Tri-Li group followed up by hosting Morénike Giwa Onaiwu, a founder of the Autistic Women and Nonbinary Network, for a discussion on inclusion, intersectionality, and libraries.

While the staff trainings we introduce here are excellent examples of what can be done, each one by itself is insufficient. Staff training should never be one and done. Staff will benefit from exposure to more than one training session, and a mix of opportunities over time will be the most effective. The study by Brannen, Milewski, and Mack found that "success in this area requires consistent, on-going training . . . for all employees in order to remain efficient at the point of need."[10] Also, don't forget that new staff also need to be trained as they are brought on board.

Keep in mind, too, that library programs rely on more than just library staff; volunteers and outside presenters are often central to their success. Their comfort and skills with people with DD can make all of the difference in the quality of the programs your library offers.

Orientations for Volunteers

Many programs for adults with DD work best with more than a single staff person in the room. The needed support can be provided by a second staff member, caregivers, aides who accompany participants, volunteers with disabilities, or other library volunteers. If you use volunteers, they do not have to be disability experts, but some training is always useful to help them understand their role. Before training volunteers, determine whether you'll want all of them to do the same thing. Consider if you'll need help with setup, room management, or both. Decide if you want volunteers to participate in activities or circulate to answer questions. Come up with guidelines for dealing with behavior issues like someone dominating a conversation or monopolizing craft supplies. Make sure that the training you offer touches on all of these issues.

Plan to meet with volunteers before programs begin to lay out your expectations and provide some basic information and guidance. If you have carefully screened your volunteers to avoid those who embrace the charity model, this training doesn't need to be long. It can take place immediately before the program if that is easiest to schedule. If an in-person training is not possible, try to arrange a phone call or virtual meeting beforehand to go over this information. Written materials can also be useful, but if you use them stick to simple tip sheets rather than long articles your volunteers might not read or be able to comprehend. For a more detailed discussion on volunteer programs for adults with DD, see chapter 17.

WHAT TO COVER IN VOLUNTEER TRAINING
- basic facts about the program's target audience
- communication strategies
- an introduction to ableism and microaggressions
- the structure and conventions of the program
- information about the volunteer role

Orientations for Presenters

Inclusive programs and more focused ones will go more smoothly if the presenters you use are prepared to work with patrons with DD. Sometimes, you can find presenters who already have some experience, so they will need little extra preparation. For them, a brief description of who will be in attendance, including triggers and special interests if you know them, may be sufficient. But even presenters who lack that experience can do a great job for your adults with DD if they are willing to try and open to some input from you.

When planning for her focused programs, Candice Casey at Hart Memorial Library, part of the Osceola Library System in Florida, first looks to her library's existing presenters to see if they are open to doing a second session of their program for her group. She has found that many of them are. She has an informal conversation with them, briefly describing the audience and their needs.[11] Renee

Grassi from Dakota Library System in Minnesota does a more formal orientation, and she has developed these guidelines for libraries working with presenters who need some training before they feel prepared to program for adults with DD.

- Explain why you are offering this program.
- Tell presenters what you want the program to cover, how long it will last, and other relevant information.
- Describe any verbal and physical behaviors the presenter might encounter and why they occur.
- Stress the importance of setting boundaries, the need to offer explicit instructions, and how structure can support participants.
- Reassure presenters that library staff will be in the room during the entire program and that they will support the participants.
- Explain the role of caregivers and group staff.
- Introduce presentation styles that work well for this particular group.
- Let them know what room setup to expect and why.
- Ask for the information you need to prepare any handouts, visual schedules, and social narratives.
- Encourage presenters to allow for interactions and conversations between attendees and caregivers and to not expect silence and full attention from attendees.
- Thank the presenters for their willingness to try something new at the library and for their contribution to the lives of community members with DD.[12]

Adults with DD are like everyone else in their humanity, but they may face a number of challenges and barriers as they try to navigate through life and participate in library programs. If the members of the library team—staff, volunteers, and presenters—are all grounded in a knowledge of best practices and helpful strategies and confident that they can work with these patrons in an equitable and respectful way, everyone is bound to have a better time and programs are more likely to be successful.

NOTES

1. Justin Davidson, "The Important Thing I Didn't See at the New Hunters Point Library," *New York Magazine*, October 4, 2019, http://nymag.com/intelligencer/2019/10/iffy -accessibility-at-hunters-point-community-library.html.
2. Davidson, "Important Thing I Didn't See."

3. Michelle H. Brannen, Steven Milewski, and Thura Mack, "Providing Staff Training and Programming to Support People with Disabilities: An Academic Library Case Study," *Public Services Quarterly* 13, no. 2 (May 2017): 61–77, particularly 63–64, https://doi.org/10.1080/15228959.2017.1298491.
4. Brannen, Milewski, and Mack, "Providing Staff Training," 64.
5. Anti-Defamation League, "Understanding and Challenging Ableism," www.adl.org/education/educator-resources/lesson-plans/understanding-and-challenging-ableism.
6. Michelle Kowalsky and John Woodruff, *Creating Inclusive Library Environments: A Planning Guide for Serving Patrons with Disabilities* (Chicago: ALA Editions, 2017), 62.
7. Sharmin Faruque (@SharminFaruque), Twitter, November 6, 2019.
8. SABE, "About SABE," www.sabeusa.org/meet-sabe/.
9. Amy Little, personal communication, November 14, 2019; quotes used with permission.
10. Brannen, Milewski, and Mack, "Providing Staff Training," 62.
11. Candice Casey, personal communication, September 13, 2019.
12. Renee Grassi, personal communication, February 12, 2020.

CHAPTER 8

Funding, Marketing, and Evaluating Programs

Before and after programs happen, a lot of behind-the-scenes work takes place. Unless we can raise the money and get the word out, our programs will not get off the ground. And until we evaluate them, we won't know if we've gotten them right.

FUNDING PROGRAMS

All programs cost something to develop and implement. Here are some of the ways you can get the funding you need for programming for adults with developmental disabilities.

Advocating for Inclusive Budgets

Ideally, funding for programming for adults with DD should come from a library's regular funding stream. If overall programming is covered in the regular budget, these programs should be included because equal access for people with disabilities is the law. Library staff should not have to argue for budget allocations to serve these patrons any more than they do for others, and yet we do. When we must, these are some arguments we can make and strategies that can be effective:

- *Find the sympathetic person in management.* One in four people has a disability and that person's friends, families, and coworkers are also impacted by disability. Find the person at your library who belongs to one of these groups. Often people with direct and indirect experience with disabilities are more open to funding these types of services.

- *Remember, this is not a special request.* We do not have similar discussions about funding for other services. Can you imagine someone saying, "We do not have enough money to maintain our women's bathrooms this year" or "I think we shouldn't spend so much on biographies because only men read them" at a budget meeting?
- *Services for people with disabilities generate goodwill and positive publicity and avoid bad will and negativity.* No library wants to find itself a hashtag on Twitter for throwing an autistic person out of the library or opening a new building that is inaccessible.
- *Libraries can leverage a commitment to basic funding to help get additional grant funds.* Many of the private sources of funds for services for people with disabilities fall outside of traditional library funding streams. If you have a demonstrated track record, those funders will be more open to your requests.
- *Embracing universal design makes the library more accessible for everyone.* Older adults and veterans are among the groups of voters that libraries often need to win over, and the things we do for people with disabilities will benefit them as well.

Making the case for funding sometimes takes a carrot-and-stick approach. The carrot is great service, good publicity, and additional funding. The stick is lawsuits and bad publicity. If you make your case well, your administration should be able to identify pretty quickly which of the two they prefer.

Grant Fundraising

Grants are often a good way to fund innovative, unproven programming of all kinds, and winning a grant can help demonstrate the worth of a new idea. The process of applying for and managing grants is easier for large systems because they often have dedicated staff; however, the good news is that almost anyone can write successful grants if they understand a little about granters and the application process.

Granters are obligated to give their money away; your job is to find the right fit and make a compelling case. Your application is a sales document, so it is important to answer what is asked, describe clearly what you plan to do and what the impact will be, and make sure that the application is well-written and professional. Whether it is asked on the application or not, be sure to indicate how your library plans to continue the program if it is successful because funders also like to see that your project will be sustainable after the grant period. If you do not meet the criteria, fully answer the questions, adhere to the format, and meet the deadlines, your proposal will not succeed.

To find potential funders, start by looking at some of these traditional funding sources for libraries:

- corporate foundations
- community foundations
- independent foundations
- library-specific grants
- government grants

Resources like the Grantsmanship Center (www.tgci.com), the *Library Grants* blog (http://librarygrants.blogspot.com), and the Visualizing Funding for Libraries data tool from the Foundation Center (https://libraries.foundationcenter.org) can help you identify some grant-making entities that fund libraries.

Targeting Autism, an initiative of the Illinois State Library created by Suzanne Schriar, was supported by two large grants from a traditional library source, the Institute of Museum and Library Services (IMLS). The first, a National Leadership Grant, paid for two stakeholder forums where librarians and advocates worked together to identify best practices and inspire librarians to develop programs and services for autistic people in their communities. Phase two involved the development and implementation of replicable training programs throughout Illinois and the United States. It was funded through a Laura Bush 21st Century Librarian Program grant. Targeting Autism has had a significant impact, and Illinois State Library was awarded a 2016 Demco Library Innovative Award for this project.

Providing programming to people with disabilities can expand your pool of potential funders beyond these sources to those that fund disability issues. Look for funding opportunities from these resources:

- disability-specific organizations
- fraternal organizations
- advocacy and self-advocacy groups
- government programs that support people with disabilities

For example, Dakota County Library in Minnesota was the first public library in that state to be awarded a Disability Services innovations grant from the Department of Human Services. Awarded in 2018, the two-year $100,000 grant was coordinated by librarian Renee Grassi. These funds were used for everything from training to sensory tools and programs to accessible library technology and program kits.[1] Inclusive Services at Brooklyn Public Library has received funding from autism groups such as the Doug Flutie, Jr. Foundation for Autism.

IS THIS GRANT A FIT?
- Does your project align with the funder's mission?
- Is your library in the geographic area covered by the funder?
- Is the application process manageable?
- Can you meet the application deadline?
- Can you do what you say you will do?
- Can you handle the required record keeping and reporting?
- Will the dollar range of awards given by this funder cover your program needs?
- How many grants are awarded each year? In other words, is there a chance you'll get funded?

The book *Winning Grants: A How-To-Do-It Manual for Librarians*, Second Edition, by Stephanie K. Gerding and Pamela H. MacKellar (ALA Neal-Schuman, 2017) offers more detailed information about grant fundraising for libraries. You can also take advantage of blogs, webinars, and articles on the subject. However you identify grants or learn how to complete applications, as you look for funding, don't lose sight of your ultimate goal, which is to improve the lives of adults with DD in your community.

MARKETING PROGRAMS

Funding, planning, and scheduling programs will not get people in the door. Promotion is also essential, and that promotion needs to go beyond what the library regularly does to market what it offers the community.

Develop a Specialized Marketing Strategy

Libraries typically use a variety of marketing strategies, including fliers at the library or other locations, brochures, calendars, library newsletters, listings on the library's website and Facebook page, posts on Instagram, and e-mail blasts to library users. Although these may reach some adults with DD or their caregivers, they are not sufficient. Some adults with DD will not understand the fliers. Others do not have access to computers or electronic devices. Those who are not already library users will not see hard-copy notices that are available at library locations or receive library e-mails. Reaching these potential patrons requires a marketing strategy that includes outreach to individuals with disabilities and community partners, specifically designed promotional materials, the use of currently accepted language, usable accessibility pages on library websites, and websites that are accessible.

Prioritize Outreach to Individuals with Disabilities

The best way to market library programs for people with DD is to be embedded in their communities. More than a one-time outreach effort, being embedded requires regular communication and showing up. You can find these communities through the resources we discuss in chapter 7's Finding Presenters section. If yours is an academic library, you can reach out to your institution's disability services office in order to connect with students with DD. You can also look to relevant blogs produced on campus to find student self-advocates. Reach out to these entities and individuals. Go to their meetings. Become part of the community. Use the contacts you make to keep current with the DD community and its members.

Once you have established relationships with some individuals with DD in your community, start to build a mailing list so it is easy to stay connected. Invite the people on the list to bring their friends to programs. When they come, add the friends to your mailing list. Remember "Nothing about us without us!" and involve these patrons in program design and implementation.

Reach Out to Community Partners

Partnerships are critical to the success of marketing efforts, and libraries that program successfully for adults with DD conduct regular outreach to community partners as part of their marketing plans. For example, Candice Casey, from Hart Memorial Library in Kissimmee, Florida, found that it doesn't work just to advertise her programs. She also conducts outreach to places in her community where adults with DD spend their days. This also generates valuable feedback that helps her plan future programs.[2] Vicki Karlovsky of Deerfield (IL) Public Library sends fliers to partner agencies and lists events in a partner agency's newsletter.[3] If you send out fliers, be sure to use snail mail as well as e-mail to ensure that those without computer access are kept informed. If you plan to send promotional materials outside of your library's catchment area, make sure that practice is allowed by your library.

Market Focused Programs

Describing your programs in a friendly, accurate way is important for success. For programs aimed at only people with disabilities, be specific, detailing exactly whom you want to attend, and make sure that your terms are the ones your patrons use. You can refer to chapter 1 for guidance on this point, or do some outreach to find out what people in your community prefer.

Bloomfield Township (MI) Public Library's program descriptions are both specific and current. Their sensory storytime program for teens and adults is described as "for adults and teens with intellectual and/or developmental disabilities and a support person."[4] This library goes beyond using correct terminology in program descriptions; they are careful to use it in all aspects of programming and service delivery. In fact, they renamed what was once the Special Needs Collection for youth and the parallel collection for teens/young adults to reflect changes in accepted terminology, rebranding them as Accessibility Support Collections.[5]

Whether your programs are inclusive or focused, event listings on the website are another place to highlight accessibility. For example, the Hennepin County (MN) Library's Webber Park Library includes information about building accessibility in theirs. A typical statement reads:

> ADDITIONAL DETAILS:
> **Accessibility:** 1st floor, no stairs, low pile carpet. All gender bathrooms available. Please contact library staff to request ASL interpretation.

The listing for this program also says that it is "inclusive of all."[6]

Integrate marketing into your library's social media strategy. Make sure the agencies and individuals you work with are aware of your Facebook, Instagram, Twitter, and other accounts. Follow their accounts and share as appropriate. When using online calendars, tag your events to allow them to be picked up in online searches.

Keep your hoped-for audience in mind as you design fliers and other promotional materials. Design for the adults with disabilities themselves, not for agency personnel or caregivers. That means using plain language, short sentences, and lots of white space. Avoid cluttered designs, fonts with serifs, idiomatic language, and double entendres. Restrict any illustrations to photographs or other images that are suitable for adults, rather than using cutesy clip art that might have more appeal to children.

Market for Inclusion

An attendee at a Brooklyn Public Library staff meeting asked how to get adults without disabilities to want to come to programs primarily for adults with disabilities. That is a good question, and Candice Casey from Hart Memorial Library provides one possible response. She suggests giving programs specific, fun names and picking topics that are appealing and fun for a broad audience.[7] You can also encourage inclusion by scheduling programs at a desirable time when alternative programs are not offered. Barbara did this for the Ferguson Library's inclusive sensory storytime for children, scheduling the program on Saturdays when there were no other storytimes. This made the program attractive to families who can't come to the library during the workweek in addition to families whose children have disabilities. Although this inclusive program was for children, the principle can be applied with equal success to adult programming. To drive home the point, promotional materials should highlight the fact that these are the only programs offered at that desirable time. Holding interesting-looking programs in a visible place is yet another strategy, one that worked for BPL's Adaptive Gaming Arcade.

When your programs are meant to be inclusive, you can convey that fact in a number of ways. Some librarians like Casey avoid directly saying that the program is for people with disabilities. She worries that people without disabilities will be dismissive. Instead, she suggests using language that is more broadly welcoming but that alerts potential attendees with disabilities that their needs will be met; for example, "This is an inclusive activity for all skill levels."[8] BPL's Inclusive Services takes a different approach, describing programs as "for people with and without disabilities." This language clearly defines the audience and acknowledges the pride many people take in their identity as disabled. During Barbara's time at the Ferguson Library in Stamford, Connecticut, fliers indicated that the library was "inclusion friendly." Some libraries' marketing materials include a number to call or an e-mail address to use if accommodations like an ASL interpreter will be needed. Providing this information sends the message that the library will make an effort to include all community members who want to attend programs.

Reach out to people who speak languages other than English and integrate them into your publicity efforts. Inclusive Services programs at BPL offer Spanish interpretation upon request, and publicity materials are in Spanish as well as other languages. Some programs are intentionally bilingual; others are Spanish only. Be sure to ask a native speaker to proofread any marketing materials you create in languages other than English. This is essential if you want to be sure what you put out is culturally as well as linguistically accurate. If you do not have anyone on staff who can do this, ask a community member. This has the added benefit of creating another stakeholder who can help you spread the word among their networks.

Offer Accessibility Web Pages

One of the things we discovered in researching this book was how difficult it can be to find out what libraries offer for adult patrons with DD. Carli Spina, associate professor and head of Research and Instructional Services at the Gladys Marcus Library at the Fashion Institute of Technology, says, "An important part of making your library accessible is advertising that your library's spaces and services are accessible and inclusive."[9] That means highlighting this information on the library's website.

An easy-to-find, comprehensive, and well-designed accessibility web page should always be part of your marketing strategy, regardless of whether your library hosts inclusive programs, focused ones just for people with DD, or both. The Deerfield library web page is a good model that includes elements that can be replicated. The first of these is its placement on the home page (https://deer fieldlibrary.org). Accessibility is the first item on the About Us dropdown menu, so it is easy to locate. The top of the web page offers an e-mail address and phone number to use to request accommodations, making that information easy to find. The page itself is divided into four intuitive sections: Building Access, Materials, Programming, and Services. Visuals are used in many areas of the web page, showing everything from what the elevator looks like to the contents of the library's sensory kits. Social Stories, one for children and one for adults, appear as links in the Services section and directly through a separate link in the About Us menu. The Adult Social Story, while not excluding the Youth Services Department in its introduction to the library, focuses primarily on how to get to Adult Services and the many materials and services to be found there. The story uses photographs and simple language in a large font to provide a comprehensive introduction to the library. Bloomfield Township library organizes its Accessibility Services web page differently, but it also contains a lot of information. Found in the Services drop-down menu on the home page (https://btpl.org), it begins with a link to the library's "Americans with Disabilities Act Policy Statement on Library Programs." Then it moves on to supports provided, organized by specific disabilities. The page also provides links to some special collections and to an excellent social story for children.

Another item to consider including on your library's accessibility web page is an introduction to personnel whom a visitor with disabilities will encounter at the library. A photograph accompanied by a brief, friendly description can go a long way toward making a patron with DD feel more comfortable approaching someone. Some libraries provide photos and information about library staff in other areas of their websites but not on their accessibility pages.

Libraries that offer sensory items for use in-house or during programs, a designated sensory area, or other useful services should mention them also on their accessibility web pages.

Ensure Websites Are Accessible

A library's website should not only provide information about the accessibility of programs, services, and physical facilities; it should be accessible itself. In fact, web accessibility is mandated by the ADA and other laws. The most basic requirement under these laws is that people with disabilities be able to navigate a website. This means meeting the following criteria:

- The structure and software are compatible with common screen-reading technology.
- Text and background have high contrast.
- Information is comprehensible in black and white.
- The font used is sans serif and larger than twelve point.
- The website is navigable by keyboard.
- Headers are used.
- All images are described.
- Information is available in both visual and audio formats.
- The accessibility functions or alternative web page is easy to find.

Also keep in mind that any information intended for people with DD should be in plain language at no higher than a fifth-grade reading level.

It is tempting, once you move beyond basic design and structure, to add lots of bells and whistles to make a website more enticing. If you do, try not to make it overwhelming, or people with learning and attention issues will have difficulty navigating it. Furthermore, some commonly used features like animations can be triggering or even cause sensory overload. Finally, whatever enhancement you add will need to meet accessibility standards. Remember these tips:

- Blinking and flickers at the wrong frequency can trigger seizures.
- Images may not be seen.
- People will interpret visual information in a variety of ways, in part depending on their level of comfort with inference and understanding of social cues.
- Automatic audio can be overwhelming.
- Slide carousels can appear to be a blur or be too fast to follow.
- Links embedded in an image are not available to screen readers.
- Scripting can be glitchy for screen readers.
- Captions that don't sync with audio can be confusing.
- Timed activities exclude people with executive functioning issues.
- "Help" pages are only useful if they are easy to find.

This all gets very technical very quickly, so we are just introducing the basics. To ensure that your website is accessible, we suggest you look to the experts and refer to sources like these:

- W3C, the World Wide Web Consortium, has accessibility standards for the novice web designer and the most experienced: www.w3.org/standards/.
- The U.S. Access Board website hosts the "Section 508 Standards for Electronic and Information Technology": www.access-board.gov/ict.html.
- The General Services Administration website lists places to test your website for accessibility: www.section508.gov/test/web-software.
- Medium offers tips on using Java scripting so it works for accessibility, including the 2017 article "Writing JavaScript with Accessibility in Mind," by Manuel Matuzovic: https://medium.com.

Even the best information is useless if the people you want to see it are unable to access it. Websites, like front doors, are the portals to your library. The extent to which people with DD are welcomed is immediately evident at both, so follow these suggestions to create an accessible and welcoming website and library.

EVALUATING PROGRAMS

It is important to build an evaluation strategy into your program planning because not everything you try is going to succeed. Some libraries start a program that becomes an instant hit, while others do the same thing and can't get more than one or two people to attend. Looking at programming as a process of trial and error will soften the blow of failures. When something isn't working after a reasonable period, move on to something else until you find the programs that resonate with your community. Regular input from self-advocates, agencies, and caregivers can make it easier to identify in advance what is likely to work well, and developing a means of evaluating programs you try will help you know what succeeded and what should be modified or abandoned. A good evaluation plan can also help sell a program to a funder.

The metrics for evaluating programming for adults with DD are different in some ways from the ones used to evaluate other library programs. For many public libraries, attendance numbers are the key indicator of program success. That criterion, however, is not relevant to programming for adults with DD because these adults do better in smaller groups that allow for more social interaction, less environmental distraction, and greater support. So, set some other goals and see if you meet them.

These were the goals of Kayla Kuni's programming for adults with DD at New Port Richey (FL) Public Library:

> Keep this group involved in the library. Make them aware that the library is for them. Make them feel comfortable. Let them know where to ask questions. Finish with a smile. . . . It's not just big numbers, it's are they actively engaged in the program.[10]

Contra Costa County (CA) Library calls their program for adults with DD Insiders for a reason. Their goal is to take members of a group traditionally on the outside of community life and turn them into library insiders. Progress in achieving these kinds of goals can be measured only qualitatively not quantitatively, so ask yourself, other staff members, and the participants themselves questions like these:

- Do adult patrons with DD report that they enjoy programs and look forward to them?
- Do they seem to be more comfortable with staff because they come to programs?
- Do staff see these patrons around the library at nonprogram times?
- Do they seem to feel at home in the library?
- Do they access library materials and services?

If these things are happening, congratulations! Your programming is a real success and a testament to your fundraising, marketing, and evaluation as well as your program design.

NOTES

1. Renee Grassi, personal communication, January 20, 2020.
2. Candice Casey, personal communication, September 13, 2019.
3. Vicki Karlovsky, personal communication, November 6, 2019.
4. Jen Taggart, personal communication, October 29, 2019.
5. Jen Taggart, "The Importance of a Name: Updating a Collection's Identity," *Adaptive Umbrella* (blog), January 9, 2020, https://adaptiveumbrella.blogspot.com/2020/01/the-importance-of-name-updating.html.
6. Hennepin County Library, "Healing Heart Wounds" (event description), https://hclib.bibliocommons.com/events/search/q=%20%20webber%20park/event/5dc1df3c6af94d440055705b.
7. Candice Casey, "Inclusive Activities for Adults" (handout); material used with permission.
8. Casey, "Inclusive Activities for Adults."
9. Carli Spina, "Accessibility Information on Library Websites," *Library User Experience Community* (blog), November 17, 2017, https://blog.libux.co/accessibility-information-on-library-websites-cda5c46a7f4b.
10. Kayla Kuni and Linda Hotslander, presenters, and Sarah Osman, facilitator, "You Belong @ Your Library: Programming for Adults with Intellectual Disabilities," *Programming Librarian* (webinar series, ALA Public Programs Office), originally recorded September 15, 2015, posted to YouTube on March 10, 2016, 54:14, , www.youtube.com/watch?v=fuSRAuX_FEc&feature=youtu.be; see also the Programming Librarian website at http://programminglibrarian.org/learn/you-belong-your-library-programming-adults-intellectual-disabilities.

PART III

Programs to Try

CHAPTER 9

Virtual Programs and Services

On January 19, 2020, a man walked into a clinic in Washington State with a cluster of symptoms that led doctors to suspect he had been infected with a then novel coronavirus, COVID-19. He became the first confirmed U.S. case of the new disease.[1] His diagnosis and the pandemic that quickly followed ushered in a new era and a new paradigm for library services.

In response to the pandemic, in mid-March ALA's Executive Board recommended that library facilities close until there was no longer a risk of staff or patrons catching or spreading the virus. Libraries quickly developed virtual programs. The Association of Specialized and Cooperative Library Agencies (ASGCLA) developed a virtual accessibility toolkit. However, developing virtual programs and services doesn't always mean that libraries can reach their intended audiences. Individuals with developmental disabilities face a variety of barriers when they want to access virtual content, and these barriers need to be addressed for virtual programs to effectively serve these patrons.

BARRIERS TO ACCESSING VIRTUAL PROGRAMS

The first barrier is that many adults with disabilities do not have access to the needed technology. Of adults with disabilities, 23 percent report they are never online versus 8 percent of adults without disabilities; 30 percent fewer have access at home to desktop or laptop computers, smartphones, tablets, or broadband Wi-Fi.[2] It is widely assumed that adults with intellectual disabilities, who are more likely to live in congregate care settings, are even less likely than those with other disabilities to have regular access to a device or the internet.

Another barrier is a lack of access to the materials needed for participation in programs or the money with which to purchase them. Particularly if they live in congregate settings, adults with DD will not necessarily have at their disposal the common household items that a librarian might think to use in a craft, such as egg cartons, beans, glue, scissors, or different types of paper. It may also be harder for adults with DD to get materials for book discussions on their own. To enable them to participate, you must find a way to get materials to them prior to your programs.

KEYS TO VIRTUAL ACCESSIBILITY

To address these barriers and make sure that virtual programs are more broadly accessible, you should take care as they are designed, keeping in mind these guidelines:

- Use UDL principles in planning.
- Use an accessible platform.
- Make sure staff and patrons know how to use the platform and its accessibility features.
- Make sure your program is comprehensible if patrons can't see or hear it.
- Read out the chat during the programs for those with print disabilities or who are on the phone.
- Ensure that the viewer's attention is not pulled away by nonessential features during the program. Consider the background and how you focus attention on presenters or key program elements.
- Provide an agenda or outline to make the program easier to follow.
- Include only graphics, background sounds, and music that support the program and are not overwhelming for some patrons. See if these features can be modified or turned off.
- Build in a way for participants to connect with you and one another, such as allowing private chat.
- Have a plan for getting needed materials to patrons before the program.

These guidelines are based in part on ASGCLA's virtual accessibility toolkit, one of the last projects done before that ALA division disbanded in September 2020. The toolkit, which can be found on the Reference and User Services Association (RUSA) website (www.ala.org/rusa/virtual-accessibility), can be used to help you make any virtual program accessible. If you have the technical expertise, you might also consider creating your own guidelines and sharing them with library staff who do virtual programming. The Hennepin County Library in Minnesota did just that. As soon as the library shifted to virtual programming, the staff's Accessible Libraries Team created accessibility best practices that were then shared throughout the system. For detailed information about creating accessible virtual programs, check out *Pivoting during the Pandemic: Ideas for Serving Your Community Anytime, Anywhere,* edited by Kathleen M. Hughes and Jamie Santoro (ALA Editions, 2021).

IS YOUR VIRTUAL PROGRAM PLATFORM ACCESSIBLE?

Does it:
- work with screen readers and AT?
- allow phone-in connections?
- have one-click joining?
- enable captioning?
- have obvious ways to request help?
- offer flexibility in displays and settings?
- make advanced features like polling accessible?
- integrate keyboard-only navigation?

Source: Claudio Luis Vera, "Which Video Conferencing Tools Are Most Accessible?," *Smashing Magazine,* July 15, 2020, www.smashingmagazine.com/2020/06/accessible-video-conferencing-tools/.

Perhaps the most important aspect of virtual accessibility is helping people use it. You can use one technology to assist people with another one; for example, you can use the phone to help patrons get started with Zoom. The Grapevine (TX) Public Library does telephone tutorials on how to use library services, and they include guidance on virtual ones. Once patrons can access the platform, you can use the platform itself to teach them how to navigate it. Every program should start with a review of how to use the platform and of the community accessibility standards. For example, people need to be alerted to say their names each time they speak and mute themselves when they are not speaking.

REAL-TIME ONLINE PROGRAMS

Real-time programs using a video-conferencing platform are the most like traditional library programs. Cynthia Hosang at the West Hempstead (NY) Public Library moved the library's weekly reading program to Zoom after the shutdown. Done in partnership with the Jewish Union Foundation, this program involves reading aloud with adults with disabilities. When they moved to Zoom, they picked up right where they had left off in Roald Dahl's *The BFG*. Hosang uses a screen-sharing app to display the book as she reads to the group.[3]

Inclusive Services at BPL took its ASL class online and doubled the attendance! The class, which usually meets at the Kensington Library, is a partnership with a nearby day habilitation program at the Adapt Community Network. The day habilitation participants both learn and assist the teacher, who works at Adapt. The classes start with the leader distributing the lesson plans for the day. Visual supports are part of each lesson, and some participants share their own languages, such as Spanish and Cantonese, during the programs. Both in person and online, this is a wonderfully inclusive program. At one session were an older couple from the community who were studying ASL so they could speak with their Deaf grandchild, a local businessman, library staff wanting to learn ASL, and the participants from the day habilitation program and their friends.

ARCHIVED VIRTUAL PROGRAMS

Libraries that already have videos of programs with live participants can expand their reach by posting these online for future viewing. If you want to do this, be sure to instruct participants to use made-up screen names and to keep their video cameras off. This avoids the issue of having to get permission from participants, which can be tricky because some may have guardians who would need to give their permission as well. Because they don't require permission, performance-only videos on platforms like Facebook Premier are simpler to share online.

You can also create and film programs specifically to share online and post them on the library's website or on a streaming platform like YouTube. One exciting example that predates the pandemic comes from San Francisco Public Library. In 1984 they worked with several state and national partners to create American Cultures the Deaf Perspective, a four-part series. One session titled "Deaf Minorities" was described in this way:

> Bay Area residents, including a Cuban émigré, an African-American woman, a Native American woman, a Japanese-American man, a feminist, a gay man, a lesbian and an older adult share their personal experiences as members of minority communities within the larger Deaf [*sic*] community.[4]

The video has several basic features that make it broadly accessible:

- a posted agenda
- simple background that lets viewers focus on the speaker
- static camera shots
- voice and ASL narration with accurate captions
- the ability to be viewed again and again

The fact that this series was written and coproduced by members of the d/Deaf and hard of hearing community helped ensure accessibility.

TELEPHONE PROGRAMS AND SERVICES

During the pandemic, while many libraries moved their existing in-person programs to an online platform, some moved theirs to the phone. For example, for four years BPL had a monthly program called Navigating Your Child's Disability: One to One Assistance, offered in partnership with the local federally sponsored parent center. An experienced Navigator helps patrons with individualized education plans, the transition to adulthood, and accessing community services. The program was moved to the telephone in May 2020, six weeks after BPL closed its physical locations. Patrons called a librarian who then scheduled an appointment time and gave their contact information to the Navigator. The Navigator then called the patron at the scheduled time. Moving the library program to the phone, one of the few options for people without reliable internet access, was a success. In one instance, for example, an autistic adult got help with community services during a Navigator phone appointment. In another, a Spanish-speaking mother with a disability got referrals to help her challenge the cut-off of her and her children's Supplemental Security Income benefits. BPL also launched telephone reference services and telephone-based story and poetry readings shortly after closing its brick-and-mortar facilities.

Other libraries also started new types of telephone initiatives to meet different needs. For example, Vicki Karlovsky from Deerfield (IL) Public Library created Library Lifeline to bring new programs and services to seniors and the adults with DD whom she serves. The program was designed to provide what services were possible during the pandemic, reaching out to regular patrons and offering free one-on-ones and check-ins. Library Lifeline offers help "accessing e-materials and e-resources, basic technology assistance, read-alouds with discussion, or . . . just . . . a friendly voice over the phone."[5] Karlovsky also reads poetry to patrons over the phone because some folks don't have computers.

THE IMPORTANCE OF OUTREACH

Karlovsky's Deerfield library initiatives exemplify the value of virtual outreach. Not content to wait for people to call her, she reached out to her patrons with disabilities. "A lot of what I am doing is checking on people to see what they need," she explains. She e-mails and calls local organizations, high school transition programs, recreation programs, and individual families to promote the phone services. She also participated in virtual programs that day and residential programs provided for the people they serve. "I've been able to help them with their programs," she says, "like dropping in on virtual book discussions, [and] helping staff find free resources for e-books and e-audio."[6] One challenge she faced was that participants in these programs come from all over the area, not just Deerfield, and are served by a variety of libraries. Since they all needed the same book for discussions, Karlovsky helped them navigate their own library systems, and she identified free resources that day and residential programs could use to find multiple copies of books for the programs.

Continued outreach and staying in touch with individuals and agencies were also mainstays of IS/BPL's virtual programming during this time, and the head of Inclusive Services continued attending and presenting at community meetings throughout the closure. Her goal was to publicize library programs and ensure that they would be tailored to community needs. Another outreach effort resulted from a collaboration between Inclusive Services, BPL's Business and Career Center, and the Queens Public Library. The three entities developed a presentation based on shared resources and designed for students eighteen years of age and older with DD who were aging out of the school system. It was delivered to school transition staff and at a city-wide conference. A version was also developed for students. Microsoft Teams was used for these presentations because it is the preferred platform of New York City's Department of Education.

PROGRAMS DESIGNED FOR OTHER AUDIENCES

As with in-house programs, inclusive virtual programs should make up a major part of a library's repertoire. These can be specifically designed to be inclusive or ones developed for other audiences that also work well for adults with DD. The Tales and Travel program, developed by Mary Beth Riedner for the Gail Borden Public Library in Elgin, Illinois, is a good example.[7] Created for adults living with dementia and originally offered physically in libraries, the program moved online in May

2020. Using a video made up of PowerPoint slides, the first virtual Tales and Travel program toured Chicago. Each slide has both text and a full-color photograph. Riedner reads all of the text on the slides aloud and offers a verbal description of the images. The tour starts with the poem "Chicago" by Carl Sandberg and a map of Chicago; it then takes viewers on a Chicago riverboat ride, pointing out and describing important buildings along the way. Next, the tour heads to Navy Pier where viewers watch a virtual Ferris wheel ride. The last stop is AT&T Plaza in Millennium Park to see Sir Anish Kapoor's sculpture *Cloud Gate*, affectionately known as the bean. After the tour, Riedner leads participants in singing "Chicago, My Kind of Town." Finally, she offers some conversation prompts and provides suggestions for extension activities such as word search puzzles and coloring pages, instructing patrons about how to find these resources online. The use of a variety of modalities, the reading aloud, and the close connection between pictures and text all made this a fun and accessible program for people with DD. In-person versions of this program are available online at http://talesandtravelmemories .com/for-librarians/.

VIRTUAL PROGRAMS THAT WORK FOR ALL AUDIENCES
- music performances
- movie showings
- some speakers
- travelogues
- cooking demonstrations
- gaming

Specific programs that convert well to a virtual environment will be introduced throughout the following chapters in part III.

The move to virtual programs began with the pandemic but promises to be a regular part of programming going forward. A hybrid model of virtual and in-person services is flexible, meets the need of a wide variety of patrons, including those who are not available during traditional open hours, and is an important part of a library without walls. For this reason, as we describe programs throughout the remaining chapters of this section, we will note some that would translate especially well to a virtual environment.

NOTES

1. Michelle L. Holshue, Chas DeBolt, Scott Lindquist, Kathy H. Lofy, John Wiesman, Hollianne Bruce, Christopher Spitters, et al., "First Case of 2019 Novel Coronavirus in the United States," *New England Journal of Medicine* 383, no. 10 (January 2020): 929–36.
2. Monica Anderson and Andrew Perrin, "Disabled Americans Are Less Likely to Use Technology," *FactTank* (online publication, Pew Research Center), April 7, 2017, www.pewresearch.org/fact-tank/2017/04/07/disabled-americans-are-less-likely-to-use-technology/.
3. Cynthia Hosang, personal communication, May 17, 2020.
4. Freda Norman, host, "Deaf Minorities," episode 4 in the four-part series *American Culture: The Deaf Perspective* (San Francisco Public Library and D.E.A.F. Media, 1984), YouTube, posted January 8, 2018, www.youtube.com/watch?v=iYbgKUy_-Ls&t=1511s.
5. Deerfield Public Library (DPL), "Accessibility: Library Lifeline: Serving Senior Citizens and Adults with Disabilities," https://deerfieldlibrary.org/accessibility/.
6. Vicki Karlovsky, personal communication, April 25, 2020.
7. Mary Beth Riedner, "Program Model: Virtual Tales and Travel Adventures," *Programming Librarian*, July 29, 2020, https://programminglibrarian.org/programs/virtual-tales-travel-adventures.

CHAPTER 10

Library and Literature-Based Programs

The point of entry to the library is often programming, and for the adults with developmental disabilities in your community, library and literature-based programs can be the gateway to the library's core services and mission.

INTRODUCING THE LIBRARY

One goal of any program for adults with DD is to welcome them to the library. While all programs should familiarize patrons with the library in general, encourage attendance at other library events, and make them comfortable with accessing library materials, some initiatives are especially helpful in this regard. One of these is library tours.

Library tours are a surefire way to introduce everything the library has to offer, so it is always a good idea to offer tours to visitors who come regularly. Tours can be done specifically for agency groups or for the public at large.

Vicki Karlovsky regularly hosts tours of Deerfield (IL) Public Library for people with disabilities. In addition to the physical tour, Deerfield library also offers a social story for adults with DD on its "Accessibility" web page (https://deerfieldlibrary .org/accessibility/). Both the social story and the tours encourage the use of adult services even if materials are procured from youth services.[1] When Lisa Hagen was at Germantown Community Library in Tennessee, she also conducted regular library tours for patrons with disabilities that she called Library Boot Camp. Hagen created a color-coded map of the library to guide participants as they went from area to area and designated each area with a sign in the same color as the map section for these adults to discover as they toured. In this way, she incorporated visuals, made the tour accessible to nonreaders, and offered an experience in map reading—all while introducing the library.[2]

BEST PRACTICES FOR LIBRARY TOURS

These guidelines can help you create successful library tours. You may not be able to incorporate all of them, but each one you can do will make your tour more engaging and accessible:

- Advertise the event in advance.
- Have registration for the tour but also accept walk-ins.
- Create a social story about the library and have it available for the tour and on the library's website.
- Hold the tour outside of regular library hours or at quiet times to avoid sensory distractions.
- Make the tour as interactive and hands-on as possible. Ask simple questions as you tour and allow participants to make and decorate name tags. Have stickers, including alphabet stickers, and markers on hand to spell out names.
- Make the tour predictable. At the beginning explain where you are going and how long the tour will take.
- Use a variety of communication strategies.
- Incorporate visuals like Hagen's map.
- Make sure all areas are physically accessible. If there is an elevator and stairs, offer both options so those with mobility issues aren't singled out.
- Show where participants should go if they have questions and talk about whom to approach for help.
- Cover library rules and behavioral expectations. Use positive statements to describe what people should do in the library.
- Explain how to request accommodations.
- Assume that participants will be utilizing all of the library's services, so cover them all in the tour.

REGULAR GROUP VISITS

People with DD who spend their days in day habilitation programs or who live in residential settings often come to the library on a regular basis in groups accompanied by agency staff. Sometimes these groups want to be left on their own, but others appreciate some assistance in using computers or finding materials. Still others are open to programming during visits, and some library staff have seen these visits as an opportunity to encourage broader participation and library use. Libraries can enhance these visits, even for groups that pretty much want to be left on their own, by offering an introduction to the library and its services.

Materials and Sensory Kits

A simple thing to do for groups that want to be on their own is to keep some materials on hand for their visits. For example, the Bloomfield Township Public Library in Michigan keeps puzzles, board games, coloring sheets with packs of colored pencils, and simple activity sheets at public service desks in both youth and adult services specifically for the in-house use of groups of adults with disabilities.

A cart or shelf of books and other materials that meet the needs and interests of regular visitors can also be preselected by library staff. In addition to activity resources, Bloomfield Township library keeps a small stack of hi-lo fiction and age-respectful nonfiction books for emergent readers at both public services desks. They change the selection weekly. Many libraries also offer sensory kits at public service desks and during programs. These include items like fidgets, noise-canceling headphones, and weighted lap pads. We discuss these kits at length in chapter 3.

Computer Help

Group visits are a great time to introduce one-on-one computer assistance, schedule group computer lab time, or share iPads. You can introduce websites of interest and demonstrate apps. Consider including coloring apps and simple jigsaw puzzle or word game apps that allow users to adjust the level of difficulty. Be careful to avoid apps that are obviously for children. Check with patrons and the agencies that visit to see if they have favorites.

Library Card Sign-Up

Group visits are good times to encourage these patrons to become regular library users by helping them get library cards. Before you do this, talk to agency representatives to make sure that group members live in your service area. Ascertain if residential agencies allow the people they serve to check out materials or if they are a barrier to this happening. If the latter, try to discuss their concerns with an agency representative to see if you can address them. This may involve offering to waive fines or extend loan periods. If group members are eligible to get cards, see if you can talk to them for a few minutes during a visit. Describe in simple language what cards offer and help them apply. Also spend some time introducing other things they might want to do at the library in addition to their group visits. If you offer library card applications virtually, be available to talk patrons with DD through this process on the phone.

Group Visit–Based Programs

Group visits can morph into a program that takes the place of more informal library time. Rebecca Wolfe from Allen County Library in Ft. Wayne, Indiana, notes, "It's great that agencies bring adults with IDD to the library, but sad when they aren't fully utilizing the library in ways we know they can with some simple programming help from us."[3] Kelsey McLane came to the same conclusion at Arapahoe Library District in Colorado after noticing that on most days from one to five day program groups came to the library, and "mostly, they would sit around for an hour, look at books, some would get on the computer, etc. And I started thinking about how much we were failing this population."[4] Her observation led to the Library for All program, based on one at nearby Jefferson County Public Libraries. Within a year this program was held monthly at three branches with as many as forty to fifty people attending each session. At Truro Public Library on Cape Cod in Massachusetts, a regular group visit from clients of Cape Abilities became a Next Chapter Book Club that has been running for several years, thanks to a similar observation and a suggestion made by Barbara.

Jen Ripka developed a new program at Naperville (IL) Public Library for Community Access Naperville during the group's infrequent but regular library visits. Using basic supplies like tape, a foam pool noodle, a ball, and a construction paper finish line flag, she created fun and meaningful library programs.[5] For example, a sports-themed program included these elements:

- short videos: people and animals on an obstacle course
- activity: running an obstacle course consisting of
    - going under a pool noodle limbo stick,
    - walking a balance beam marked with painter's tape on the floor,
    - picking up and tossing a foam ball into a basket, and

      – crossing the finish line!
- scavenger hunt: looking for sports equipment hidden throughout the room
- unstructured computer time
- library time

You might consider extending the scavenger hunt into the stacks and placing the sports equipment in the sports section to help familiarize participants with the library outside of the programming room.

    As with any focused program for adults with DD, having more than one program leader can help things run more smoothly. Flexibility is also required, as participants can come to the library later or earlier than planned, and program elements may need to be adjusted to accommodate these schedule changes.[6]

LITERATURE-BASED PROGRAMS

Once patrons are familiar with the library, there is a world of possibilities for literature-based programs. You can try one of the options given here or develop your own.

Story and Activity Programs

This type of programming is more common in youth services than in adult services, but a number of libraries have created successful focused models for their adult patrons with DD.

Sensory Storytime

Bloomfield Township library youth services librarian Jen Taggart and adult services librarian Ed Niemchak designed a storytime for teens and adults with DD that combines elements from the library's sensory storytime for youth with age-respectful elements for teens and adults. Their adult-appropriate themes include music, government, nutrition, in the garden or kitchen, going places, folktales, and STEAM (science, technology, engineering, arts, and mathematics) topics. They read picture books published for children that have simple, rhythmic, or interactive texts and age-appropriate illustrations. Titles are predominantly nonfiction. The program is held in the library's large community room where chairs are arranged in a semicircle with spaces left open for wheelchairs. Additional tables and chairs are located in the back of the room for use during the sensory experience/craft.

Generally, each storytime consists of eight to ten steps:

1. Greeting
2. Theme introduced by a visual schedule that includes program activities
3. Seated or adapted yoga pose. Favorites include "reach for the sky" and "forward bend."
4. Rhyme with ASL or active movement
5. 1st story
6. Interactive song
7. 2nd story
8. Theme-related music or video clip
9. Sensory experience/craft. This is a social time and the highlight of the program.
10. Goodbye[7]

Music and Movement Storytime

Allen County Library's Music and Movement Storytime is an outreach program run by Rebecca Wolfe. Each session has a theme, and as many as forty people attend. The participants like to hold stuffed animals during the program, so Wolfe brings an assortment that fits the theme. The program includes

- hello song
- greeting
- movement songs (Jim Gill songs and hip-hop from Mr. Chris are popular.)
- reading or readers' theater (Wolfe does echo reading with nonreaders: first she reads a word or phrase, and then the participant repeats it.)
- music with egg shakers or scarves
- closing song, often calming new age music or a guided meditation[8]

This type of program incorporates many of the components of UDL and multiple intelligences theory. There are linguistic, musical, and kinesthetic presentations. There is intrapersonal engagement with the stuffed animals and interpersonal engagement with the hello song, readers' theater, and singing together. Changing topics increases the engagement. The action and expression are musical, verbal, and spatial. This type of musical program could easily go virtual on a platform such as Zoom, Microsoft Teams, or RingCentral.

Literature and Craft Program

The more traditional literature and crafts programs offer similar UDL possibilities. Vicki Karlovsky's PLACE (Public Library Access and Community for Everyone) quarterly program at Deerfield library is a good example. In Karlovsky's model, the reading section, usually a short story or poem written for adults, is followed by a discussion and then a craft. She places sensory kits in the room so items like fidgets and noise-canceling headphones are available for those who want them. The craft time always has three to four options that vary in difficulty, an application of UDL. Coloring sheets also vary in level of difficulty. People participate in the program in whatever way they are comfortable. Some read aloud; others don't. Some do other activities like coloring during the reading; some retreat to a quiet space if needed. Some make one craft; others make all four of them.

Participants receive a packet containing these items:

- a cover introducing the theme
- a program schedule
- information about the author and some context, like the period or setting
- the text of the poem or short reading
- discussion questions that Karlovsky finds online
- step-by-step instructions for each craft option[9]

Although her programs require a lot of preparation, Karlovsky likes them because she believes they offer something for everyone.

Virtual Read-Aloud

At the request of partner agency the Arc, Moline (IL) Public Library used Zoom to take their read-aloud program online during the pandemic. The biweekly virtual program is structured like a storytime. Librarian Lisa Powell Williams reads to the group from picture books that match the program theme and ones with humorous elements. "So much of the group was about laughter and the group preferred things that were somewhat silly," she says.[10] As she reads, she stops to point out things in the art, and if the art is visually busy, she might ask the attendees to find something in the images. One regular attendee of the in-person program liked to find colors in the art that matched her outfit.

The virtual program includes most of the elements of the in-library read-aloud:

- opening counting rhymes
- catching up on what is going on in the lives of participants

- introducing the theme
- picture books
- a discussion about what they did at that session
- promotion of the next program

The virtual version eliminates the craft that is part of the in-library program. Williams reads more books instead. There is also less interaction in the virtual program, but the participants still enjoy it. During a beach-themed program, one man looked up with a big smile on his face as he held up a blue-and-green drawing. His caregiver said it was a picture of the waves in the book that had just been read. Seeing that, Williams knew the man was engaged in the program and it was a success.

Book Clubs

Books clubs are the bread and butter of adult services programming, and there are some great models for adults with DD.

Next Chapter Book Club

The most widely adopted book club model for adults with DD is by far the Next Chapter Book Club (NCBC), created by Dr. Tom Fish in 2002. Entities that sponsor NCBCs are called affiliates, and many are libraries, often working in partnership with direct service agencies. In 2018 40 percent of the total clubs and 70 percent of new clubs formed that year were associated with libraries.[11] This trend makes sense because libraries are a natural fit for this program. The NCBC model's three elements—social connectedness, community inclusion, and literacy learning—all tie in well with the values and use of public libraries.

The NCBC model consists of a weekly session of an hour or so for a group of four to eight members plus two facilitators. Members take turns reading a book selected by the group; facilitators assist emergent readers and elicit conversation about the reading and about the lives of club members. Food and drink are usually a part of the mix, and getting to purchase a snack can be a highlight for members whose group meets at a coffeehouse or restaurant.

In some libraries staff serve as club facilitators; in others community volunteers fill these roles. Many facilitators love the experience and grow very attached to club members. Sophia-Louisa Michalatos, longtime facilitator of the NCBC at the Ferguson Library in Stamford, Connecticut, had this to say about her club experience: "Next Chapter Book Club has enriched my life in immeasurable ways. I consider being part of our book club as my great good fortune. Reading, and engaging in our book group is the highlight of my week."[12] Club members feel the same way. One member, a sixty-year-old named Gary, had this to say about his club: "This is what I've wanted to do all my life. Since I've been in the book club I've been learning."[13]

Some libraries go beyond the basic model. Glen Cove Public Library in New York, for example, uses a small item that matches the theme of the current book as a turn-taking item that is passed from member to member, making it easy for everyone to know who has the floor and giving members something to hold on to or fidget with as they speak. They also host an annual winter holiday party and sing-along for their NCBC members. The Germantown (TN) Public Library enriched its NCBC experience with field trips to a sensory-friendly play and to the screening of a film based on a book read by the club. If this book club model is something you want to try, check out "Become an Affiliate" on the NCBC website (www .nextchapterbookclub.org/become-an-affiliate).

Silent Book Club

Silent Book Clubs are being hosted by a growing number of libraries, and the trend was featured in an article in the May 2020 issue of *American Libraries.* Each club has its own structure, or lack thereof, and most require very little planning. This type of book club can work well for many adults with DD, as demonstrated by a successful club started by autistic self-advocate Janine Brooks and hosted by Omaha's Autism Society of Nebraska (ASN). It is called Silent Book Club for Au-some Readers and Introverts, although so far all of the attendees have been autistic. As Brooks points out, the lack of pressure to read a shared book or to participate in the discussion can be a draw for some who love reading and want a bit of social connection without the obligation to read aloud or be part of a discussion.

The club meets monthly for two hours with the following structure:

- introduction: members sharing something about themselves and showing the books they plan to read
- silent reading
- discussion

The final discussion isn't literary analysis. For example, a member might say there was a swordfight in the chapter they read that day, and another member might add that their book had a swordfight as well.

Members sometimes bring books to exchange, and snacks are available. Someone has a chance to win a $20 gift card at each session. About five to nine people attend each meeting, although they are not always the same people. They tend to read material for adults, including audio formats and magazines. During the COVID-19 pandemic, the club switched to bimonthly meetings on Zoom that lasted an hour instead of the usual two. The format remained essentially the same in an abbreviated form.[14]

Here's how to make existing Silent Book Clubs inclusive:

- Incorporate a regular structure into meetings.
- Offer visual supports.
- Manage transitions between program segments. The ASN–Omaha club uses a chime to indicate when the reading period begins, when there is five minutes left to read, and when it is time to transition from reading back to talking.
- Structure the discussion period so that it is clear when it is someone's turn to speak, but be sure to emphasize that participation in the discussion is optional.
- Have fidgets and other sensory supports on hand.
- Leave space in the room for people who need to pace or stim.

When care is taken to let everyone know that their choice of reading material will be respected, so those reading graphic novels or books written for children are not shamed in any way, a Silent Book Club can bring together your community's introverts, adults with DD, English language learners, and others—all of whom can read together in peaceful and silent harmony.

Library-Created Book Club Models

The Dakota County Library in Minnesota is one of several libraries that have created their own book club models. In partnership with the Autism Society of Minnesota, their AuSM Book Club meets monthly. Instead of reading the same book together, attendees select a theme or genre they want to focus on the next month, choosing from options provided by a special education literacy teacher and a librarian. Past themes have included classic authors, mystery, history, action/adventure, sci-fi/fantasy, and sports.

Meetings follow this format:

- Greetings and social time.
- Book share: Attendees share five things they liked, didn't like, or learned about the book they read that month. They also comment on and ask questions about others' books.

- Genre review: The facilitator reviews the month's genre and introduces related movies and TV shows.
- Book selection: Attendees are guided to use the library's catalog to find books in the next month's genre. Interests, reading level, and preferred format are taken into account.
- Book checkout: Participants take their selected materials home to read and prepare for the next meeting.

Some attendees come with copious notes; others need to be prompted to elicit their thoughts. Some read at an advanced level; others are nonreaders who need supports or access to their books in audio. Participation and communication are individualized. This format allows people with a wide variety of reading skills and interests to join together, share books, and get reading suggestions from one another. Anywhere from two to ten people come each month, and because the majority are regulars, they are known to each other and to staff on a first-name basis. The club creates connection and community, fosters a love of books and reading, and builds comfort with using the library.[15]

In 2017 library assistant Jeny Wasilewski Mills created the Read-Ability Book Group for the Evanston Public Library in Illinois. Many participants of this program for adults with intellectual and cognitive disabilities are members of partner agency Center for Independent Futures. Read-Ability participants read one book every four months. New members register at the beginning of the cycle. At the end of the trimester, members vote on a new book from a list created by staff. Titles are predominantly young adult or adult fiction, mysteries, or science fiction. According to Mills, this choice was made so "members can experience books aimed at their actual age level, books they might not have gone to the library to get on their own."[16]

The group meets weekly for one hour. Sessions begin with a review, followed by Mills reading aloud to the members, who follow along with print or audio copies. At the end of the reading there is a discussion. As with all of the book club models, everyone involved has wonderful things to say about the program. Member Claudia Joehl says:

> I look forward to seeing what happens in the books we read and talking about it in the book club. I like being part of a group of people who like to share what they think about things. I also like the way we vote to choose the book we'll read and that we can ask questions about things we don't understand that we read.[17]

The focused Books for Dessert program began at the Port Washington (NY) Public Library in 2003. There is an advisory board comprised of parents, professionals, and program leaders. A comprehensive manual includes everything from book lists to guidelines for recruiting program leaders, all of whom are education professionals. Leaders and assistants are paid for each session, and the responsibilities of the library staff, advisory board members, and program leaders are clearly defined. The program is funded through the library's foundation. When each book, usually a hi-lo title, is completed, the group watches a movie based on that book. Members get their own copies of each title to keep. The program meets weekly for about an hour and a half, with a hiatus during the summer.

Leaders may modify the plan based on the participants in each group, but in general the sessions are similar to those of other clubs, with a review followed by reading and a discussion. This club also spends time learning vocabulary from the books they read and, of course, given the name, eating dessert together. As the manual states:

> The clubs...have become an integral part of participants' lives, as well as having expanded their horizons (and their caregivers' awareness of their abilities and potential). All involved . . . have been surprised and delighted by the response. We've all learned to forget all the warnings about plateaus and inability to perform beyond a certain ceiling. We haven't found that ceiling yet.[18]

WRITING WORKSHOPS

Library book clubs for adults with DD dispel the myth that they aren't interested in reading. Another myth is the idea that these adults can't or don't want to write, yet best-selling books have been written by authors with DD, including Temple Grandin's *Thinking in Pictures: My Life with Autism* (Doubleday, 1995) and John Elder Robison's *Look Me in the Eye: My Life with Asperger's* (Random House, 2007); and the publication in 2016 of *The Reason I Jump: The Inner Voice of a Thirteen-Year-Old Boy with Autism,* by Naoki Higashida (Random House, 2016), demonstrated that you don't have to be verbal to write a powerful memoir.

Bryan Boyce wanted to change the way we think and talk about people with disabilities, so he founded a company in the Twin Cities area in Minnesota called Cow Tipping Press. He offers writing workshops for people with disabilities in partnership with agencies and organizations like libraries and publishes the work created during these workshops. Boyce named his company after "Cow Tipping in the Dark," a poem written as part of his first class. He selected it because he wanted the writers' voices front and center.[19] His approach is unique, even among neurodiversity publishers.

A number of libraries, including Ridgedale Library, part of the Hennepin County system, and the Dakota Library, both in Minnesota, hosted these workshops. The Dakota library one was virtual. The workshops are literary, not literacy, programs. No one's spelling or grammar is corrected, and no one directs what someone should write about. Scribes assist attendees to get their ideas on paper, but they write down people's exact words and do not guide the writing process in any way. The anthologies of workshop writings published by Cow Tipping Press are also unfiltered and unedited in the conventional sense, with spelling and grammar left as is.

The Grapevine (TX) Public Library has a different virtual writing program. Librarian Ruth Chiego shares story starters with a Facebook group, and because "they can't write, but they do pictures," they respond with those. She explains:

> It's created a sort of pen pal synergy that we didn't have before. Their personalities are seeping out through their words in ways that we haven't seen before. It is just kinda wonderful to see that the connections are holding even though they are not seeing each other. They like "thumbs upping" and "liking" each other.[20]

Encouraging group members to tell stories with pictures incorporates AAC into the program, and Facebook's icon-based feedback encourages additional communication.

AUTHOR TALKS

Author talks, another staple of library programming for adults, are ideal programs for adults with DD. As we mentioned earlier, there are authors who openly talk about their developmental disabilities, and some are happy to speak to groups to promote their work. Temple Grandin spoke at a 2013 ALA conference about her then new book *The Autistic Brain: Thinking across the Spectrum* (Mariner Books, 2013) to a standing-room-only crowd. That same year, when Harilyn Russo's book *Don't Call Me Inspirational: A Disabled Feminist Talks Back* (Temple University Press, 2013) was published, BPL's Inclusive Services, then the Child's Place for Children with Special Needs, hosted a book launch and signing. IS/BPL advertised it heavily in the disability community in Brooklyn, including among people who shared Russo's diagnosis of CP. The event was held in a fully accessible showcase space at the Central Library.

Finding out what accommodations authors need is critical to making these programs work. When Michael John Carley, author of three books, including 2021's *The Book of Happy, Positive, and Confident Sex for Adults on the Autism Spectrum . . . and Beyond!* (Neurodiversity Press, 2021), spoke at BPL he requested a lapel mike so he could walk around as he spoke. Autistic author Morénike Giwa Onaiwu talks about her speaking style on her website:

> I might wear noise canceling headphones and/or sunglasses while presenting; I might cosplay . . . ; I will most likely have some sort of stimming tool/fidget device with me (it might be a discreet, small one embedded in my fist that's invisible to the audience . . . or it might be something wearable that I will only touch as needed); I will probably use fillers such as "um," or "like," or "you know," while speaking; I might not make eye contact with your audience . . . etc.[21]

Onaiwu is a powerful virtual speaker, something BPL found out when her flight to NYC was canceled because of snow in 2018. She coached us through setting up her conference keynote speech on intersectionality via Zoom. This was Inclusive Services' first Zoom program!

All of the author talk programs discussed here were inclusive, with self-advocates making up a significant part of the audiences.

TIPS FOR INCLUSIVE AUTHOR TALKS

When planning for inclusive author talks, make sure to do the following:
- Use an accessible venue.
- Let the speaker know to expect an inclusive audience.
- Involve people with DD in the planning.
- Get the word out in the disability community well in advance.

In addition to hosting published authors, consider organizing programs featuring the adults with DD who attend your writing workshops or plan a book launch for local authors with DD. All types of author programs can easily be inclusive, and they can offer a showcase for often underrepresented writers. These speakers with

DD can be important role models for other individuals with DD, who are often told what they are unable to do. By organizing inclusive author talks, we can support both the authors and our communities.

SUMMER READING CLUBS

Summer reading clubs (SRCs) are commonplace for youth, and many libraries also have clubs for adults, but only a minority of these are inclusive, designed to accommodate the interests and abilities of patrons with DD. Germantown Public Library has a different model, a focused SRC for adults with DD for which they create a modified version of their adult summer reading booklet. They market the program to adults with DD with a kickoff dance. The decorations at the dance reflect the summer reading theme, and the attendees often wear costumes.

Some summer programs go beyond reading. Glen Ellyn (IL) Public Library's adaptive Summer Reading Challenge is based on multiple intelligences theory, acknowledging that patrons have a variety of learning styles. To make the program more appealing, teens and adults with disabilities contributed to a list of suggested activities that count toward the challenge, including these:

- Read.
- Bake.
- Color.
- Find the birthdate of your favorite author.
- Look up a book in the catalog.
- Walk on the Prairie Path.
- Play catch.
- Take the dog for a walk.
- Look at the sky at night.
- Gaze at clouds.[22]

San Francisco Public Library's summer program, which is similar in structure to Glen Ellyn's, was designed to be inclusive. The library's Inclusive Programming Committee suggested a change from SRC to Summer Stride, which focuses on learning more broadly. Time spent in learning activities, including reading and attending programs, counts toward earning club prizes. Kickoff events are held at two area agencies that serve adults with DD, the Arc of San Francisco and the Janet Pomeroy Center.

No matter what library or literature-based programming you do, your library can become a source of community engagement, connection, and books for adults with DD.

NOTES

1. Vicki Karlovsky, personal communication, November 6, 2019.
2. Lisa Hagen, personal communication, September 26, 2019.
3. Rebecca Wolfe, personal communication, October 31, 2019.
4. Kelsey McLane, personal communication, November 14, 2019.
5. Jen Ripka, personal communication, January 21, 2020.
6. Jen Ripka, personal communications, January 20 and 21, 2020.
7. Jen Taggart and Ed Niemchak, "Sensory Story Time for Adults" (guest post), *It Takes a Village, but It's Nice to Have a Blog,* September 27, 2018, http://brycekozlablog.blog spot.com/2018/09/sensory-story-time-for-adults.html
8. Wolfe, pers. comm.
9. Vicki Karlovsky, personal communication, November 3, 2019.
10. Lisa Powell Williams, personal communication, August 18, 2020.
11. Tom Fish, personal communication, January 14, 2020.
12. Sophia-Louisa Michalatos, personal communication, March 22, 2019.
13. Next Chapter Book Club, PowerPoint training document; quoted with permission.
14. Janine Brooks, personal communication, May 30, 2020.
15. Renee Grassi, personal communication, October 27, 2019.
16. Jeny Wasilewski Mills, personal communication, November 4, 2019.
17. Evanston Public Library, "Introducing the Read-Ability Book Group," www.epl.org/introducing-the-read-ability-book-group/.
18. Port Washington Public Library, *Books for Dessert: Program Manual*, 4; for more information about the program, see https://pwpl.org/books-for-dessert/.
19. Bryan Boyce, personal communication, October 28, 2019.
20. Ruth Chiego, personal communication, March 31, 2020.
21. Morénike Giwa Onaiwu, "Speaking/Training (& Consulting)," https://morenikego.com/speaking/.
22. Josh O'Shea, personal communication, October 31, 2019.

CHAPTER 11

Materials for Adults with Developmental Disabilities

A collection that is diverse in both content and format will be an extension of the library's culture of inclusion. It will be more accessible to people with DD and can provide a solid base for programs. In this chapter we focus on how to ensure that a diverse collection meets the needs of those adults with DD who are not readers or not fluid readers.

COLLECTIONS TO SUPPORT PROGRAMMING

Programs are the gateways to books, so adults with DD, like other users, will want to borrow materials related to programs they attend. After they hear an author speak, they might check out that author's books. After a program on organic gardening, they might look for books on heritage tomatoes. Your library will probably already have books like these that many adults with DD will want and can use. For others, particularly those with ID, you will need to purchase more specialized materials.

When planning to broaden your collection, look to what you already buy and the interests of your patrons with DD. You might focus on adding material that directly supports your programming, or you might want to expand the collection overall. In either case, buy a variety of nonfiction subjects and fiction genres in a mix of formats, including print, graphic, hi-lo, audio, and e-book. Purchase these materials in the languages included in your adult collection. Be sure to have books by authors with lived experience to ensure diversity and take care to avoid material that is ableist, just as you would avoid racist materials.

Don't forget to involve the intended audience in materials selection! Ask adults with DD what they want, and chat about what they are reading. Suzanne Williams, librarian at the College of Adaptive Arts, takes this a step further: "I eavesdrop on conversations," she says. "Every time I hear someone say, 'I would like to know' or 'that's my favorite,' I buy it. The introduction to the library is: 'anything you want to read; just tell me . . . I will buy it.'"[1] It works! Her students with DD are excited to go to the library, often for the first time in their lives.

Books by People with DD

Having materials by people who write from their own experience, called *own voices* materials, is central to the inclusion of people with DD. These authors' perspectives can be validating for your patrons with DD, and these books can introduce the disability experience to people without disabilities. You probably already have some in your collection, such as books by autistic scientist Dr. Temple Grandin and the popular memoir *Funny, You Don't Look Autistic: A Comedian's Guide to Life on the Spectrum,* by Michael McCreary (Annick Press, 2019). To identify less well-known titles written by neurodiverse authors, use a resource created by Lei Wiley-Mydske, who is autistic, a disability activist, and the parent of an autistic child. Her Ed Wiley Autism Acceptance Lending Library of books by neurodiverse authors is available twice monthly at the Stanwood-Camano Community Resource Center in Washington State, and her website lists the books in her collection (https://neurodiversitylibrary.org/book-list/).

An important example of this type of material, one that focuses on the experience of autistic people of color, is *All the Weight of Our Dreams: On Living Racialized Autism*. In the preface, Morénike Giwa Onaiwu, an autistic, nonbinary woman and mother to autistic children speaks to the importance of these materials. The daughter of immigrants from Nigeria, she says:

> I was a minority group within a minority group within a minority group. There was no place that I belonged. . . . Even those who accepted me, cared for me, loved me still did not understand me. Having something of my very own, like the anthology [*All the Weight of Our Dreams*] by people and for people who were like me . . . just as different . . . would have been inexplicably meaningful.[2]

Other *own voices* materials come from Cow Tipping Press, a unique company that publishes anthologies of works created by adults with DD during their writing workshops. These anthologies are described in "Use Our Books" on the company's website (http://cowtippingpress.org), and they are available from Amazon. The workshops, offered as a program series in some libraries, are featured in chapter 10 of this book. These anthologies would be a wonderful addition to many library collections, and they can also be used in programming.

Types of Books to Collect

It can seem especially challenging to find materials for adults with ID, but some books that you might already have in your collection or ones that you can easily acquire can fit the bill, even though most of these are intended for other audiences. Explore these options:

- *Books for children and teens:* Crossover reading should not be dismissed, but be careful in selecting titles and stick to choices that are respectful of adults.
- *Hi-lo books:* These books with low reading levels are of high interest to teens or adults.
- *Books for new adult readers:* These titles are developed specifically for adult literacy programs.
- *Books for English language learners:* This material is written for those who read in their native languages but not in English.
- *Books for English speakers learning other languages:* Similar to materials for English language learners, these books are leveled and progressive. Publishers of these books may be your best source for Spanish and other non-English language hi-lo books.
- *Books with visual supports:* Pictures can help readers decode meaning from unfamiliar words and situations.

Buying these types of materials will ensure that your collection to serve adults with DD includes a range of reading or Lexile levels. Lexile levels were originally developed as a more nuanced way to match a student's ability with an appropriate book, but they have become a stand-in for reading levels in popular use. Each grade level contains an overlapping range of Lexile levels. For example, second grade ends at 795L and third grade begins at 645L.[3] Some books, especially those published for children, will list suggested grade levels on the copyright page or the back cover as a way to indicate the complexity of the text. For adults with ID, collect as broad a range as possible, up to 1260L or fifth grade, but focus on the first through third grade range.

Books Written for Children and Teens

Collaborate with youth services librarians to identify books for the collection that were written for children and teens. Like many adults without disabilities, some adults with DD enjoy these titles. We suggest starting with nonfiction because it can reach across age groups more easily than fiction. A book on whales can have more or less detail and more or less textual complexity while still conveying the same basic information. It may be less obvious that a nonfiction book was intended for children than it is for a fiction title. Pay attention to the tone before adding a book to your collection. Avoid texts that patronize or lecture readers. Look at the illustrations. They should appeal to adults. Photographs can work well, so long as the photographs are age appropriate and focus on adults not children.

Remember to include books for youth that portray the disability experience. A good source for finding titles is Disability in KidLit (http://disabilityinkidlit.com), a website and authoritative source that analyzes the portrayal of disability in middle grade and young adult books. On Goodreads (www.goodreads.com), pay particular attention to the hashtag #OwnVoices, created by Disability in KidLit senior editor Corine Duyvis, which indicates books written by someone who identifies as part of a traditionally marginalized group, including people with disabilities. The Schneider Family Book Award winners are also choices to consider because the intent of the award is to recognize books that accurately portray the disability experience. To find winning titles, visit www.ala.org/awardsgrants/schneider-family-book-award.

Hi-Lo Books

Abridged books or hi-lo adaptations of well-known historical novels are popular choices for librarians buying for people with DD. If you have these, we suggest you also make sure to have the unabridged versions so they are available for those adults with DD who read at a higher level.

Some of these books are versions of classics or canon titles, and those can be problematic. Author Padma Venkatraman discusses this issue in a *School Library Journal* opinion piece, saying that because sometimes "racism, sexism, ableism, anti-Semitism, and other forms of hate are the norm" in these books, we need to take a second, critical look at using them.[4] As Venkatraman says, "Challenging old classics is the literary equivalent of replacing statues of racist figures."[5] Consider instead purchasing high-quality books that reflect diverse experiences.

Books for New Adult Readers and English Language Learners

These books are written for adult audiences, so the content will be age appropriate for adults with DD. The language, however, will be simpler than that found in books written for more proficient English readers. Books for English language learners often cover issues of importance to new Americans, and these can therefore be a good source of information about topics like the U.S. Census and voting.

Books with Visual Supports

Materials with visual supports are already well integrated into your collection, and they are popular with all audiences, including adults with DD. These books are not only pleasurable to read; they are easier for some adults with DD to understand. A small-scale study published in 2018 found evidence that using straightforward text with illustrations improved comprehension for adults with ID.[6] Picture books for adult audiences, coffee-table art books, and many magazines are common materials with inherent visual supports. Graphic novels and comic book–style nonfiction also provide visual supports, telling a story through both pictures and words. Be careful of manga, though, when considering graphic formats for adults with DD, those with print disabilities, and new adult readers. Often these stories read from right to left and have content that is more suited to teens than adults. If you are considering purchasing or using manga, take a second look to make sure it works for your audience.

Providing books with visual supports along with parallel audio editions greatly improves accessibility for patrons with DD, but buying the same title in multiple formats is the ideal because it allows users with a wide variety of reading strengths to access and discuss the same material. Shakespeare's plays and other well-known works can often be found in print and graphic novel formats, as filmed performances available on DVD and through streaming services, as well as in audio and e-book formats. We suggest that you collect them all.

From time to time, books are published in different editions for multiple audiences and all of the editions would be worthy additions to a collection, especially if your users with DD have a wide range of reading abilities. For example, Nobel Laureate Malala Yousafzai's 2013 autobiography, *I Am Malala: The Girl Who Stood Up for Education and Was Shot by the Taliban* (Little, Brown, 2013), was published in both an adult's and a children's version. A picture-book edition was added in 2017. Jason Reynolds published an interpretation of Ibram X. Kendi's scholarly work on the history of U.S. racism for a younger audience called *Stamped: Racism, Antiracism, and You* (A Remix of the National Book Award–Winning *Stamped from the Beginning*). These books are also all available in audio.

MATERIALS FOR USE IN PROGRAMMING

Having a rich, diverse collection will enhance your programming options. To guide you as you pick books for a specific program for adults with DD, consider the nature of the program, the interests and abilities of the participants, and how they will interact with the materials. For storytimes geared to adults, picture books and others with visual supports tend to work best. For reading clubs, longer works are usually selected. For art programs, you can use both children's picture books and highly illustrated coffee-table art books. Here are some types of materials to consider for a variety of programs.

Books Written for Adults

Many titles in your existing adult collections can work well in book clubs if the participants are cognitively able to deal with the length and content. Some of the specialized, more accessible materials for adults that we discussed earlier are also good reads and worth considering. However, if your group reads adult books, be prepared to watch for a lack of understanding, even among those who can decode the words and grammar. You may need to explain cultural concepts and words some participants may not be able to figure out from the context. An example of a book club that successfully reads adult books is the Read-Ability Book Group at Evanston (IL) Public Library. *House Rules* by Jodi Picoult and *Finding Dorothy* by Elizabeth Letts are two adult novels the group has read together.[7]

Other Types of Materials for Adults

The graphic format books that we discussed earlier as well as audiobooks can be used in programming, as can short stories, plays, and poems. Vicki Karlovsky has had success with both short stories and poetry in her PLACE program at Deerfield (IL) Public Library. The collections by Thomas Fish and Jillian Ober from the Next Chapter Book Club organization include short stories and plays that are good to use in programs. Written for NCBCs, which are for adults with DD, the stories and plays feature adult characters with DD and the plots touch on romance, personal appearance, jobs, and similar topics that interest adults with DD as much as they interest other adults. The available collections are *Something's Brewing: Short Stories and Plays for Everyone* (Proving Press, 2020), *New Love, Spilt Milk, and Potbellied Pigs* (Proving Press, 2019), and *Lucky Dogs, Lost Hats, and Dating*

Don'ts (Woodbine, 2012). These books have a place in many collections as well as in programs.

Picture Books

Although picture books are associated with young children, some can be sophisticated and of interest to many adults, not just those with DD. The key is to pick ones that are respectful of adult readers. Jen Taggart and Ed Niemchak of Bloomfield Township (MI) Public Library do this when choosing books for their adult sensory storytime. Try some of these categories when selecting titles to use:

- nonfiction about the natural world, the arts or performing arts, history, vehicles, or famous people
- folktales, which often have repetitive and simple texts and adult characters and are derived from traditional oral literature
- stories that introduce a culture or country
- fiction that appeals to all ages

SELECTING PICTURE BOOKS FOR ADULT PROGRAMS

Look for picture books that:
- avoid condescension
- have a subject or story of interest to adults
- feature adults in central roles in the narrative and illustrations
- use a serif-free font
- have uncluttered spreads and lots of white space
- have text and illustrations that work well together

Middle Grade or Young Adult Chapter Books

Many NCBCs read middle grade, young adult, or abridged novels. Some other book-related programs described in chapter 10 also use these types of books. Hi-lo books written for teens can also work well with some groups. If you intend to select children's or teen chapter books for programs, keep these thoughts in mind:

- Select some titles with protagonists who have disabilities, but not exclusively.
- Look for books that portray the wide range of backgrounds and experiences that reflect your community.

- Choose books with simple plots and avoid those with complex relationships.
- Choose books with fully developed adult characters as well as children.
- Try fantasy books. Autistic adults often like them because the world building describes the ground rules of society, something they don't get in realistic fiction.
- Superhero stories and series like *Star Wars* are often popular with adults with DD, as well as those without disabilities, because the characters and stories are familiar from TV and movies.
- Animal stories can also have appeal. Choose ones that focus on the animals rather than a young child protagonist.
- Consider young adult fiction or nonfiction titles from YALSA's annual Quick Picks for Reluctant Young Adult Readers lists. You can find these lists on ALA's website (www.ala.org/yalsa/quick-picks-reluctant-young-adult-readers).

Follow these guidelines, and if you have an established group, let the members pick the book themselves. This is important, both to ensure that they are committed to the choice and to support their agency and ownership of the program. To make the choice a little easier for the participants, try booktalking a few to pick from in advance and then facilitate a discussion of the options and let the members vote.

ACCESSIBLE READER'S ADVISORY

The nature of your readers' advisory service for patrons with DD can affect the accessibility of materials. The first thing to consider is whether your library's practices in this regard are stigmatizing or welcoming. One way to minimize stigma is by introducing both youth services and adult services librarians together on the library's website, along with information about their favorite reading genres. Deerfield library does this, including an informal photo of each librarian to make them easier to identify. Listing adult and youth services staff together makes it easier for adults with DD to approach youth services staff if they need help finding reading materials intended for younger audiences.

Readers' advisory should always be nonjudgmental, regardless of what material is desired. It should respond to requests for specific types of materials while also offering options that could introduce patrons to new choices. It should offer books at the level the reader has been comfortable with but not exclude some that might be a bit of a stretch. This can be especially helpful for those adults with DD who have underestimated what they can read or enjoy. Readers' advisory can be used to introduce some of the types of books we discuss in this chapter, many of which the average patron with DD may not have previously encountered. And communication during readers' advisory, like all communication with adults with DD, should be in the patron's preferred manner, whether that is verbal, written, or using AAC.

Reading recommendations can also come through program theme-based displays and book lists. They can be featured in reviews or provided as lists offered at public service desks, during programs, and on the library's "Accessibility" web page. There are many ways we can get the right book into the hands of a patron with DD.

SHELVING FOR INCLUSION

Shelving can be an extension of readers' advisory, facilitating browsing and introducing new materials by their proximity to old favorites. Both can play a role in making your library inclusive. Libraries generally either interfile the materials we have discussed in this chapter throughout the collection or they create a stand-alone collection. If you choose the latter approach, the challenge is to shelve materials in an attractive, welcoming way without stigmatizing users of the collection. Special reader collections are often marginalized, shelved in back areas or even behind closed doors, reinforcing the stigma of using them. The Nashville (TN) Public Library addressed this problem by creating their Fresh Reads collection. "Our goal was to provide [adult new readers] . . . access to the same types of titles and materials offered to established readers . . . just . . . on a lower Lexile level."[8] First, they ditched the labels, and then they moved the collection to a more central place in the library and displayed it in freestanding units. Finally, they branded the collection Fresh Reads and created a recognizable logo. Adult new readers were involved throughout the process, and the new concept worked! When asked in an e-mail if circulation of these titles increased, Meg Godbey responded, "Yes, definitely! The titles were rarely used before Fresh Reads, [and] now they often circulate."[9]

An entire neurodiversity collection is another possibility, or you could inter-shelve these books and highlight them in displays or book lists. If you already have a collection that focuses on disability-related issues, make sure that it includes at least some materials actually written by and reflecting the perspective of people with disabilities. If you call it the Special Needs Collection, consider renaming it following Bloomfield Township library's lead. Theirs is now called the Accessibility Support Collection, which is currently considered a less stigmatizing name. Their collection includes sensory items and other materials as well as books. You can learn more about it on the library's website (www.btpl.org).

Another thing to consider is shelving some picture books written for children but suitable for adult readers in adult services. Or shelve some adult and children's materials together in a neutral area of the library. Not only could a variety of adults with DD use such a collection without embarrassment, parents and children could use it to access books together.

You can also curate carts of materials that reflect the reading interests and abilities of library regulars with DD and have these available when they come for group visits. This can be a way to introduce new titles and allow for browsing. This practice will also minimize the need for them to spend a limited library visit hunting for preferred materials on the shelves. However you shelve your books, remember when you do displays to include a wide variety of formats.

People with DD have a wide range of interests, preferences, and reading levels. Some read at an advanced level, while others do not. Some have very specific reading interests; others enjoy a variety of genres. Some are not print readers or enjoy audiobooks. Others lean toward highly visual materials and prefer graphic novels. All of these types of materials and more should be made available to adults with DD when they visit the library.

NOTES

1. Suzanne Williams, personal communication, October 14, 2019.
2. Morénike Giwa Onaiwu, "Preface: Autistics of Color: We Exist, We Matter," in *All the Weight of Our Dreams: On Living Racialized Autism,* ed. Lydia X. Z. Brown, E. Ashkenazy, and Morénike Giwa Onaiwu (Lincoln, NB: DragonBee Press, 2017), xiv.
3. Georgia Department of Education, "Lexile Framework for Reading," www.gadoe.org/Curriculum-Instruction-and-Assessment/Assessment/Pages/Lexile-Framework.aspx.
4. Padma Venkatraman, "Weeding Out Racism's Invisible Roots: Rethinking Children's Classics," Opinion, *School Library Journal,* June 19, 2020, www.slj.com/?detailStory=weeding-out-racisms-invisible-roots-rethinking-childrens-classics-libraries-diverse-books.
5. Venkatraman, "Weeding Out Racism's Invisible Roots."
6. Meredith Saletta and Jennifer Winberg, "Leveled Texts for Adults with Intellectual or Developmental Disabilities: A Pilot Study," *Focus on Autism and Other Developmental Disabilities* 34, no. 2 (2019): 118–27, first published October 4, 2018, https://journals.sagepub.com/doi/10.1177/1088357618803332?icid=int.sj-abstract.citing-articles.3&.
7. Jeny Wasilewski Mills, personal communication, November 4, 2019.
8. Meg Godbey, personal communication, June 2020.
9. Godbey, pers. comm.

CHAPTER 12

Art, Craft, and Maker Programs

We all can enjoy creating art and crafting objects. When these types of programs are created using UDL principles, everyone, including those with fine motor and cognitive issues, can participate. Arts-and-crafts programming is frequently offered in libraries and deserves a place in any listing of programs for people with developmental disabilities. As with all other program types, the secrets to success are communication, an understanding of what patrons need and are capable of doing, and partners to assist.

ART MAKING AND SHARING

A number of libraries offer adults with DD the opportunity to create their own art. Some of these opportunities come in the form of structured programs, for example, Grace Walker's Beyond Ability Art Club program at the Pickerington Public Library in Ohio. This program introduces participants to a range of artistic media, including watercolor, paint, mixed media, chalk, oil pastels, and clay. Each hour-long session starts with a brief explanation of the medium, tailored to the comprehension level of the attendees. For example, when introducing watercolor painting, Walker cautions that the paper will tear if it is too wet. Sometimes she shows works by famous artists and points out aspects of their techniques, like Claude Monet's use of cool colors and small lines in his painting *Bridge over a Pond of Water Lilies.* After the introduction, participants are free to create whatever they choose. Some copy the style of the featured artist; others go off in a different direction.[1]

In 2013 Kayla Kuni started arts programming at New Port Richey Public Library in Florida after noticing that the adults with disabilities who were students at Red

Apple School were not library users. Her research, building of library administrative support, and outreach to the school led to a productive relationship between the two institutions and ongoing programming mostly, but not exclusively, based on art. The programs she started continued even after Kuni left the library.

Kuni built her programs around a simple art project with no more than three or four steps. That way projects could be completed in the allotted time or at home or a day program. Keeping projects simple allowed participants to experience the self-esteem that comes from successfully completing something challenging but not impossible. Kuni notes, "Around step three several students wanted to quit, they want[ed] to give up, but when they worked through that process and finished, they felt really proud of themselves." Even if these patrons find simple projects a challenge, she says, "Don't treat it like a kid's program! They are adults."[2]

As you do arts programming, keep in mind that structure is good, but so are flexibility and room for creativity. Consider offering options that can appeal to a variety of interests and skill levels, and let participants choose materials and ways to personalize the project. Have alternatives for those who want to do their own thing. Make sure that artwork produced is the unfiltered creation of people with DD regardless of ability and that library staff, caregivers, and volunteers offer only encouragement and support. Remember to provide visual supports and transition reminders. And, last, set up the room to avoid distractions and help participants focus. After some trial and error, Kuni arranged her space with the art-making tables in an open square, allowing participants to see one another and show off art work after it is completed. With this setup, program leaders and volunteers can move easily between participants and stand in front instead of behind them when offering assistance.[3]

Coloring

A simple way of making art is coloring, and many of the librarians we spoke to provide coloring supplies for adult patrons with DD to use in an unstructured way. These supplies are offered during programs or made available for group in-library use. If you offer coloring sheets, choose ones with age-appropriate images and a variety of difficulty levels so that there is something for everyone. Like Bloomfield Township (MN) Public Library, you can purchase coloring sheets designed for adults with dementia, which also work well for adults with ID, but any simple ones that are not childish are good choices. These can be paired with the more intricate and easily available adult coloring sheets.

Offering a variety of coloring materials also makes this activity more inclusive. Some adults with DD have difficulty with fine motor skills, so having grips for colored pencils and markers in a variety of sizes can be helpful. Colored pencils and crayons of different sizes work well too. Mix it up with markers, Cray-Pas, watercolor pens, and pastels, each of which has a different resistance and texture. If you have iPads, let patrons use them to access coloring apps independently or during programs.

Art Exhibits

San Francisco Public Library (SFPL) in California and Hennepin County Library in Minnesota have both held exhibits of art created by people with disabilities. The HCL program ART-Abilities Gallery has been in existence since 2005. Lori Merriam from partner agency Homeward Bound coordinates the month-long annual exhibit of art created by adults served by local residential programs. The responsibilities of all participants are clearly delineated:

The library:
- provides exhibition space
- hosts an opening event for artists, family members, and agency representatives:
    - prints invitations
    - provides a small stipend for a performer with a disability for the opening
    - offers light refreshments at the opening
    - markets the exhibition

Homeward Bound:
- coordinates
- sends invitations to partner agencies for distribution
- pays for wall labels that identify the artist and piece

Participating agencies:
- solicit artwork from adults they serve
- select the pieces to submit
- frame and mat the artwork

The program is considered a real success, giving the artists a chance to showcase their work in a public venue and offering the community exposure to their work. Originally held at the Ridgedale Library, it moved to Golden Valley Library when Ridgedale closed for renovations. The exhibit was so well received there that Golden Valley continued hosting after Ridgedale reopened, with the exhibit starting at Ridgedale, then moving to Golden Valley for a second showing.[4]

The Disability Changemakers exhibit, brainchild of Marti Goddard, access services manager and ADA coordinator at SFPL, was the culmination of a program created with IMLS grant funding in partnership with the San Mateo and San José library systems. Community members nominated people with disabilities who they felt are Bay Area change agents, and artists with disabilities were tasked with creating portraits of selected Changemakers. An exhibit of the artworks and information about the subjects was held from January to March 2020 at the San Francisco Main Library. An exhibit of posters based on the artworks was exhibited in San Mateo. The San Francisco exhibit was supplemented with programming by a number of the featured Changemakers.[5]

If you are short on wall space or your physical facility is closed, consider doing a virtual art display complete with an online opening. Host the exhibit itself on the library's website and then schedule an event, using Zoom or another platform, to introduce the art and artists. Brooklyn Public Library did the 34th Annual Ezra Jack Keats Bookmaking Competition in this way in May 2020, putting both the citywide winners and the full gallery of entries online along with related activities.

CRAFT PROGRAMS

The creation of crafts is an element in or the focus of a number of programs for adults with DD. The PLACE program at Deerfield (IL) Public Library described in chapter 10 is a literature-based program that includes a craft. Public service specialist Mary Barnes describes the monthly focused offering at Tuckahoe Area Library, part of the Henrico County (VA) Public Library system, as including sensory activities, building, coloring, crafts, and time for socializing. Coloring books and pages, colored pencils, and twist-up crayons are also available. Activities are arranged in stations, and the program is run open-house style. Participants choose which activities they want to do, and staff and caregivers offer assistance and support as needed.

Arapahoe Libraries' Library for All program is different in that it has crafting as its centerpiece. Typically, there are four stations: two with takeaway crafts, one coloring station, and a sensory station. Music requested by patrons is played throughout the program, encouraging the fun, social atmosphere that is the program's goal.

Over time that goal has definitely been met:

> When the program originally began, groups would file in quietly, sit
> down, wait for the crafts for the day to be explained, and then begin
> work. Now . . . it is a place to be creative, connect with other people,
> and just relax. The energy in the room is contagious, and we have so
> much fun. Lately . . . folks just pick a table that looks interesting and
> start grabbing supplies. . . . It is the most wonderful kind of chaos,
> because I take it to mean that program participants feel like they can
> take some ownership of the space . . . like feeling comfortable . . . at
> a friend's house.[6]

Fidgets or sensory tools can be fun and functional to make during crafting
programs. We make jewelry and key fobs, so why not fidgets? You can create
some easily from chenille sticks and beads. Try these:

- Wrap a short chenille stick loosely around a pencil. The stick can be rubbed
  or played with.
- String a single bead on the chenille stick before wrapping it loosely around
  the pencil and securing the ends with tape so the bead will not slide off.
  Washi tape is a good choice because it comes in a range of colors and
  patterns. Patrons can slide the bead up and down the chenille stick spiral.
- String a number of beads on a short chenille stick and secure the ends to
  either end of a craft stick. Slide the beads up and down the stick or twirl
  them on the chenille stick. Use beads with a variety of colors and textures.[7]

Or take a page from the Blount County (TN) Public Library and make fidgets out
of felt squares and marbles. Just glue, tape, or sew three of the edges of two felt
squares together, making a pouch. Insert the marble and close up the fourth
side. This library also makes fidgets out of nonlatex, see-through cleaning gloves
by filling the gloves partway full of items, like small pom-poms or rice, and tying
them closed.[8]

ART AND CRAFT PROGRAM TIPS

Art and craft programs involve advance preparation, and the program time can
be intense. But as librarians who have done them say, these programs promise to
be extremely rewarding for you as well as for your patrons. Remember to involve
the participants in the selection of projects and planning. They are more likely to

HOW TO MAKE A SENSORY GEL PAD FIDGET

You need these supplies:

- a large bottle of hair gel
- heavy-duty sandwich bags with zip closures
- duct tape, preferably colored or patterned
- an assortment of beads, buttons, and small toys like googly eyes

Fill the bags about a third full with gel. Add several items. Leave room so you can squish and move the items around in the gel. Press out most of the air in the bag and zip it closed. Use the duct tape to securely tape the zipper side so it doesn't open. You can also tape all around for an attractive appearance.

Source: Kathryn Sneed, "Homemade Sensory Gel Pad," *Singing through the Rain* (blog), March 20, 2013, https://singingthroughtherain.net/2013/03/homemade-sensory-gel-pad.html.

attend if they have a vested interest, and it will be a better program. To make these programs go more smoothly, consider these suggestions as you plan:

- Plan well in advance and set up early.
- If you are working with agency groups, don't duplicate programs the agencies are already doing.
- Warn people about the potential for mess.
- Choose projects that are easy to transport.
- Select age-appropriate projects.
- Allow for people working at different speeds.
- Keep the program moving to keep from losing participants' attention, but allow for breaks for those who need them.
- Create projects that can be completed in only a few steps, yet offer a range of possibilities to embellish or change the basic project.
- Make an imperfect model of each project.
- Create a handout with basic instructions in plain language and/or visuals of the steps involved.
- Recruit helpers to offer guidance and assistance as needed.

You need to pay particular attention to materials. Materials should be safe, easy to use, and interesting. You can make art with almost anything, so try things like sponges, toothbrushes, cut potatoes, or even damp tea bags or bubbles made with bubble solution mixed with food coloring. Using these types of materials will also make it easier for participants to repeat projects at home or to follow along if the program is virtual. Specifically, you should do the following:

- Have adaptive tools like scissors and pencil grips on hand.
- Offer project choices so that those with limited fine motor control can join in.
- Offer alternative materials in case any are problematic for participants.
- Avoid using materials that commonly trigger allergies or have strong scents.

Art and craft programs do not have to take place only at the library. Kuni suggests doing outreach programming as well. You can also offer these types of programs online. Ruth Chiego at the Grapevine (TX) Public Library runs a program during which patrons with DD make pictures in response to a story starter she posts on Facebook. The participants share their creations in comments. To make it easy for people to participate in virtual art or craft programs, offer a grab-and-go supplies pickup at the library, do a project that uses materials that people commonly have at home, or coordinate with program staff so they can supply the materials.

Whatever program model you choose, follow Arapahoe Libraries' example and engage in the activities along with patrons. They also train their crafts program leaders to "put on their friendliest and most outgoing face and focus on making conversation and getting to know patrons as people [and to] . . . keep in mind that sometimes friendly means companionable silence or respecting someone's boundaries and giving them some space"[9]—good suggestions for any interaction, not just during art and craft programs.

PHOTOGRAPHY PROGRAMS

The availability of digital cameras on phones combined with the ability to quickly share photos makes photography easily accessible for adults with DD. Photography can be done anywhere, is primarily solitary, and requires little planning. Libraries can introduce adults with DD to this potentially fun and engaging activity and can provide the needed technology for those who don't have access to it at home.

Photobooth

Libraries can introduce photography in a number of ways through programs for adults with DD. A simple way that pairs crafting with photography is a photobooth activity like the one used by Arapahoe Libraries in Colorado as part of their Library for All program. Library for All meets three times monthly for an hour and usually features four activity stations. At times, the photobooth is a fifth option. At one photobooth session, the *Ghostbusters* theme song played while an Arapahoe librarian kicked things off by striking a silly pose in a mask and challenging participants to take a picture. "Challenge accepted. . . . I hand my phone over [to] the patron who dared test my willingness to look silly. 'Take my picture!' I tell him."[10] Throughout the room, patrons make their own props and experiment with costumes. Another librarian "in goggles and a lab coat is snapping Polaroid pictures in front of colorful backdrops. Folks are taking selfies with their phones, or offering to take photos, and making new friends in the process."[11] And though they don't say it directly, everyone is clearly having a good time.

Photography Art Walk

Another possibility is an Art Walk program like the one Westlake Porter Public Library in Ohio runs annually. In April and May, the library schedules meetups in public spaces and markets the events to local group homes and day programs. Promotional materials describe the event this way:

> Capture pictures of scenery you find beautiful and inspiring with a smartphone. The Library will print, mount, and display photographs to the public at our pop-up gallery. This is an opportunity for persons with disabilities to explore nature and share your unique perspective with friends, family and the Westlake community![12]

Participants are asked to provide their own transportation and to bring a companion and a smartphone or tablet. If devices are not available, the library has several for patron use. Everyone is given time to photograph whatever appeals to them, and librarian Natalie Bota assists if needed. Afterward the photos are uploaded and Bota works with an expert, like an art librarian or a volunteer photographer, to select some to display. These are printed, matted, and hung in the library's gallery for a month. At the end of the exhibit, a reception with refreshments is held for the photographers, their family members, and the participating agencies.

Photography Classes

Candice Casey incorporates instruction into her photography programs at the Hart Memorial Library in Kissimmee, Florida, teaching adults with DD how to take better pictures and encouraging them to take photographs for display. An even more structured photography program can be based on the one for teens with autism previously taught at Queens Museum in New York City and featured in Barbara's 2014 book *Programming for Children and Teens with Autism Spectrum Disorder* (ALA Editions, 2014). The goal of that program was socializing, and participants had a chance to share and discuss their works with others using the taking of pictures as the focus of their interactions. If you are comfortable and know a little bit about composition, lighting, and simple editing, you are qualified to lead this program; or you can recruit a community partner with expertise to run the weekly group, with a staff member serving as coleader.

As adapted for adults, the first meeting could introduce photography and the series, teaching the basics in a rudimentary way. Define common terms such as *shoot*, *focus*, *closeup*, and *edit*. Cover photography etiquette explicitly and include discussion of the following:

- asking permission to take someone's picture
- respecting physical boundaries
- avoiding taking embarrassing pictures

It is helpful to talk openly about behavior guidelines in the beginning, and to have them available in writing, using clear, simple language.

Subsequent sessions need to be similarly structured and could start with everyone introducing themselves and reviewing the etiquette rules. Build each class around a theme like whole and part of a person, vertical and horizontal, light and dark, movement and still. Other possibilities are straight and curved, big and small, smooth and textured. After describing the theme and showing examples, give a set time of twenty to thirty minutes for picture taking. Provide objects to photograph and areas inside or outside the library where participants can take photos. Circulate to answer questions or assist participants. Warn everyone when five minutes are left for taking photos.

Come back together to share favorite photos, projecting them if possible. Discuss the day's theme and the participants' experience as they took pictures. While viewing the photos, allow participants to comment on one another's work in positive ways. Model constructive comments and how to praise the efforts of peers, or give specific guidelines, such as asking participants to say two things they like about someone else's work.

ACCESSIBLE MAKER PROGRAMS AND ACTIVITIES

Accessible makerspaces celebrate the positive aspects of hacking and making. "Makerspaces are about community. We need to ensure everyone from the community can participate," says one student in the University of Washington's guide to creating accessible makerspaces.[13] One way to do that, by applying UDL principles to create inclusive makerspaces, was suggested by librarian Amanda Hovious in a blog post. Multiple means of presentation can be achieved with simple instructions offered in multiple languages supplemented by visuals and audio. For multiple means of expression, consider offering a variety of projects and materials, both digital and physical. Have assistive technology available and offer touch screen devices. To engage people in multiple ways, work in a quiet space, draw in people who are not active, appeal to a wide range of interests, and give positive, constructive feedback.[14]

Adaptive gaming technology can be made at an inclusive hackathon program like the one offered by Jeff Edelstein when he was at the University of Michigan Shapiro Library. This event focused on working with gamers to create controllers and other accessible equipment. His program drew an inclusive crowd, including people with autism and CP. Edelstein suggests, "Get as many pieces of equipment as you can, just having the bits and pieces that you can mix together . . . be comfortable with trial and error, [and] remember that the work is collaborative between the librarian and the user."[15]

An accessible makerspace that focuses on empowering people to make their own tactile illustrations is the Dimensions Lab at the Andrew Heiskell Braille and Talking Book Library in New York City. Heiskell does workshops on the software, which offers visual and nonvisual interfaces, 2-D and 3-D printing, and one-to-one tutorials. After learning the how-tos, patrons can make appointments to use the lab's equipment. The multiple means of action and expression delivered by the software, multiple means of representation demonstrated by different types of instruction, and the lack of restriction on what people can produce all make Heiskell's model an accessible makerspace. The library also hosts workshops on how to use the circulating 3Doodlers, pens that write 3-D images. The Dimensions Lab is open to the entire community, and one of its superusers is autistic.

When the Grapevine library went virtual, so did its makerspace programs. "We are trying to teach them how to make them at home, from making your own gel boards [to] stress balls. We've done those programs in the library before," says librarian Ruth Chiego.[16] As with craft programs, make sure to either provide materials or use ones that are readily available in most people's homes or residential settings. Demonstrate the maker process online and provide a way for participants to ask questions and share their work. For example, enable comments and chat and encourage photographing and sharing products using those features.

No matter what you make together, you and your patrons can find fun, connection, and accomplishment through art, craft, and maker programs if you follow the suggestions in this chapter. As Kelsey McLane, formerly of Arapahoe Library District says:

> I think the tricky thing is [not] underestimating the patrons. They are very enthusiastic and willing to learn everything they need to in order to finish. . . . [A]fter each program, I was usually so exhausted! But they were always so patient, and I absolutely LOVED seeing their faces with their LED card lit up for the first time, or their science experiment worked. We wanted to empower them to take these projects and do them how they wanted and have ownership.[17]

Concord (CA) Library's Kimberli Buckley sums it up:

> [It] is really a fun time for me to sit down with them. . . . They can spend time letting their creativity take over and when they are done, they are so proud of what they have created. This is a really special time for [me] as well when I can bond with them and learn more about their lives, their families, where they go on vacation and things like that. Crafts are kind of magical like that[;] they give you time to sit down, talk, and share.[18]

NOTES

1. Grace Walker, personal communications, January 12 and 17, 2020.
2. Kayla Kuni, personal communication, December 20, 2019.
3. Kayla Kuni and Linda Hotslander, presenters, and Sarah Osman, facilitator, "You Belong @ Your Library: Programming for Adults with Intellectual Disabilities," *Programming Librarian* (webinar series, ALA Public Programs Office), originally recorded September 15, 2015,

posted to YouTube March 10, 2016, 54:41, www.youtube.com/watch?v=fuSRAuX
_FEc&feature=youtu.be; see also the Programming Librarian website at http://programming
librarian.org/learn/you-belong-your-library-programming-adults-intellectual-disabilities.

4. Lori Merriam, personal communication, September 9, 2019.

5. Marti Goddard, personal communication, December 6, 2019.

6. Arapahoe Libraries, "Community Impact Outside the Library (ish): Library for All and
New Day Storytime," staff handout provided by Elena Cabodevilla, December 16, 2019,
quoted with permission.

7. Counselor Keri, "Pipe Cleaner Crafts for School Counseling." *Confident Counselors* (blog),
April 30, 2018, https://confidentcounselors.com/?s=pipe+cleaner+crafts.

8. Barbara Klipper, notes from "Sensory Screenings: Movies for Everyone at the Library," session at the 2019 ALA Annual Conference, Washington, DC, June 24, 2019.

9. Arapahoe Libraries, "Community Impact Outside the Library (ish)."

10. Arapahoe Libraries, "Community Impact Outside the Library (ish)."

11. Arapahoe Libraries, "Community Impact Outside the Library (ish)."

12. Natalie Bota, personal communication, May 29, 2020.

13. AccessEngineering, "Making a Makerspace? Guidelines for Accessibility and Universal Design," University of Washington, Disabilities, Opportunities, Internetworking, and Technology (Do-It) (website), www.washington.edu/doit/making-makerspace-guidelines
-accessibility-and-universal-design.

14. Amanda Hovious, "Making Makerspaces Accessible with UDL," *Designer Librarian* (blog),
May 20, 2015, https://designerlibrarian.wordpress.com/2015/05/20/making-maker
spaces-accessible-with-udl/.

15. Jeff Edelstein, personal communication, September 19, 2020.

16. Ruth Chiego, personal communication, March 31, 2020.

17. Kelsey McLane, personal communication, November 14, 2019.

18. Kimberli Buckley, personal communication, December 12, 2019.

CHAPTER 13

Performing Arts Programs

The performing arts play a large role in our libraries. Circulating CDs or DVDs and streaming video are often extremely popular. Film showings and live performances are staples on many program calendars. These can also be highlights of your programming for adults with developmental disabilities. Beyond passive programs, workshops and classes offer additional benefits for participants with DD, increasing the possibilities for fun, learning, and engagement. Programs can be centered around film, dance and movement, music, theater, or storytelling, as well as other performing arts. The possibilities are many. This chapter offers some ideas.

FILM-RELATED PROGRAMS

Film screenings are a staple of public library programming for good reason. They do not require a lot of financial outlay or staff time to organize and run, and movies are popular with audiences of all ages and abilities. Film showings can easily be designed to be naturally inclusive and welcoming to people with disabilities. One way to do this is to make your library's film showings sensory friendly.

Sensory-Friendly Films

In 2007 AMC Theaters, in partnership with the Autism Society, began sensory-friendly film showings at select theaters. At these screenings, the sound is turned down and the lights up and people are allowed to talk, walk around, and even dance during the film. However, in the commercial theater environment, these programs are fee based, which creates a barrier for some people. It was therefore only natural that the concept would come to libraries.

TIPS FOR MAKING FILM PROGRAMS SENSORY FRIENDLY
- Use a link in the program announcement to offer a social story–like narrative.
- Keep the lights up and the volume down.
- Offer fidgets.
- Allow attendees to walk around.
- Permit snacks from home.
- Let attendees talk and sing during the movie.

Some libraries add to the basic model. Brooklyn Public Library displays related books in a variety of formats at the entrance to the screenings. The Paseo Verde Library in Henderson, Nevada, designates an open seating area for people who bring blankets or pillows from home. Librarian Erin Silva of the Iowa City Public Library and her community partner from the Iowa City Autism Community also suggest these approaches:

- using non-fluorescent lights or covers on fluorescent ones
- having seating options like wiggle chairs or stools, stabilizing balls, and disks
- providing noise cancelling headphones
- offering [large foam shapes called] crash pads, for those who "need to stimulate themselves . . . by crashing into them.[1]

Vicki Karlovsky encourages dancing during her film programs at Deerfield (IL) Public Library, and she sometimes uses the karaoke feature on DVD or Blu-ray discs to turn the viewing into a sing-along. She always uses the closed-captioning feature, and she equips a quiet area outside the room with coloring sheets and crayons for those who want a calming activity. Applying UDL principles, she presents "the programs on three different screens which are in three different areas. They all play the movies but they have different levels of lighting and volume."[2]

Deerfield library's movie programs show that inclusion can go both ways. Although marketed for people with DD, other library visitors who notice that a film they are interested in is being shown will join the audience. They are always welcome.

Musicals and comedies are the most popular genres at Deerfield library, and *Mama Mia* and *Hairspray* were big hits. In general, these genres work well with an audience that includes adults with DD, so long as care is taken to avoid films, like *Gigi,* that are now considered offensive. Marcela Chiarandini of the Whitney

Library in Las Vegas, Nevada, goes outside of that genre box from time to time, showing different types of films, including the R-rated horror flick *House of Wax*.[3] Bloomfield Township (MI) Public Library shows documentaries, often pairing them thematically with their adult sensory storytimes. Whatever types of films you decide to show, make sure they represent diverse communities and that some portray the disability experience authentically. Include films made by people with disabilities and other underrepresented identities.

Film Discussions

Deerfield library includes a craft or structured discussion in its film programs. A refreshments break gives staff the chance to rearrange chairs into a circle. When the group reconvenes, Karlovsky is ready with questions to prompt discussion. But once she starts things off, the discussions often take on a life of their own. "I usually come prepared with a ton of questions," she says. "Sometimes I fly through them and sometimes I only get through three because there is so much discussion. . . . Sometimes you just hit a nerve and it goes really well." The discussion piece is one of her favorite things about the programs, and the insights shared by the adults with DD "always surprise" her."[4]

Participants in Janine Myers's film discussion program, held several years ago at De Soto Public Library in Missouri, watched the film at their day program and then came to the library for a moderated discussion. These guidelines are based in part on her experience:

- Involve participants with DD along with partner agency representatives in planning and movie selection.
- Arrange for participants to watch the movie together before the program.
- Start discussions by asking what participants liked or didn't like. If someone didn't like a part or a character, ask how the movie would be different if that element was removed.
- Be flexible. Have prepared questions but be ready to improvise based on responses.
- Base questions on participant interests. Myers would ask students who liked computer games how they would make one from the movie being discussed.
- Involve participants further by recruiting some to serve as program assistants.[5]

Film showings and discussion programs can be easily adapted to a virtual environment. All you need is a film with public performance rights from your collection that can be streamed and a format that allows people to interact, such as Microsoft Teams or Zoom. Dedicated apps like Squad, Screner, or TwoSeven also allow you to share films and discuss them at the same time. Regardless of the platform, you can employ the same prompts you would have used in person. E-mail attendees in advance to share links to song lyrics or the lyrics themselves and to encourage sensory-friendly involvement, such as singing and dancing during the passive parts of the program. You can also e-mail guidelines for making simple fidgets at home and even a recipe for popcorn! An alternative way to prepare attendees is to make resources and sensory tools available through your library's curbside pickup service or by delivering resource kits directly to participating day habilitation and residential programs.

Even if you provide song lyrics, you should always use the closed-captioning feature when you screen movies, whether in the library or virtually. This makes it easier for participants to sing along and follow the auditory portion of the movie, which might otherwise be inaccessible to those who have hearing impairments or those who have difficulty processing auditory input at the speed of speech.

Participatory Film Showings

Anyone who has ever attended a late-night showing of *The Rocky Horror Picture Show* will recognize the idea of dressing in costume and interacting with the movie that Susan McBride built into her December 2019 showing of *Elf* at the Hinsdale Public Library in Illinois. This fun event took place during the library's twice quarterly social club for adults with disabilities, which grew out of its successful Next Chapter Book Club. At both book and social club meetings, teen volunteers assist attendees, often with a ratio of one volunteer to one participant, so there is plenty of support to help the program run smoothly. For the participatory movie, enthusiastic volunteers were acquired through the high school's Peer Buddies Club, which pairs regular and special education students for activities during the school year. McBride provided a variety of props and simple costumes so people could get into the spirit of the film. Attendees were cued by the volunteers so they could use their props and call out lines to the characters during the action.[6]

McBride adapted he script from one that was shared in a programming librarian Facebook group. You can find these scripts online by searching for "interactive movie scripts." Many of these scripts would be suitable for an audience of adults with DD if simplified. In addition to modifying an existing script, McBride created her own for an interactive showing of *How the Grinch Stole Christmas*.[7] Whether you adapt a script or write your own, this is a fun program to build around a film, and waiting for a chance to interact with some of the scenes can help attendees focus as well as feel like they are truly part of the group.

Another way to introduce participatory movie watching in a small group is to show one of Netflix's interactive films, which are like choose-your-own-adventure books. *Black Mirror: Bandersnatch* or *You vs. Wild* are two that could work well. You need a Netflix account to access these movies. Showing Netflix content in a public setting usually violates their terms of service, but they have a special policy for certain films shown in educational environments like libraries. Search for "Educational Screenings of Documentaries" at https://help.netflix.com for more information on this exception and "Interactive TV Shows and Movies on Netflix" for a list of films. If your patrons have Netflix accounts, you can do this program virtually using Netflix's Teleparty app. One benefit of going online with patrons who have the service themselves is that it avoids the fair use issue.

Disney-Themed Movie Programs

Disney movies are well-known and many adults with DD enjoy them, so a number of libraries offer programming based on Disney. Rebecca Wolfe from Allen County Public Library in Indiana shows Disney films at her monthly program for adults with DD called Walt's Magic Movie Club.[8] Andrew Plait gives his patrons at Medicine Hat Library in Alberta, Canada, a chance to demonstrate their Disney knowledge by interspersing some of his programs for adults with disabilities with Disney movie trivia.[9] But Disney films may not appeal to all of your adult patrons with DD, so also think outside the Disney box. Ask your regulars which movies they enjoy, and show some of those. You can also give some of the other genres we mention a try.

Film Festivals

There are two major disability-related film festivals, the Superfest International Disability Film Festival and ReelAbilities Film Festival. Some Superfest festival films are made by people with disabilities and feature characters with disabilities. Festival films all have audio descriptions as well as closed-captioning, making them accessible to people with a wide range of disabilities. Since the festival originated in California, the San Francisco, Berkeley, and Sacramento Public Libraries have all had screenings. Libraries elsewhere can show the films by hosting a showcase, which is a great way to spread disability awareness and acceptance. One attendee at the Berkeley Public Library showcase explains it this way: "Superfest told me stories about people and issues I don't hear anywhere else. It gives me empathy for a wider range of experience and continues to challenge my assumptions about disability."[10] Both Brooklyn Public Library and San Francisco Public Library were early and consistent partners with the annual ReelAbilities Film Festival, held in seventeen locations, mostly in the United States. For more information on that festival, go to https://reelabilities.org.

DANCE AND MOVEMENT PROGRAMS

Programs that include dancing or movement activities are another good choice for adults with DD because they are fun and offer physical activity, which is not always built into their day. Build movement into existing programs by adding a stretch break or a time for moving to music, or build an entire program around a movement activity. Yoga, which we cover in chapter 15, is one example. If you do movement programming, be sure to offer activity choices so that the session will be accessible for everyone, including those with physical disabilities and seniors.

Dance Party

The annual kickoff event for the disability track of the summer reading club at Germantown Community Library in Tennessee is a dance based on the year's summer reading theme. When the theme was Out of This World, the library held a sci-fi dance, with themed decorations and costumes. Dressing up or wearing costumes for these types of programs provides an opportunity for creativity and adds to the fun and excitement of the event.

Party Dancing

Medicine Hat Library teaches party dancing as one of its weekly programs for adults with disabilities. Librarian Andrew Plait projects music videos on a large screen as a source of dance music and a visual guide for participants who need support. He uses videos from YouTube's Just Dance channel.[11] In the videos, songs play, dancers perform, and lights and colors flash in the background. If you have autistic patrons or others in your program who might be overstimulated by such busy visuals, another option would be to start the program by showing one or more simple dance move tutorial videos, so everyone can work on their moves. Erick Bassan's videos are a good resource because he demonstrates dance moves repeatedly and even in slow motion, making it easy to master them while viewing. His tutorial "3 Simple Party Dance Moves for Beginners: Basic and Easy Steps" is available on YouTube (www.youtube.com/watch?v=-KjWiVD-nUE). After practicing some steps, just put on some popular music and let the dancing begin.

Ballroom Dancing

Ballroom dancing can also be an easy-to-do library program. One example is Candice Casey's Swing Dance program at Hart Memorial Library in Kissimmee, Florida. Participants are taught a few basic ballroom dance steps like swing, jitterbug, and Lindy Hop. They practice together and then watch a video of professional dancers performing the same steps.[12] If you have *Dancing with the Stars* fans and someone who teaches ballroom dancing in your community who can run a basic workshop at your library, this program could be a big hit.

ACCESSIBLE MUSIC PROGRAMS

In a book for colleagues, music therapist Maria Ramey says that music programs succeed with people with disabilities in part because of "the inherent social nature of music, its strengths as a tool for memory establishment and the order it creates from chaos."[13]

The activities and principles put forth in Ramey's book are respectful of the life stages and capabilities of adults with DD. Adapted for a library setting, the guidelines she offers include these:

- Control the environment by minimizing distractions.
- Expect success. Adults with DD can respond well to higher expectations. People often expect less of them than they are able to do.
- Recognize what they do well. Adults with DD are often used to being told what they can't do.
- Keep directions clear and simple. Use few words. Avoid multiple directions. Demonstrate each step.
- Keep the pace patron driven, even if it means you don't get to do everything in your program plan.
- Be prepared to improvise and adapt as you go along.

With these thoughts in mind, you can adapt or create a range of musical programs that will be enjoyed by your adult patrons with DD.

Drumming and Percussion

As part of the Insiders program for adults with DD, the Concord Library in California tried an easy-to-replicate program they called Drummm. During the program, participants join in an interactive drum circle using many different percussion instruments. Your library may already have some of these instruments in the children's department, or you can try reaching out to music teachers at your local school to see if it is possible to borrow some. If these aren't options, you can make your own percussion instruments, like shakers made from plastic Easter eggs: fill them partway with small beans or rice and glue the halves together with superglue. Empty oatmeal containers and coffee cans make good percussion instruments, and paper plates filled partially with beans and glued together make good tambourines when shaken. Adult services librarian Addie Spanbock says, "This type of program is always well received by our Insiders because it gets them up and moving around or dancing and allows them to experience the joy of making music and feeling the vibrations of the instruments."[14]

Music Lessons

Many people with DD do not have the opportunity to study music, so Inclusive Services at Brooklyn Public Library helped fill this gap by offering music lessons to young adults with DD. Over six weeks, a preregistered group received voice lessons from community partner Daniel's Music, culminating in an impromptu group performance. Two series were offered before the agency shifted its catchment area. In addition to vocal training, drums and rhythm instruments could be safely and easily taught in the library. Slide whistle or recorder lessons are fun and could be therapeutic for adults with DD who could benefit from oral input and breath control exercises. Ukulele, frequently taught in libraries, could also be fun for some, but not all, adults with DD.

A library is not the best place to teach every instrument, but other types of music lessons make wonderful library programs for adults with DD. For example, Lisa Powell Williams from Moline (IL) Public Library was awarded a grant in 2017 that funded her inclusive visual arts and music Artability programs for adults with ID. The music program consisted of a series of weekly classes led by music therapist Emma Vogel. Classes offered a variety of musical experiences, including listening to and then discussing favorite songs; making improvisational music with rhythm instruments accompanied by singing; musical games; and group songwriting.

In the songwriting session, the group took a well-known song and changed the lyrics to create a new song about a different subject.[15]

Interactive music making was the favorite of the eight classes. Vogel played guitar or downloaded music while participants played along on drums, rhythm sticks, or bells. The session that worked least well was music Bingo. Participants were asked to match pictures of instruments on flash cards to ones on bingo cards, but they found the pictures too complicated. For example, there were a number of types of drums and the attendees had trouble telling them apart.

Sensory-Friendly Concerts

Since 2010 IS/BPL has been offering sensory-friendly concerts in partnership with Music for Autism (MFA). Some features of this program support people with autism:

- consistent structure
- cap on audience size
- social story–like narrative sent to registrants in advance
- picture schedule used throughout the concert
- the expectation that audience members can make noise and leave their seats
- musicians who are comfortable with the audience
- interactive sections
- nearby room for breaks

Each concert has the same three sections: music, conducting, and percussion time. During music time, the musicians are introduced and they play, usually describing the type of music and their instruments between songs. Volunteers help the audience members engage with the music, often by dancing with them. During conducting time, the performers describe the role of a conductor and demonstrate basic conducting movements, and then they let the audience conduct the show. During percussion time, volunteers hand out instruments and the audience plays along. Two community agencies, My Time Inc. and New York Cares, recruit volunteers for the concerts.

The response is joyful. Carrie describes an early concert:

> Children and adults, with and without autism, danced in the aisles, conducted the trio and played along with percussion instruments. One man in his late 50s got on stage with the performers and conducted the audience! . . . [Another] young adult who came with his group home wowed the audience with his take on the Charleston.

The musicians are professionals, and the cast of a Broadway show and a brass quintet have been among the performers. Spanish language social media spread the word far and wide about the first bilingual concert, and people came to Brooklyn from all over New York State for that program. MFA wrote it up in its Winter 2013 newsletter:

> Music for Autism's very first bilingual concert . . . was an unprecedented success! Every seat was filled and over one-third of the audience spoke primarily Spanish. Willie Martinez and La Familia Sextet wowed the audience with beautiful and engaging Latin jazz sung and introduced in both English and Spanish. And all of the printed and publicity materials were also in both [languages]. . . . It was a spectacular day![16]

Starting in April 2020, BPL supported MFA's shift to virtual concerts without any loss of format, musician quality, or energy. There have been some changes though. The social story was updated. People register on the MFA website, as before, but are sent the link to an invitation-only YouTube platform the day of the concert. Instead of a written concert schedule on the stage, a banner runs along the bottom of the screen announcing the sections of the concert. Everyone misses the live interaction between the audience and the musicians, but MFA finds ways to compensate. A highlight of one concert was the singer suggesting that people improvise rhythm instruments using sticks, spoons or even a cell phone case! Audience members sent in pictures showing their instruments. A benefit of the virtual programs is that they can reach a wider audience.

Sing-Alongs

Music therapist Maria Ramey says, "The power of the sing-along to enhance focus, participation and other areas should not be overlooked."[17] Singing in a group is also lots of fun. We have already mentioned a couple of programs that can incorporate sing-alongs: movie screenings and holiday parties. You can also do a sing-along as a stand-alone program. Include songs that regular participants already know and like, but also try introducing one or two new ones that are simple and easy to learn. Ask your regulars to name their favorite songs and note ones that seem to be known by a number of them. Before your sing-along, print out lyrics for readers to follow or display them on a screen. If the group will include nonreaders, keep to well-known songs or ones that are easy to do as call-and-response. Try to be age appropriate, but if what the participants know and love are kids' songs, follow their lead. For songs with multiple verses, you can try making simple props, like the Old MacDonald cubes that librarians from Alvin Sherman Library at Nova Southeastern University in Florida created for their sensory program for children. Take a square tissue box, cover it with plain paper, and glue a picture of a different animal or object on each side. Participants throw the box like a die, and then the group sings the verse again, each time inserting the name and/or sound of the animal or object that lands face up.

Rebecca Wolfe's Music and Movement Storytime at Allen County library, featured in chapter 10, offers some other suggestions for music programming. That program mixes literature, music, and movement—always a winning combination.

THEATRICAL PROGRAMMING

For many people, experiencing live theater is a transcendent experience, unlike watching a movie, TV show, or streaming video. Because it takes place in front of you in real time, anything can happen. Unfortunately, opportunities for people with disabilities to enjoy theater, from both sides of the footlights, are limited. Lack of financial resources, transportation issues, and other barriers often make live theater out of reach, and opportunities to see themselves represented in theater are even rarer. Even roles for people with disabilities are often played by people without disabilities. During the 2019 season, however, an actor in a wheelchair won a Tony Award for the first time. After winning for her portrayal of Ado Annie in *Oklahoma!*, Ali Stroker said, "This award is for every kid who is watching tonight who has a disability, who has a limitation or a challenge, who has been waiting to see themselves represented in this arena—you are." [18]

Brooklyn Public Library addressed this imbalance by booking the Identity Theater. The troupe is led by Nick Linnehan, who has a traumatic brain injury (TBI), and it features other actors and crew members with disabilities. They make magic! Their series of performances of fractured fairy tales drew people of all ages to the library, many for the first time. Another popular program at BPL came from the YAI Players and the Berkeley Carroll School. They teamed up to create an inclusive performance group called Theater of Dreams. Funded by the Ann C. and LeRoy Warner Foundation, the theater group performed multiple times at two of BPL's flagship libraries. Seeing actors with disabilities on stage is powerful, and for some it is life changing. Their show-stopping performance of Maya Angelou's poem "Phenomenal Woman" was haunting and memorable, and a review in *Exceptional Parent Magazine* described the impact of the group in this way: "The

Players' performances are a powerful reminder that all people—with or without disabilities—share aspirations for self-expression, growth, and exploring new horizons. . . . The YAI Players convey an important message: dreams can come true."[19]

These types of inclusive theater programs are no more complicated to arrange than a typical library performance. If your library wants to work with an inclusive community theater group, keep these things in mind:

- Have a contract that clearly defines expectations for the library and the theater company.
- Ask specifically about and plan for any accommodations the company needs.
- Make audience building the responsibility of both partners.
- Go bigger than you usually would with publicity. For example, local press might be interested in this type of event.
- Reach out to people with and without disabilities.
- Keep communication open with your liaison.

Virtual Programs

The experience of watching theater on a device is not the same as viewing a live in-person performance, but it is better than no theater at all, and bringing theatrical performances to the virtual sphere is fairly easy. Simply decide on a platform to use and record a performance as it happens at the library. You can stream it live, archive the recording on your website or a third-party site like YouTube, or do both.

VIRTUAL THEATER PROGRAMS TO-DO LIST
- Get written permission from all of the actors to make and show the recording.
- If audience members are included in the shot, get waivers from them too.
- Use a wide-angle lens to capture the entire scene.
- Use a tripod when filming to keep the camera stable and prevent shakiness.
- Captions are not optional. Make sure to use them and edit ones that come from a captioning program when necessary.

Using Theater in Book Clubs

If you run a book club for adults with DD, consider integrating theater into the program. Try readers' theater to help members engage with books and to make reading programs more interactive or consider adding plays to the novels and nonfiction titles the group reads. Any short, simple play can be read and acted out. Try the ones in *New Love, Spilt Milk, and Potbellied Pigs* (Proving Press 2019) and *Something's Brewing* (Proving Press, 2020), two story and play collections written by Tom Fish and Jillian Ober for Next Chapter Book Club members and other readers with DD. If you add props and even costumes, these theatrical readings can be even more entertaining. Kate Monsour has read plays with her Books for Dessert program participants at Port Washington (NY) Public Library, and they really enjoy it. She is also considering having group members read a play that is scheduled to be performed in the library and then hosting a performance or question-and-answer session with the actors just for Books for Dessert attendees.[20]

Theater Arts Workshops

Hosting a workshop series that culminates in a performance is another way to go. PLAI (Performers Linked by Able Imaginations) Theatre's Helena Gleissner Judd was eager to expand her work teaching theater arts to people with disabilities, so she reached out to Inclusive Services at BPL. The inclusive program she organized for the library was simple: over the course of six weeks, young adults with and without DD would write, rehearse, create the set for, and then perform a show at the library. BPL recruited the cast and crew and PLAI Theatre provided the expertise. The young adults worked together over six Saturdays, and their culminating performance went so well they did it again the following year. The library would have continued this program indefinitely had PLAI Theatre not moved to Great Britain.

STORYTELLING

Oral storytelling is a performing art that is deeply connected to youth services in public libraries, and Antioch Public Library, part of the Contra Costa County Library system in California, brought in a presenter to teach personal storytelling to adults with DD as part of its Insiders program. After telling some personal stories, the presenter told participatory action tales, asking everyone to say aloud words or phrases that repeat in the stories. Afterward several attendees told personal stories of their own. This type of program would be easy to replicate in libraries that have storytellers among the staff or access to storytellers in the community.

Other performing arts workshops can also be brought to the library. Some to consider are puppetry, simple improv, and even some clowning techniques. If you can find someone with expertise who is able and willing to make their program accessible, you can give any of these a try and see if they resonate with your community.

NOTES

1. Erin Silva, personal communication, March 30, 2020.
2. Vicki Karlovsky, personal communication, May 16, 2020.
3. Julie Wootton-Greener, "Las Vegas, Henderson libraries offer sensory-friendly movies," *Las Vegas Review-Journal,* December 12, 2019, www.reviewjournal.com/local/henderson/las-vegas-henderson-libraries-offer-sensory-friendly-movies-1913028/.
4. Karlovsky, pers. comm.
5. Leslie Lea Nord, "Reaching Out: Library Services to the Developmentally Disabled," *Public Libraries Online,* January 5, 2015, http://publiclibrariesonline.org/2015/01/reaching-out/.
6. Susan McBride, personal communication, March 10, 2021.
7. McBride, pers. comm.
8. Rebecca Wolfe, personal communication, October 31, 2019.
9. Andrew Plait, personal communication, September 25, 2019.
10. Superfest Disability Film Festival, "Showcases" (web page), www.superfestfilm.com/showcases.
11. Plait, pers. comm.
12. Candice Casey. "Inclusive Programming for All Ages," presentation poster shared via e-mail, September 13, 2019.
13. Maria Ramey, *Group Music Activities for Adults with Intellectual and Developmental Disabilities* (Philadelphia and London: Jessica Kingsley, 2011), 18.
14. Addie Spanbock, personal communication, December 12, 2019.
15. Lisa Powell Williams, personal communication, August 18, 2020.
16. *Music for Autism Newsletter,* Winter 2013.
17. Ramey, *Group Music Activities,* 18.
18. Mahya Salam, "Ali Stroker Makes History as First Wheelchair User to Win a Tony," *The New York Times,* June 9, 2019, www.nytimes.com/2019/06/09/theater/ali-stroker-oklahoma-tony-awards.html.
19. Joel M. Levy, "Theater of Dreams: Showcasing the Talents of People with Disabilities (Lively Arts)," *The Exceptional Parent* 31, no. 5 (May 2001), 47+; accessed March 17, 2012, via Gale Academic OneFile.
20. Kate Monsour, personal communication, March 30, 2020.

CHAPTER 14

Gaming, Board Game, and Escape Room Programs

Games and gaming bring people together in a number of ways, from playing tabletop or board games around a table to participating in multiplayer games online. Gaming offers opportunities to practice skills, craft an identity, and interact with others. As the AbleGamers Charity founder Mark Bartlet puts it, "[W]e make friends via shared experiences," whether those experiences are at school or work, as part of a religious institution, or during gaming.[1] Gaming in the library is an exciting way to provided inclusive, shared experiences for adults with developmental disabilities.

ACCESSIBLE GAMING IN LIBRARIES

A number of accessible gaming programs are offered at libraries. Some, like those featured at the DC and Minot (ND) Public Libraries, rely on a dedicated gaming area. The Access Center at the DC library, developed in partnership with Able-Gamers, has two adaptive gaming stations in enclosed carrels. One addresses visual needs, the other physical needs. Appointments are not required. Patrons can game whenever the library is open with guidance from staff members. The library also incorporates accessible gaming into its monthly game night. Gaming is popular with autistic patrons, those who are blind, and those with CP. According to librarian Patrick Timony, one of the best aspects of the program is that the "games bring people to the library and they find out what we do."[2]

The Minot library created a dedicated accessible gaming space after a local disability service organization offered the library a free Xbox adaptive gaming controller. Librarian and gamer Pam Carswell seized the opportunity. Use of the space is appointment based, and staff can customize the equipment for a patron. "I had to make that adaptive equipment work for multiple users, so we used Velcro, 3D printed clips and cord organizers" to create more flexibility, explains Carswell.[3] Carswell notes an important benefit of the program for users: "[T]hey live in group homes and do a lot of things in groups. It is nice to have something that is just for them."[4]

Brooklyn Public Library had two types of inclusive accessible gaming programs that emphasized the social side of gaming. The first of these, Inclusive Services' monthly Adaptive Gaming Arcade (AGA), was designed as a place where teen gamers could congregate at specific times. Librarian John Huth worked with Able-Gamers and a focus group of young adults with disabilities to develop the AGA, which had a variety of controllers, screens, and gaming systems in addition to PC games. Like the Minot library staff, Huth helped gamers create a setup that worked for them. Gamers could play individually, cooperatively, or competitively, and volunteers with and without disabilities helped with the extensive setup, checked on the gamers, and assisted with customizing games and supporting players when necessary. The second BPL program, Wii Bowling, was also a group experience. Created by the Services to Older Adults department working with senior centers and the city's department on aging, Wii Bowling consisted of competition among branch-based teams. Of course, each team had its own bowling shirts. The weekly games culminated in an annual tournament.

Inclusive Gaming

Neither BPL program saw adults with DD as the intended audience. The arcade was designed for teens with disabilities, but its visible location off the Central Library's Grand Lobby enticed adult gamers with and without disabilities as well. Adults with DD often joined in on Wii bowling because the programs were accessible to them. They took place on weekday mornings when adults with DD could attend and in the same visible location as the arcade. The application of UD principles made both of these programs naturally inclusive.

University of Michigan's Shapiro Library developed two linked gaming programs in partnership with the Medical School's physical therapy program and the university's Computer and Video Games Archive (CVGA). The first, a workshop on creating adaptive gaming technology, echoed work done by Carswell. The second was a gaming showcase where players were able to try the CVGA's equipment. Both programs attracted gamers with disabilities and their allies, including those with CP and autism. The events were organized by Jeff Edelstein in response to the lack of adaptive gaming equipment at retail game kiosks.[5]

Bringing Gaming Online

Adaptive gaming programs could also be done virtually. The Spartanburg County (SC) Public Libraries have taken a first step by circulating controllers, including adaptive ones, and offering virtual Brawlhalla and Jackbox Games meetups. Both allow for online gaming partners and communities, and Jackbox Games has both streaming and videoconferencing options. By combining the two services and curating the games, it is possible for libraries to host a virtual gaming program for adults with disabilities.

Making It Work

Making gaming accessible means looking at both physical and content access.

Physical Access

Ensuring physical accessibility takes people with a variety of needs into account, enabling gamers with CP, spinal bifida, autism, and other disabilities to play. To help ensure physical accessibility, have a variety of gaming systems, displays, and controllers on hand. A 2018 survey found that gamers with disabilities preferred PCs, in part because they are easy to adapt. Available PC features include customized controllers, PC mouses, subtitles, and key remapping.[6] Dedicated gaming systems are also popular. BPL's accessible arcade had Xbox 360, PlayStation 4, Nintendo Wii, and Atari 2600. Each system has unique features that meet an accessibility need. For example, the Xbox and Wii systems allow for hands-free play, and the PlayStation 4 has text to speech, color inversion, and enhanced text options.

Controllers are the key to accessibility. Start with the standard controllers, which have some accessibility features. Next, look at commercially available adaptive controllers. Finally, think about getting additional adaptive equipment to modify the controllers. Puff and blow switches, chin-mounted joysticks, and button switches, all of which can operate a basic toggle function, can work well. Both BPL and Minot library found it helpful to adapt switches using Velcro, play dough, cord organizers, and 3-D printers. If this all seems beyond your staff capabilities, follow Jeff Edelstein's example and partner with disabled gamers or an occupational therapist in your community to develop accessible equipment options. You can find people to help at your local Assistive Technology Center program (www .at3center.net/stateprogram).

One benefit of having a variety of gaming options is that it allows gamers to experiment to see what works best for them before buying equipment. That is why the CVGA suggests, "Get as many pieces of equipment as you can, [have] the bits and pieces that you can mix together[, and] . . . more importantly know and be comfortable with trial and error[;] remember that the work is collaborative between the librarian and the user."[7]

COMMERCIALLY AVAILABLE ADAPTIVE CONTROLLERS
- Microsoft
  - Adaptive Controller
  - Specs Switches for Adaptive Controller
  - Leg Mounts for Adaptive Controller
  - One-Handed Joystick for Adaptive Controller
- 3dRudder Foot Controller
- CronusMAX PLUS
- ASCII Grip Controller for PlayStation 1 and 2
- Adroit Switchblade
- Razer Atrox
- Gooseneck Joystick

Content Access

A central contradiction in gaming complicates making some content accessible. Access is usually about eliminating barriers, but in some games, barriers, like the oscillating toadstools in the Mario Brothers games, are intrinsic to game play. The saving grace is that since these games are designed to entice the broadest possible audience, they have some built-in flexibility. Many games build in UDL: levels get progressively more difficult, allowing players to master skills before they move on, and some offer two ways to do things, such as monitoring timed levels with a visual timer and a countdown clock. These types of features make the games more inclusive.

A deeper dive takes us to cheat codes. These are "lines of code which when entered into a game can be used to change the game's behavior, alter a character's looks and abilities, skip levels or access other hidden features."[8] Although sometimes dismissed by gamers without disabilities, according to Huth, these codes can "open a door so that a person with a physical disability can . . . drive a car 100 miles per hour; a person with an intellectual disability can . . . master the martial arts; or a person with an emotional disability can . . . become a superhero."[9]

The leap from playing a stand-alone game to online gaming is a big one. Talking about his experience at BPL, Huth says, "[O]ne of the big things we confronted was that we were accessible on the physically adaptive level, we were successful. . . . Once the game got more complex and moved online, social adapting got harder."[10] This social barrier can be big for people with ID, those with communication issues, and neurodiverse people. Huth puts it this way: "[P]layers need social acuity to not be blocked by the other gamers" and to prevent bullying.[11] Bartlet suggests two work-arounds: one is to use online house rules to find players like themselves; the other is to use a socialization ramp-up model where a player masters skills in a single-player version of the game and then graduates to the online version.[12] Another way to support neurodiverse gamers is to further scaffold by having two people or a closed group play in the same room. Carswell suggests disabled gamers bring a buddy: "We set it for the two of them. Maybe they are one character. In Minecraft . . . [for example,] one navigates the game and the other mines."[13]

Gaming is getting more accessible, which makes it easier to provide accessible gaming programming now than it was in the past. Major gaming companies have been working with disabled gamers and organizations like AbleGamers Charity to broaden their reach to disabled gamers and consequently increase their sales. PlayStation 5 and Xbox Series X, both released in 2020, are the most accessible platforms released to date. These companies learned what libraries are learning: universal design is good business.

Despite the benefit of improved platforms and equipment, what forms the core of successful programming is being a gamer and *getting* gaming, as Carswell demonstrates. If you know how it works, what draws people to it, and where the flexibility is, you are well on your way to being able to adapt gaming. You can then use commercially available products, your gaming knowledge, and available community support and tools to create accessible gaming programs at your library.

Disabled gamers, occupational therapists, gamers who work in the DD fields, your local Assistive Technology Center, and siblings of people with DD who game are all potential partners you can approach for help in adapting gaming. In addition to assisting with the planning and running of programs, these partners can also be a source of program volunteers. This is important because gaming programs are labor intensive and often rely on volunteers for their success. The volunteers at IS/BPL's Accessible Gaming Arcade, some of whom have disabilities and all of whom are gamers, help set up and take down the equipment, check people in, assist individuals as they play along with and against program participants. They also help get the word out about the programs. Gaming can be hard to sell to administrators and caregivers, but explaining the role gaming can play in people's lives may help. Gamers with disabilities have many reasons for gaming. First and foremost, they find it fun and challenging. They play to manage stress, manage pain, and combat depression. Gaming also helps many improve hand strength and build skills.[14] But the social benefits are what really sells gaming. Bartlet has "seen lives change when a person with disabilities is given access to the amazing communities created around gaming. The shared experiences that they have will open up the world to them."[15] BPL's chief librarian Nick Higgins puts it this way: the Wii Bowling League is "truly intergenerational and multicultural programing. Everyone enjoys playing together. . . . [It creates] comradery between participants of all backgrounds and abilities . . . [and] some trash talking when necessary."[16]

BOARD OR TABLETOP GAMES

Board games, also known as tabletop games, also offer unique opportunities for socializing and incidental learning. Board game play can impart cultural capital, increasing players' general knowledge base and mastery of popular culture. This can be useful for some adults with DD who have TV and movies as their primary sources for knowledge acquisition. Mostly, however, tabletop gaming is just plain fun. As Bucks County Free Library Youth Services Assistant Pat S. says, "There is something about the co-location of physical items, sitting across from each other at a table, sharing pizza."[17]

Board Game Nights

Public libraries often keep board games on hand for casual in-house use, but some formalize board game play in a program, often called a board game night. John Pappas talks about this type of program in a blog post, and he offers some tips for success:

BENEFITS OF PLAYING BOARD GAMES
- "brings people closer, strengthens relationships, and can help you meet new people"
- "teaches you how to set goals and be patient"
- "is great for reducing stress and makes for laughter"
- "creates more happiness"
- "enhances creativity and self-confidence"

Source: Pat S., Youth Services Assistant, "Benefits of Playing Board Games," Bucks County Free Library (website), January 28, 2019, https://buckslib.org/benefits-of-playing-board-games/.

- Teach one game at each session, and demonstrate all games that are provided.
- Have enough volunteers and staff to maintain a one to four or five ratio.
- Partner with a local game store as a possible source of games, volunteers, and expertise.
- Get multiple copies of the games you buy.
- If you do a series of programs, introduce a different game each time but also have games played earlier on hand.
- Include some classic games like chess, checkers, and Monopoly and decks of cards.
- Also try some newer gateway games, ones that are simple and easy to learn. A good example is Ticket to Ride by Alan R. Moon, published by Days of Wonder.
- Play in an open area of the library if possible. This makes it easier to attract spectators and for participants to leave or join the group.[18]

Board game nights can easily be inclusive, as the program at St. Charles (IL) Public Library demonstrates. Everything from dominos to role-playing games are available for participants to choose from. Games are played at tables in open areas of the library or in meeting rooms, for people who want a quieter place to play. A library staff member facilitates, engages attendees, and makes sure there are enough patrons in each group to play the selected game. Parents and caregivers work and play with the gamers with disabilities, but you could recruit volunteer assistants instead. The program primarily attracts families with autistic children, but the basic structure could easily work for a group that includes adults with DD, hopefully without their parents! San Francisco Public Library also runs an inclusive gaming program, offering theirs annually during International Games Week. Uno, Connect Four, and mancala games have all been popular at these events.

Game night programs are fun for participants, and they can be done in a way that is not labor intensive for staff. However, with a little more advance preparation, the possibilities for fun, socializing, and learning all increase.

Board Game Classes

Susan Rozmiarek, who teaches a class on board games for adults with DD at the University of Texas (UT) at Austin, provides guidance on how to run a more structured inclusive board game class. Hers is one of several courses created by neuroscience professor Dr. Jon Pierce in recognition of the fact that learning opportunities for adults with DD are scarce once they leave school. Rozmiarek likes the way Pierce designed these courses to foster inclusion:

> What is so cool and unique about this program is that topics are chosen to be of interest to both UT students and adults with IDDs. The material is presented in such a way that these students learn alongside under-graduate and graduate student volunteers, providing an enriching and integrative experience for both groups.[19]

Because of this feature of the program, student volunteer assistants have as much fun playing and learning about games as the students with DD who are enrolled in the class.

Based primarily on Rozmiarek's experience and expertise, here are some things to keep in mind as you develop an inclusive board game class:

- Require registration and set a limit on the number of participants.
- Plan a series to give attendees a chance to get to know one another.
- Increase the challenge as players develop skill and learn to work together.
- Determine how many games and how many copies of each you need by the number of sessions and participants you expect.
- Pick games that can be played together by people with a variety of literacy, math, and problem-solving skills. Modify some games if needed, or create shortcuts for the players with DD to level the playing field.
- Create simplified visuals of game rules for players with DD.
- Host game programs at times when players with disabilities are available and can get to the library.

- Allow space in the room setup for nonplaying aides or staff to move freely among the gamers to unobtrusively offer assistance.

Seating can either be assigned or by choice. Assignments enable new groupings each week and help gamers meet new people. Letting gamers decide allows people who feel comfortable with each other to sit together. The downside is that it can lead to some people feeling left out, as former friends hurry to pick seats next to each other. If you aren't sure, try it one way and modify if needed.

Program Elements

Each of the six sessions of Rozmiarek's UT Austin class runs two to two and a half hours. Each session starts with a thirty-minute social time followed by a short (fifteen-minute) interactive lecture and about thirty to forty-five minutes of game play. The last segment is a group discussion. Rozmiarek teaches her classes the actual structure of board games, assigns homework, and works with students on writing reviews of the games they play. If this is more than you are prepared to do, it is easy to simplify the session contents. Start with a short snack/social time that is followed by a brief presentation focused on the session's game. Go over the rules and introduce possibilities for modification, such as lengthening time limits, making the game cooperative rather than competitive, or simplifying play by eliminating steps or game pieces. Also be sure to have the rules available in plain language. Follow game play with a discussion of the participants' personal experiences, asking questions such as these:

- Did players enjoy the game?
- What did they like about it?
- What didn't they like?
- Would they want to play it again?
- Would they recommend it to others?

Admittedly, a board game series like this can be labor intensive, requiring some serious prep in the beginning. Over time that will diminish, as games that have already been modified are replayed, volunteers return and don't need training, and participants grow in skill. But the program also promises the opportunity for lots of fun and inclusive social interaction. So, as you consider this programming option, remember that those rewards can make the prep worthwhile, and board game program day may end up being one of your favorites.

Selecting Board Games

According to Rozmiarek, these are some of the features to look for when selecting games for an inclusive audience:

- simple rules
- an element of luck that somewhat levels the playing field
- strategy possibilities for those who are into more complex game play
- the opportunity for friendly or cooperative play, so players can assist each other as needed[20]

Additionally, look for games with these qualities:

- appeal to all ages and to the nondisabled as well as disabled gamer
- are not childish (although some children's games, like Guess Who? and the Game of Life, can work)

Also consider games that come in fun, life-size versions.

For help in selecting games, you can look to your local game store or websites like Board Game Geek (https://boardgamegeek.com), which is a rich source of information, reviews, and commentary on a huge number of board games. The "Tabletop" web page of the ALA Games and Gaming Round Table website (www.ala.org/rt/gamert/tabletop) is library specific and contains many resources. A source for information on tabletop gaming for people with disabilities is Meeple Like Us (https://meeplelikeus.co.uk). This website offers what they call an *accessibility teardown* on many games. These are extensive reviews and ratings focusing on several areas of accessibility, including visual, cognitive, physical, communication, emotional, intersectional, and socioeconomic. For more information on these categories, refer to the chart at www.meeplelikeus.co.uk/meeple-like-us-results-to-date/. Meeple Like Us reviews also contain ideas for simple modifications to play that can make specific games more accessible. Using this searchable site, it is possible to find games that are playable by a wide variety of people with and without DD. Two games that get high ratings on this site for people with cognitive impairments are Santorini and Ice Cool, so they might be good ones to try in your program.

Bingo

Bingo is a perennial favorite, and a number of libraries offer regular games for patrons with DD. You can play traditional bingo with numbers and letters, or you can play the way they do at Hart Memorial Library in Kissimmee, Florida, where

Bingo for Books has been a highlight of this library's monthly programming for adults with disabilities for several years. Adult services librarian Candice Casey introduces a literary component through thematic cards she creates using a free online Bingo card generator. For example, for a music theme, the word choices included song titles, musicians, and band names. To do this type of Bingo, generate the card and print the word choices on a sheet of cardstock. Cut the sheet into strips with one word or phrase on each. During the game, randomly select a strip and read the word slowly, clearly, and repeatedly, giving all participants time to see if the word is on their cards. Since participants will vary in their reading and game play ability, have volunteers on hand to make sure that no one misses a word or is confused by the game. At Hart library, winners get prizes consisting of simple adult books, children's titles, cookbooks, CDs, DVDs, and so forth, selected from donated materials. You can add to the program with a book or video on the theme or a brief discussion.

Jigsaw Puzzle Programs

Completing jigsaw puzzles as a group, like playing board games, is a social, fun, and popular activity. You can easily make this activity inclusive by offering a variety of puzzles with different levels of difficulty. Or try ones that have a variety of challenges built into the same puzzle, which allows puzzlers of differing ages and abilities to play together. Look for inexpensive 400-piece Three Generations puzzles, whose pieces are in three sizes. The puzzle images are suitable for adults, and a 400-piece puzzle, although large, can be completed by a mixed group in one session. White Mountain's What's for Breakfast puzzle also has pieces of varied sizes, and the picture of cereal boxes should be fun for both disabled and nondisabled puzzlers.

ESCAPE AND PUZZLE ROOMS

Escape rooms have become something of a phenomenon over the past decade. Invented in Japan and derived in part from gaming, escape rooms are locked venues in which people have to work cooperatively to collect clues and find the key that frees them. Puzzle rooms are similar, but they remain unlocked, and instead of figuring out how to escape, participants work together to find clues and solve a puzzle.

A number of libraries do escape room programs. They are fun, and they also offer lots of opportunities for learning and skill building. There is a literary component, as clues must be read and deciphered, and such skills as critical thinking, problem solving, cooperative math, and teamwork are developed in game play. If your library already does escape rooms, they may be suitable for adult patrons with DD as is, especially if they are for patrons of all ages. If not, some modification may be needed to make them accessible. To make escape rooms inclusive follow these guidelines:

- Use simple puzzles or offer ones with a variety of difficulty levels.
- Provide visual supports.
- Decrease the amount of time it takes to solve the room.
- Pay attention to sensory issues and the potential for overstimulation.
- Make sure people with fine or gross motor challenges are accommodated.
- Pair participants with DD with buddies, either one-on-one or one per small group.

With all of these options available, every library should be able to find games and ways of gaming that work for both their patrons and their institutions. This is good because these programs can be consequential as well as fun. As Michael James Heron notes:

> Games exist not just as entertainment products but powerful tools of *social integration*. When we can share our experiences of participation with the people around us, we build cultural capital. That cultural capital permits us to feel included in the wider conversation of society.[21]

NOTES

1. Mark Bartlet, personal communication, September 11, 2020.
2. Patrick Timony, personal communication, September 18, 2020.
3. Pam Carswell, personal communication, September 14, 2020.
4. Carswell, pers. comm.
5. Jeff Edelstein, personal communication, September 19, 2020.
6. Emerging Technology from the arXiv, "The Secret World of Disabled Gamers," *MIT Technology Review*, July 3, 2018, www.technologyreview.com/2018/07/03/240440/the-secret-world-of-disabled-gamers/.

7. Jeff Edelstein, personal communication, September 16, 2020.
8. John Huth, e-mail correspondence, August 21, 2015.
9. Huth, e-mail corr.
10. John Huth, personal communication, September 10, 2020.
11. Huth, pers. comm.
12. Bartlet, pers. comm.
13. Carswell, pers. comm.
14. Emerging Technology from the arXiv, "Secret World of Disabled Gamers."
15. Bartlet, pers. comm.
16. Nick Higgins, "Gaming for All: Level the Playing Field for People with Disabilities," presentation at the 2015 ALA Annual Conference, San Francisco, June 27, 2015.
17. Pat S., Youth Services Assistant, "Benefits of Playing Board Games," Bucks County Free Library (website), January 28, 2019, https://buckslib.org/benefits-of-playing-board-games/.
18. John Pappas, "A Beginner's Guide to Hosting a Board Game Night," *Programming Librarian* (blog), May 25, 2017, www.programminglibrarian.org/blog/beginner's-guide -hosting-board-game-night.
19. Susan Rozmiarek, "Games That Adults with Intellectual and Developmental Disabilities Enjoy," *Board Game Geek* (blog), December 5, 2017, https://boardgamegeek.com/ geeklist/233696/games-adults-intellectual-and-developmental-disabi.
20. Susan Rozmiarek, personal communication, September 16, 2019.
21. Michael James Heron, "Cultural Integration and the Accessibility of Gaming," *Computer Games Journal* 5 (2016): 91–94, https://link.springer.com/content/pdf/10.1007%2Fs 40869-016-0028-x.pdf.

CHAPTER 15

Social Connection and Wellness Programs

Although many library programs have wide appeal, others may be of interest to only a small number of people. Wellness programs often fit in this category; they tend to have a loyal but small following. If they are inclusive, adults with developmental disabilities might want to attend some regular library programs like these aimed at only a subset of patrons. Even within the group of programs specifically for adults with DD, there will be some that not everyone will want to attend, but these programs still have a place in our libraries. In this chapter we introduce a few types of more specialized programs for you to consider.

SOCIAL GROUPS

Many adults with DD face a range of difficulties in making social connections and developing friendships. Some arise out of the disabilities themselves, such as the social communication difficulties experienced by many autistic people, others from societal barriers that prevent access to classes, clubs, meetups, and other community experiences where adults often make connections. Even if they are able to access these events, some adults with DD find them overstimulating or overwhelming, making it hard for them to relax and connect with others.

To support adults with DD as they socialize, you can offer workshops that teach a variety of social skills, host or run groups, or plan inclusive programs. Meetups and connections happen naturally when people come together around common interests at the library.

Hosting Social Support Groups

Hosting outside groups that need meeting space is the simplest and easiest way to bring social opportunities for adults with disabilities into the library. Usually all that is required from the library is a meeting room and the listing of sessions in the library's events calendar. Libraries don't have direct involvement in these groups, but they can be used as opportunities to promote programs, collections, and services. If your library already hosts such a group or is approached by community members or partner agencies looking to start one, see if they will allow a staff member to visit for a short presentation on the library. Leave fliers and other materials at group meetings, and ask if the group would like to come early or stay after a meeting for a personalized library tour.

One example of a social group for people with DD that meets at a library is the JOY–Social and Support Group for Disabled Young Adults at Leesburg Public Library in Florida. The group started meeting monthly at the library in 2017, welcoming new participants, playing games, and planning outings. Off-site, the group has gone bowling, walked downtown to see holiday decorations, and attended an outdoor movie showing. The library provides meeting space and lists the in-house meetings on its social media pages and on the library's event calendar.

San Francisco Public Library also hosts an outside group, the AAC Conversation Club, at its Noe Valley branch. Initially, the branch manager denied the group's request to hold meetings there because it violated SFPL's limits on repeated use of meeting space. However, the parent who initiated the request persisted and reached out to SFPL access services manager and ADA coordinator Marti Goddard. Goddard realized that this group fell into a different category from others wanting to use meeting space repeatedly. It was a conversation club, and the library already sponsored conversation clubs for speakers or learners of a variety of other languages. Thanks to her awareness and intervention, the group has been meeting at the library to practice talking with their AAC devices since 2013. In 2019, as many as fifteen people attended meetings, and because an outside organization facilitates the club, it requires little to no work by library staff.[1]

The SFPL experience demonstrates the value of having staff who are trained and experienced in working with people with disabilities and who also know library policies and programming. Branch managers will not necessarily have the required breadth of knowledge and experience. Even in small libraries, designating an individual staff member as a point person or forming an accessibility team can guarantee that there are personnel equipped to meet a need like this one.

Library-Run Social Groups

Susan McBride created and runs her own social program at Hinsdale Public Library in Illinois. Her twice quarterly social club for adults with disabilities grew out of the library's successful Next Chapter Book Club, so it is called Next Chapter Social Club. Group participant Holt Mapel said, "I like the people and making friends,"[2] when asked about his experience at the club. Parents also weigh in with positive comments. One mother whose daughter attended for the first time for a showing of the movie *Elf* in December 2019 said, "There are very limited opportunities for people with disabilities in a social setting. To have this in the community is wonderful."[3] That is true not only in Hinsdale but in every community, so programs like this will most likely be gratefully received by your patrons with DD and their caregivers.

Although social groups work best in person, virtual social group programming can be successful as well. A simple, informal virtual program to consider hosting for an existing group is an Ice Cream Social on Zoom or another platform, similar to one hosted by AASCEND (Autism Aspergers Spectrum Coalition for Education Networking and Development) in California. The invitation asked members to have an ice cream treat ready in their own homes when they logged on. The host played recorded music while everyone ate their ice cream together. Some talked, others didn't, but everyone got to be together doing something enjoyable.

With a skilled facilitator, you can introduce more structure into virtual social programs. Choose a platform that is intuitive to use, make sure that potential participants have technology access, and spend some time showing those who attend how to use the technology. Keep the group small or use breakout rooms. The facilitator should begin by calling on people to introduce themselves and then be ready with some prompts to get the conversation going. Using a screen-sharing app, you can add games, movies, or virtual trips to the meetings.

FANDOM PROGRAMS

Fandoms are essentially subcultures of individuals who share a common interest and who like to interact as a community around that interest. In recent years, fandoms have become a regular part of library programming, and in "'You're Not a Real Fan!': What Libraries Can Offer Fandom," Maureen Langley discusses the positive role she feels libraries can play in fandoms and the many benefits fandoms can offer participants. These include the opportunity fandom participation provides to improve critical thinking and analytical skills, develop technical and leadership skills, and get feedback—all of which can lead to more self-confidence. She also highlights the social benefits of participation:

> [S]ocial interactions and people skills are most often cited as the reason for participation in fandom. . . . Fandom is also sometimes described as a place for social misfits, the disempowered, and the marginalized members of society. I believe that this is becoming less accurate as fandom becomes more popular; however, it is still important to note that fandom provides a safe environment full of like-minded individuals who share interests and passions.[4]

Teen Fandom and Geek Programming: A Practical Guide for Librarians by Carrie Rogers-Whitehead specifically addresses the benefit of fandoms for people with disabilities. A chapter called "How Geek Programs and Collections Can Be Inclusive" presents the multimedia principle developed by educational psychologist Richard Mayer, which says that we learn more from a combination of words and images than from just words. Rogers-Whitehead points out that graphic novels and comics, which frequently have fandoms, naturally combine images and text. Autistic people, many of whom are visual learners, are often drawn to these media, and they are perfect candidates for participation in library fandoms. Another appeal of graphic novels for autistic individuals lies in the fact that images, more than words, "convey slang, idioms, and 'hidden rules' of culture more effectively than text alone."[5] Rogers-Whitehead also says that because many comic book characters can also be found in movies, TV shows, audiobooks, and video games, comic fandom offers the opportunity to explore these characters in ways that are auditory and tactile as well as visual. They therefore work for people with a variety of intelligences.

Rogers-Whitehead offers a number of suggestions for including people with disabilities in what she calls geek programming:

- Make sure these programs are accessible for everyone who attends. Provide options.
- Have a quiet space available so people with sensory processing disorder or anxiety have a place to get away from the noise and activity.
- Use or display the captions in movies so there are multiple ways, auditory and through text, to engage with the story.
- Think about bringing cosplayers to the library to interact with individuals with DD in a focused program.[6]

If you follow these guidelines and put your favorite geek-friendly materials on display, be prepared for a fun and successful fandom program.

Basic fandom programs can also be brought online, giving participants an opportunity to show off costumes and share favorite comics, books, or other items with one another. Try using screen sharing to read an e-book or watch a movie together or just facilitate a conversation about the shared interest. Check out chapter 9 on virtual programming for guidelines on how to keep the program accessible.

WELLNESS AND PERSONAL GROWTH

When most people think about where to go for health and wellness experiences, the library is probably not high on the list. Yet libraries have been successful in offering a variety of successful health and wellness programs to their communities. Here are just a few you can consider introducing to your adult patrons with DD.

Yoga

The ancient practice of yoga is very popular, and practitioners can be found almost everywhere in the United States and Canada. Libraries offer yoga programs for people of all ages, and many people can benefit from and enjoy yoga. Library director and yoga instructor Jenn Carson says:

> If you've got a body and you can move some of it, you can do yoga. I've seen yoga done with people in wheelchairs, babies, the elderly, pregnant women, big muscly gym guys with no flexibility, high schoolers and people with developmental or cognitive disabilities. Most poses can be modified to fit a person's needs or limitations.[7]

You can bring in a local instructor to run yoga sessions or do a staff-led program, but whoever leads should have some experience working with people with disabilities. If you want to adjust your already existing yoga program to make sure adults with DD are included, try following these tips, based on ones by British yoga instructor Jan Lauren Greenfield:

- Demonstrate each pose, and then give verbal instruction while demonstrating again.
- Break poses down into three stages so students can find their own levels.

- Use the wall for support and help with balance.
- Build in rest breaks by including Child's Pose every few poses.
- Work on strength building, not flexibility, because some people, like those with Down syndrome, may be hyperflexible.
- Try different yoga styles to see what works best.
- Demonstrate proper form standing next to a participant.
- Set boundaries and behavioral expectations.
- Leave time at the beginning and end for discussion, but discourage student conversations during sessions.
- Integrate animal poses and discussion into the program.[8]

If some participants use wheelchairs or have limited mobility, you can do seated poses.

Another blogger shared her experience of teaching yoga to adults with a range of disabilities:

> [S]ome of the people who initially started did not think that Yoga was for them. . . . People are starting to take ownership of the sessions, suggesting things that they would like to do. . . . I have really noticed people starting to become physically stronger, their backs grow longer, confidence build, improvements in co-ordination and also cognitive improvements. . . . I have learned not to underestimate the ability of people. . . . [E]ach session does not have to be perfect for people to benefit.[9]

This blogger starts her yoga sessions with the "Rub Your Hands (Om Song" (by Karma Kids Yoga, from the 2008 *Come Play Yoga* album). To do this chant, start by having everyone sit on the floor on mats or in chairs. Demonstrate the actions as you introduce them verbally and again as the group performs them. You can also create a visual of the steps and use that to help participants learn the movements.

The chant and movements go like this:

[Ask everyone to hold their hands at chest height, palms facing each other.]
"Rub your hands." [Rub palms together as you speak.]
"Sit up tall."
"Take a deep breath." [Take a deep breath in as you lift arms up over your head and spread legs apart.]

"Om . . ." [Say this slowly on a long breath out. As you chant the Om bring arms down and palms together and bring legs together with bottoms of feet touching, if possible.]
[Do this sequence twice.]

Everyone ends up with their palms together, so have them bow their heads and say "Namaste," a Sanskrit greeting done in this posture. Have a variety of movements in mind for the chant so you can meet the needs of your participants in any given program.

Both of these bloggers remind us that the best practices for all programming for adults with DD apply to yoga as well. If you keep these in mind and follow the suggestions in this section, your adult patrons and you can have a wonderful experience doing yoga together in your library.

There are plenty of videos, blog posts, and virtual library programs that you can access online to help you offer a great yoga experience virtually. The trick is to make the program inclusive using the same techniques in the virtual world as in the physical, such as giving instructions one step at a time, describing while demonstrating, and making time for discussion. Also try incorporating more visuals to demonstrate poses, and emphasize safety measures like having a mat and a spotter. Keep communication open through either chat, comments, or discussion. This is important, as is getting feedback afterward to show you what to do better the next time. Consider consulting with or outsourcing the program to professionals who have training in doing yoga with people with disabilities.

Meditation

Jenn Carson's book *Yoga and Meditation at the Library: A Practical Guide for Librarians* (Rowman and Littlefield, 2019) provides some guidance for meditation in library programs. One way to introduce meditation is to include it in yoga sessions, a common practice in yoga classes. You can also introduce simple meditation techniques as a separate program or integrate them into a program with multiple elements. As with yoga, there are many types of meditation, but mindfulness meditation is popular now, so it is probably the easiest type to bring into your library programs. You can easily find simple mindfulness exercises or practices online that you can incorporate into programs you already do. Consider introducing simple relaxation techniques like body scans or try mindful breathing exercises.

Vision Boards

Making vision boards is a cross between a personal growth session and an art program. Vision boards are collages made up of words and images cut from magazines and meant to represent the dreams, goals, and vision of the creator. When vision boards are made in a group, participants share what is on their boards and what the various items mean to them. It's a great way to get people to engage with what they like and want in their lives and to share a bit about themselves with others. Adults with DD may have never been asked to explore their dreams and goals in this way, so making and sharing a vision board can offer them a unique opportunity for self-exploration and social contact.

Vision board programs are simple and inexpensive to run. All you need are a pile of old magazines, scissors (including some adaptive ones), poster boards or large pieces of cardboard, and glue sticks. You can also provide markers, stickers, or ink stamps so participants can embellish their creations. Artistic skill is not required, and people can put as few or as many items on their boards as they like. The choice of items for the board does not have to be thought out; in fact, some vision board makers contend that the best boards are made when the creators just select things that appeal to them as they go through the magazines, letting the boards they create speak to them about their tastes and interests.

Librarian Natalie Bota makes vision boards with adults with DD at an hour-long program at the Westlake Porter Public Library in Ohio. Participants enjoy it and successfully create boards, and Bota learns some new things about regular patrons through their creations.

Before Bota's program starts, she sets up the room with tables surrounded by chairs and spaces for people with wheelchairs. There is also room for people to walk or stim. Some magazines and precut images are placed on each table. You might also put stickers, stamps and ink, and drawing/writing materials on the tables. Make sure to have a variety of the types of tools needed for the activity, like scissors or glue. Sheets of cardboard or poster board should be available for participants to take as they enter the room.

The program should start with a review of the schedule and a description of vision boards and how to make them. If you like, you can suggest some types of images people might want to look for, such as places to visit, pets, jobs they might like, people they find interesting, things they'd like to own, and so on. In her program, Bota circulates as people work, offering prompts and guidance. She leaves time at the end for patrons to share what is on their finished boards, if they want to.[10]

GARDENING

Gardening can be social or contemplative. It involves exercise and requires envisioning the future. It has the added benefit of producing beauty and food. Making gardens accessible starts with design; by using UD and UDL principles, you can create both physical gardens and garden-related programs in which adults with DD can easily participate.

Sensory elements are an important part of inclusive library gardens, and the Brenda L. Papke Memorial Sensory Garden at the Staunton (VA) Public Library offers a good example. It

> fully engages visitors' senses. Many plants have strong tactile appeal, while a stone wall and a fountain provide contrasting textures. The fountain also stimulates hearing. Herbs add taste and smell, and gravel paths engage proprioception as well as provide accessibility for wheelchair users. [11]

There are also quiet spots for reading and contemplation. It is a great space in which to offer library programs.

Another inclusive garden model can be found at Gwinnett County (GA) Public Library, where all of the fifteen branches have vertical, self-contained aquaponic tower gardens that are easily accessible to wheelchair users. The tower gardens were created in response to a lack of access to fresh fruit and vegetables in the county, and library staff and patrons plant and maintain them. The library's garden-related programs focus on growing food and maintaining the towers. The bilingual programs Science in the Mexican Mother's Kitchen and Science in the Korean Mother's Kitchen are examples of how the libraries have embraced the entire community by growing food. In these bilingual programs, local mothers demonstrate cooking to an intergenerational audience. The towers are popular with everyone, including seniors and adult students with disabilities, and a school transition program brings young adults with DD to the library for garden programs.

Although nice, it is not necessary to have an elaborate garden to have a successful inclusive or focused gardening program. All it takes is some soil, seeds or seedlings, and a pot. For example, the Warren Township (NJ) Library hosted a program that taught adults with DD how to pot and care for plants. The program, led by a professional horticultural therapist, was one of an ongoing series of programs offered at that library for these patrons. It was one of the most popular programs of the series.

TIPS FOR MAKING GARDEN PROGRAMS ACCESSIBLE
- Apply UD principles when creating the space.
- Have adaptive tools.
- Incorporate sensory supports.
- Provide latex-free gloves.
- Avoid plants that are common allergy triggers.
- Focus on hardy plants.
- Explain and demonstrate.
- Follow plants as they grow.

The New Port Richey (FL) Public Library integrated its seed library into programming for young adult students with DD. Librarian Kayla Kuni showed the students how to grow their own fruits and vegetables "using library resources ranging from gardening books to the seed library. . . . We did one art project in which we painted ceramic gardening pots. Students were given a small bag of potting soil," and they chose their own packets of seeds. "They were . . . given the choice to take the pots home (most did) or leave them at school," where the program was held.[12]

Kristi Olabode of Grand Prairie Public Library System in Texas does gardening as part of her focused program for teens and adults with disabilities called First Fridays STEAM. Individuals with caregivers attend these programs along with two high school transition groups. Each session has a different theme, and the garden one, How Does My Garden Grow, is offered in the fall and spring. The session is interactive. Participants learn about how plants grow, and they explore the materials. They plant something in a pot they get to take home, along with knowledge of how to care for their new plants. Other program themes in the series include music with a music therapist, art therapy with an art therapist, and an imagination playground that involves construction with giant building materials. During the pandemic, this program moved online; materials were sent to the participating high schools, and a closed interactive session was then held on Zoom.[13]

As in the Texas example, garden programs do not have to be limited to brick-and-mortar libraries. Gwinnett library's Centerville Branch created a butterfly garden off-site in partnership with a therapeutic horseback riding center. The center's outdoor garden regularly hosts inclusive workshops on topics like growing vegetables and flowers in small spaces. Brooklyn Public Library offers virtual family gardening programs that premier monthly on Facebook. These programs include stories or poetry, some information about plants, and a gardening activity. Created using UDL principles, the programs use a picture schedule; include a mix of types of activities, such as reading, singing, and planting; employ closed captions; and build in time for reflection. At the first Garden Adventure program, beans were put in bags and jars to germinate. The resulting plants were examined at the second program to see how they had grown. By the fourth program they were potted. The success of this virtual program depends on using materials, like dried beans and baggies, that people have at home.

Emotional well-being often rests on the connections we make with one another, and having friends is the best predictor of satisfaction with life. That's why programs like the ones in this chapter are important. Adults with DD can have limited opportunities to interact with others in the community, and libraries can provide this type of connection. Warren Township Library counted their programs a success precisely because these connections were made. Their program participants "have become friends, in part because of these library programs. They have begun to develop their own social circle—a circle where they can support and care for each other."[14]

NOTES

1. Marti Goddard, personal communication, December 6, 2019.
2. Kimberly Fornek, "Libraries' Book Clubs Evolve for People with Special Needs," *Chicago Tribune,* December 30, 2019, www.chicagotribune.com/suburbs/hinsdale/ct-dhd-next -chapter-book-clubs-tl-0102-20191230-6ilbdp6alzdcleh3atj6x72bau-story.html.
3. Fornek, "Libraries' Book Clubs Evolve."
4. Maureen Langley, "'You're Not a Real Fan!': What Libraries Can Offer Fandom," Web Junction (website), March 12, 2014, www.webjunction.org/news/webjunction/youre -not-a-real-fan.html.
5. Carrie Rogers-Whitehead, *Teen Fandom and Geek Programming: A Practical Guide for Librarians* (New York: Roman and Littlefield, 2018), 133.
6. Rogers-Whitehead, *Teen Fandom and Geek Programming,* 134.
7. Jenn Carson, "Yoga in the Library," *Programming Librarian* (blog), May 11, 2015, https:// programminglibrarian.org/blog/yoga-library-0.
8. Jan Lauren Greenfield and Nicole Schnackenberg, "Ten Things I Learned Teaching Yoga to Adults with Special Needs," *Special Yoga* (blog), July 21, 2015, https://specialyoga.org .uk/blog/ten-things-learned-teaching-yoga-adults-special-needs/.
9. Lucy, "Teaching Yoga to Adults with Special Needs/The Power of Om," *Special Yoga* (blog), July 21, 2016, https://specialyoga.org.uk/blog/teaching-yoga-adults-special -needs-power-om/.

10. Natalie Bota, personal communication, July 21, 2020.
11. Carrie Scott Banks and Cindy Mediavilla, *Libraries and Gardens: Growing Together* (Chicago: ALA Editions, 2019), 39.
12. Kayla Kuni, personal communication, January 2, 2020.
13. Kristi Olabode, personal communication, November 17, 2020.
14. Pressroom, "Cultivating Special Populations Programming at the Somerset County Library System of New Jersey," *SCLSNJ News,* October 5, 2017, https://sclsnj.org/cultivating -special-populations/.

CHAPTER 16

Adulting Programs

Adulting is what we do to maintain our lives as adults. "When you buy new tires for your car, you're adulting. When you cook a meal from scratch . . . you're adulting. Paying your bills on time? Getting a loan? Adulting."[1] A generation or more ago, some of these skills were taught in school. Now new adults and teens interested in learning these skills often look elsewhere, making Adulting 101 programs popular in a number of libraries.

The skills taught as adulting behaviors are wide ranging. They can include cooking, balancing a checkbook, comparison shopping, good citizenship, dressing for success, basic sewing, packing a suitcase, and many more. For many adults with developmental disabilities, mastery of these skills can prove elusive. Cognitive challenges, sensory issues, difficulty with activities that require fine motor skills, limitations in the ability to focus and attend to a task, and the lack of opportunity to learn through practice may all play a role. Library programs can help.

Some existing adulting programs could appeal to a number of adults with DD, either as is or with the application of UDL principles and the other strategies we discuss throughout this book. However, some typical adulting programs, like car repair, may not work for many people with DD regardless of design because few of them drive or own cars. A program focused on negotiating public transportation might be more useful and popular. If you talk to your patrons with DD and explore their needs, you can easily come up with a series of adulting programs, some inclusive and others focused, to introduce skills that are both useful and fun to learn.

WHAT ARE ACTIVITIES OF DAILY LIVING?

Adults with DD may be more familiar with the term *activities of daily living* (ADLs) than with *adulting*. ADLs is the term used in therapeutic and educational environments. ADLs are everyday activities like shopping, food preparation, housework, and laundry that allow us to take care of ourselves and live independently.

FOOD-RELATED PROGRAMS

Everyone eats, and public library cookbook collections are perennially popular. Building on these interests, libraries offer food-related sessions as part of their adult programming. Some existing food programs can become inclusive, and focused programs can be created and introduced for your adult patrons with DD. This chapter presents some possibilities.

Cooking Demonstrations

With the popularity of cooking programs and the ascendency of celebrity chefs, many patrons, both with and without disabilities, will welcome the idea of watching someone cook at the library. Kate Niehoff from Schaumburg Township District Library in Illinois thought her regular group of autistic young adults would enjoy this, so she hosted the program Cooking Demonstration for Adults Facing Social Challenges. Dave Esau, a popular local chef, prepared a variety of dishes and demonstrated cooking techniques.[2]

You can also consider doing a cooking demonstration online. For people who are used to television cooking shows, virtual cooking demonstrations may seem even more familiar than in-person ones. One advantage is that everyone can get a close-up view; another is the possibility of posting the recipe step-by-step on a split screen. Of course, participants won't be able to smell the dish as it is prepared or taste it at the end, but for people with sensory sensitivities and allergies, those things could be a plus!

Learning to Cook, Cooking to Learn

Watching someone cook is entertaining, but it won't leave unskilled observers with the ability to cook at home. For adults with DD who may have had little or no access to the traditional ways people learn to cook, such as "parental or familial guidance, self-instruction, peer modeling, mass media presentations, formal training, and trial and error,"[3] the approach needs to be more hands-on. Cooking with Confidence, an offering of the Free Library in Philadelphia's Culinary Literacy Center (CLC) in partnership with A. J. Drexel Autism Institute's Philadelphia Autism Project (Philly AP), is just such a program. The library provides space, setup, and a sous chef, coordinates scheduling, and buys ingredients. Philly AP provides some funding and an intern, handles registration, collects data, and offers support. Recipes are simplified and broken down into steps. The presenter reads each step, models it, then has the students do it themselves.

The two-hour sessions are consistently structured and include these segments:

- welcome period
- talk about kitchen safety
- handwashing
- active food preparation
- cleanup and table setting
- eating together
- discussion of the meal after eating
- promotion of other library offerings

Instruction is person centered, accommodating different ability levels, and everyone gets at least some hands-on time. Some students come with an aide, some use AAC devices. Nutrition, ADLs, and social opportunities are all built into the program design.

You do not need the Free Library's impressive facility to carry out a similar program. All that is needed is running water, a sturdy table, and an electrical outlet. CLC's comprehensive *Culinary Literacy: A Toolkit for Public Libraries*, which is available online, provides guidance and has a list of additional helpful items.[4] Cathy Rietzen who runs the CLC program for Philly AP suggests substituting lettuce knives for sharper implements for this audience.[5]

Athens (GA) Regional Library worked with the CLC to develop its culinary literacy programming. An American Dream Literacy Initiative grant funded fully equipped kitchen carts for eight of the Athens library branches. The CLC trained interested staff who then started offering programs. One was for adults with disabilities and their families, conducted in partnership with a community organization. In the six-week series, instructor and chef Theresa Rice broke down her standard instruction into simple steps. Classes introduced basic kitchen concepts and followed a natural progression with each class building on the previous ones. The six sessions were as follows:

- *The basics:* The first class provided an overview of equipment, tools, and ingredients through learning how to prep and make eggs three ways.
- *Countertop and refrigerator:* This lesson covered safe storage, washing hands, labeling food, rotating items in the freezer, and so forth, while making tuna and egg sandwiches and salad.
- *Skillet:* This session focused on measurements; how to peel, cut, and chop; how to hold knives; and using cutting boards all while making tortilla pepperoni pizza.
- *Stovetop or crock pot:* Participants learned wet and dry measures with salt, lentils, and water; used a variety of cup and spoon sizes; and reviewed knife safety as they made lentil soup.
- *Oven:* Oven safety and the use of cooking spray were covered as participants made a sheet pan dinner.
- *Treats:* The final class focused on making Halloween-themed sweets.

Classes were interactive and hands-on and included additional activities and visuals. Rice used regular knives with her students, and one mom shared that she had never thought of letting her adult daughter use a knife before. The mom was surprised at how well her daughter did, and she later shared photos of her daughter at home happily preparing breakfast and baking a pie.[6]

Selecting Cookbooks

Some cookbooks work better than others for adults with DD. These are some of the elements to look for:

- simple recipes requiring few ingredients, tools, and steps to prepare
- separate lists of ingredients and tools
- clear instructions that do not chain steps
- definitions for cooking jargon like simmer and sear
- visuals that show what the dish will look like or, even better, cookbooks that demonstrate the entire process visually
- recipes that are inexpensive to make, because many adults with DD live on fixed incomes

Consider cookbooks published for people with disabilities like *Look 'n Cook Microwave Cookbook* by Ellen Sudol (Attainment, 1999) and *Visual Recipes: A Cookbook for Non-readers* by Tabith Orth (AAPC, 2006). *Good and Cheap: Eat Well on $4/Day* by Leanne Brown (Workman, 2015) is the cookbook used by the CLC. It has inexpensive recipes and some illustrated finished products. Both an English and a Spanish version, *Bueno y Barato* (Workman, 2017), are available free online as PDFs. Accessible Chef (www.accessiblechef.com) is a place to find visual recipes plus useful resources, including adaptable kitchen tools.

BEST PRACTICES FOR COOKING PROGRAMS
- Teach basic cooking terms.
- Use pictorial recipes whenever possible, and simplify the steps of each recipe.
- Involve the participants in prep as well as cooking.
- Pay extra attention to potentially dangerous situations, such as working with sharp knives or around hot oil.
- Build on skills as they are mastered, introducing more complex cooking techniques and recipes over time.
- Provide choices so dishes can be personalized.
- Create simple songs or chants to reinforce basic procedures.[*]

Before you do any cooking, check with your local board of health for certification requirements.

---

[*]Janice Goldschmidt, *Teaching Authentic Cooking Skills to Adults with Intellectual and Developmental Disabilities: Active Engagement* (Silver Spring, MD: AAIDD, 2018), 32.

MONEY MANAGEMENT PROGRAMS

People with disabilities are far from the only ones who can benefit from information about finances. Teens need the basics, but older adults may be looking to increase their savings or improve their credit scores. However, the issue is more complex for people with DD. While their ability to function independently may be contingent on their ability to master basic money skills, their financial situation may be complicated by having a guardian or on their reliance, in part or in whole, on government funding. Most books and financial training programs will not be able to meet their needs. Instead, a library program can be one way to offer them basic financial education.

Money Management Games

Learning that is embedded in game play can be more fun than didactic lessons. Try money-themed Bingo, using terms like ATM, budget, credit card, debt, and so on, for the Bingo words. You can define the terms during play or afterward. Introduce one of the readily available board games that teach financial literacy, such as Pay Day by Winning Moves Games. Attainment Company sells some money-themed games designed specifically for people with disabilities. Consider integrating these into your gaming programs, or use them as part of a series of programs on money management.

Money Management Workshops

The Hart Memorial Library in Kissimmee, Florida, offered a three-part workshop for adults with disabilities based on information in *How Money Works for Kids,* which is available online.[7] Presenter Amanda Miller covered money basics, including how to get correct change, how to tip, why taxes come out of a paycheck, and how to make sure your money lasts until the end of the month. Miller used handouts and role-plays, personalizing the learning for each attendee. Her sessions incorporated many of the best practices discussed elsewhere in this book; they were interactive, visuals were available through the handouts and a white board, and a hands-on experience was offered with play money. The twenty participants left with a basic functional understanding of how money works in their lives.

Another excellent resource you can use is a free financial literacy curriculum for adults with disabilities called *Cents and Sensibility*, available online from the Pennsylvania Assistive Technology Foundation.[8]

Financial Planning

As difficult as financial planning is, it is even harder for people with disabilities and their families who must navigate the interconnected systems of national, state, and local benefits and entitlements. Specific issues include the following:

- Supplemental Security Income (SSI) eligibility
- income and asset limits
- Medicaid waiver services
- financial and estate planning tools such as
  - PASS (Plan to Achieve Self-Support) plans
  - ABLE (Achieving a Better Life Experience) accounts
  - special needs trusts
- financial guardianship
- poverty

SSI eligibility is crucial for a significant number of people with DD, in part because it brings Medicaid eligibility with it. Medicaid is the federal health insurance program for people with disabilities. It provides basic health care and specific services such as day habilitation, community habilitation, housing, aides, equipment, and medication that allow people with high support needs to live in the community or in institutions. Adults with DD who come to libraries in groups access agency services because of Medicaid waivers. Maintaining SSI eligibility is a matter of life and death for many people, and not understanding the systems can result in tragic errors.

Adults with DD make decisions that could impact their benefits every day. To help them understand these decisions and their implications, Brooklyn Public Library partners with EmpoweredNYC, a program from the Mayor's Office of People with Disabilities, to offer workshops for individuals with DD as well as one-to-one financial counseling. These are offered at the library in partnership with BPL's Business and Career Center. One of the reasons these presentations are so popular is that they are done by individuals with disabilities who can connect to the audiences and relate to their issues. Independent living centers, agencies that support people with DD, ACCES-VR (Adult Career and Continuing Education Services–Vocational Rehabilitation), and self-advocacy groups are other places to look for potential presenters.

Families, caregivers, and guardians also need information about financial planning. Those who already have access to financial planning services need specialized advice on the long-term financial needs of the people with DD whom they love or care for. Families who do not have many assets also need financial planning, although they may not realize it. Presenters must be able to address both groups. BPL offers these types of workshops regularly and finds that panel presentations which include a parent or guardian of an adult with DD are the most popular.

To find a presenter, consider approaching a local member of the Special Needs Alliance, a professional organization of attorneys with interest and expertise in disability law. Other resources to consider include your local DD council and independent living center, agencies that support people with disabilities, affinity organizations such as the Down Syndrome Congress, and insurance or investment companies with specialized divisions. Any of them may be willing to present at your library or refer you to other local resources. State and local government agencies may also be able to help. If you end up using a commercial agency that provides these types of services, consider a panel presentation to stay focused on the financial planning options and not one company's services.

COMPUTER SKILLS PROGRAMS

Using a computer, whether a desktop or laptop, tablet, or phone, is essential to everyday life. We shop, read the paper, play games, apply for school and benefits, and file taxes online. It is often assumed that people learn at least rudimentary computer skills at school, but this is not always the case for adults with DD. Libraries have stepped into the breach.

Computer Instruction

At the New Port Richey (FL) Public Library, Kayla Kuni developed computer classes, working closely with staff from the Arc and the individuals they serve. Each class focused on a skill, such as using a mouse, while exploring a topic. Although topics ranged from the Olympics to job hunting, the structure of each class was the same: review terms and introduce new ones, turn on the computer, and explore the day's topic. Kuni kept the group to five or six people and minimized the time between sessions so people didn't forget what they had already learned. By the end of the series, participants knew how to turn the computer on and off and how to choose between a mouse and a touchpad, and they were able to look up information independently.[9]

Other libraries offer computer training for adults with DD. Staff from the Queens (NY) Public Library's Job and Business Academy travel from the Central Library to the remote Glen Oaks branch to work with a group from a prevocational center, ANIBIC (Association for Neurologically Impaired Brain Injured Children). Branch manager Younshin Kim has forged a long-standing partnership with the center. BPL has more informal computer classes; a technology resource specialist demonstrates iPad use on an impromptu basis. At Deerfield (IL) Public Library, Vicki Karlovsky offers formal classes, sometimes works individually with people on computer skills, and sometimes teaches at a local service provider, the Center for Enriched Living. Her first one-on-one at the center was with an individual who wanted to learn how to access music on the internet. Together they developed a Pandora station and navigated YouTube:

> [A]fter we finished he actually leapt up . . . to grab one of the staff members . . . brought them over to a different computer where he proceed[ed] to show them everything that he had just learned with me. . . . [He was] really excited to kind of show that off and use it on his own.[10]

San Francisco Public Library hosts an inclusive computer class that had a unique evolution. A partner agency, the Arc, began teaching basic computer skills classes in the Main Library's computer lab for the individuals they served. The program quickly evolved from a focused to an inclusive one. According to access services manager Marti Goddard, "Learners in these classes have included participants from the Arc along with members of the general public who find the classes in the Library's monthly listing of classes."[11]

Technology skills can be taught over the phone as well as in person. Deerfield library's Library Lifeline has assisted people with downloading e-books and using e-resources, and Inclusive Services at BPL has helped adults with disabilities navigate the holds process, use their phones to go online, and access a Zoom meeting. All of this support was given on the phone.

Internet Safety

Library computer education programs for children and teens often cover cyber safety, but many adults could also benefit from this information, and adults with DD may need it even more than the average adult. Although all of us are capable of making mistakes online, such as falling for phishing scams, adults with DD have less experience in the wider world and can be sucked in more easily. Without access to the resources and experiences many of us rely on to help us correct or avoid such hazards, adults with DD are vulnerable to making costly or dangerous mistakes. Libraries can fill this gap by having accessible information available on their websites or in print and offering internet safety programs for adults.

A cyber-safety workshop should also cover the potential benefits of going online for adults with DD. Ashley Ritchey, director of New Jersey Self-Advocacy Project, lists these as a series of freedoms:

- Freedom from isolation
- Freedom from immediate identification as a person with a disability
- Freedom from constraints of daily life
- Freedom to create your own persona
- Freedom to explore the world, areas of individual interest, and relationships with people they might not otherwise meet[12]

You can look to the library's staff or local organizations to find a presenter who is knowledgeable on this subject. Or you can use the material in "Staying Safe Online: Tips for Adults with Intellectual and Developmental Disabilities and Their Loved Ones," a webinar from the Arc of New Jersey. Both the slides and a video of this presentation can be found online (www.arcnj.org/information/archived_webinars.html).

Text and E-mail Etiquette

Many adults with DD, as well as others, could benefit from learning about behavioral expectations when communicating digitally, including the difference between communicating by text and e-mail. Texts are more informal and used for friends or peers; e-mails are used in professional communication or to communicate with older relatives who don't text. Because e-mail is how we communicate with schools or potential employers, understanding proper e-mail etiquette can have a bearing on getting into a program or being hired for a job. Armed with this information, adults with DD will be better equipped for participation in personal and business relationships and will have an additional set of tools for more independent living. If you do a session on this topic, be sure to cover the use of emojis, capitalization in texts, appropriate content, and what to put in e-mail subject lines, among other topics. These are things that are misunderstood and misused by many new adults, not just those with developmental disabilities.

RELATIONSHIPS AND SEXUALITY

There are many myths about people with DD and sexuality, including they are not interested in or capable of having relationships, they are not sexual like everyone else, and they are all heteronormative. The headline "Couple with Down Syndrome Told Not to Marry, Proves Critics Wrong 25 Years Later" is just one example of how wrong these assumptions are.[13] Despite the facts, adolescents with DD are not given the same information on this aspect of their lives as other teens. A young man with DD said of his time in school, "When the other kids had sex education, I had to go somewhere else."[14] His experience is far from unique, both in schools and in homes. When queried, self-advocates were clear about what they wanted instead:

- "Parents need to trust us; we are old enough to be in a relationship."
- "A couple should have a chance to get to know about each other and to talk to each other in private."
- "Caregivers should expect people to want relationships and be prepared for a potential negative impact if they do not have the opportunity to form relationships or express their sexuality."
- "Provide comprehensive sexuality education for people with I/DD that includes discussions about desire, pleasure, appropriate dating behaviors, and the interpersonal skills needed."[15]

Library Programs

Libraries have a role to play here as well. IS/BPL has been offering events on relationships, sexual health, sexuality, and gender identity since the early 2000s. Initially workshops were aimed at teaching parents and caregivers how to support this aspect of their children's lives. At the first one, a gasp rippled through the audience when the presenter suggested that to decrease their children's frustration, resulting meltdowns, and inappropriate behavior, they may need to be explicitly taught how to masturbate. Subsequent workshops covered topics such as relationships and the LGBTQ+ (lesbian, gay, bisexual, transgender, queer/questioning, plus) community.

After a BPL conference on bullying where a panelist announced that he had been bullied not because of his intellectual disability but because he was gay, it became clear that the focus needed to shift. At the next conference, an LGBTQ+

self-advocate from Columbia University conducted a breakout session for autistic LGBTQ+ people. It was the only session that was oversubscribed. Since then, IS/BPL has assumed that people with DD would be part of the audience for programs on sex, sexuality, and gender identity.

When libraries went virtual, so did BPL's programs on these topics. At a Zoom Voices of Power meeting, Planned Parenthood presented on sexual health, covering basic anatomy, hygiene, sexually transmitted diseases, and birth control. Participants saw detailed, labeled line drawings of a penis, breasts, and a vagina. They watched videos of self-advocates demonstrating the proper way to put on a condom and how to do a breast exam, modeled on a male. Throughout the presentation, presenters used gender-neutral terms like *person with a vagina* and *person with a penis* and the pronoun *they*. Participants had good questions. In some ways, having the workshop online was better because it allows for privacy and the opportunity to opt out of a section unobtrusively.

Taking on the subject of online dating, Marc Lazar taught a program called Online Dating (for Humans) to autistic young adults at the Schaumburg Township (IL) District Library. It covered many topics, including how dating has changed since the 1950s, the importance and types of dating websites and apps, the pros and cons of online dating, how to create a profile, how to communicate once a match is made, first-date safety, how to handle rejection and reject others respectfully, and more. Lazar also addressed the issue of self-disclosure, saying that the decision whether or not to reveal disability status depends on individual comfort but that no one should feel embarrassed about being autistic.[16] It is also important that no one feel excluded because of who they want to date, so if you do a program like this, be sure to mention and normalize same-sex dating.

Finding Presenters and Resources

Finding someone to conduct programs on these issues can be tricky, but it is easier than in the past because some organizations have developed and others have expanded their offerings. If you are looking for speakers try these sources:

- Autistic Women and Nonbinary Network (Among other things, AWN Network has a great plain-language pamphlet for trans autistic people on how to find a doctor.)
- DD service providers

- LGBTQ+ support groups affiliated with DD organizations like YAI: Seeing Beyond Disability or the Self-Advocacy Association of New York State
- Planned Parenthood

Other resources can also be useful. The National Council on Independent Living (NCIL) has an excellent series of sex education videos and discussion guides by and for people with DD. The guides are written in plain language that many people with DD can understand, and the videos feature people with disabilities. Find them online at www.ncil.org. Libraries can also make sure to have good books on the subject in their collections; examples include these titles: *Sexuality and Intellectual Disability: A Guide for Professionals,* by Andrew Maxwell Triska (Routledge, 2018); *The Autism Spectrum Guide to Sexuality and Relations,* by Dr. Emma Goddall (London: Jessica Kingsley, 2016); and *Gender Identity, Sexuality and Autism: Voices from across the Spectrum* by Eva A. Mendes and Meredith R. Maroney (London: Jessica Kingsley, 2019). Among other topics, all of these cover issues related to intersectionality.

A staff member who is comfortable with this content and knowledgeable about how to communicate effectively with adults with DD one-on-one or in a group could also potentially run a session on these topics. Wherever you get presenters, they need to be prepared to work with this audience and to apply these best practices:

- Consider patrons' chronological age when deciding what topics to cover.
- Consider patrons' developmental ages when deciding how to present the information.
- Use accurate visuals.
- Use accurate, clear terminology, not euphemisms.
- Address the various components under the LGBTQ+ umbrella.
- Have a sense of humor.

CIVIC ENGAGEMENT

Adults with DD are members of their communities, and like everyone else, they benefit from active involvement. Library initiatives can help get them involved.

Voter Support

Recognizing the importance of an informed and active electorate, in 2020 ALA produced a guide called *Libraries and Voter Engagement*.[17] It reminds us that libraries, as nonpartisan community gathering places that provide programming and access to accurate information, are ideal places to promote an educated and engaged citizenry. While the resources and ideas in the guide are good ones, they may not meet the needs of potential voters with DD. For example, Meet the Candidates events tend to be crowded and loud and the questions asked too abstract. To make programs like these more accessible, collect written questions in advance. This will help adults with DD get theirs addressed. You can also record the event for later playback or make it virtual so people can engage at their own pace. You can also share the NCIL's *Including People with Disabilities in Your Political Campaign: A Guide for Campaign Staff* (https://ncil.org/campaign-guide/) with candidates or their representatives and refer voters with DD to ASAN's *Your Vote Counts: A Self-Advocate's Guide to Voting in the U.S.* (https://autisticadvocacy .org/policy/toolkits/voting).

Also try hosting a voter registration drive. BPL's Voices of Power group does one every year. They also point potential voters to accessible information and guides. A good source is the Arc's "Voting" web page (https://thearc.org/vote/), with information in plain language in both English and Spanish. SABE also offers resources and workshop modules on its website (www.sabeusa.org/govoter/). Many state and local Boards of Elections also have appropriate guides or can do an in-person or online presentation.

Helping Others

By the time people with DD reach adulthood, they have long experience with being the recipients of help, pity, and charity. While some of what they receive is needed and welcomed, always being in the position of receiver and rarely in the position of giver is not a good thing because, like everyone else, they experience joy, connection, and enhanced self-esteem when they are able to do things for others. Building on that premise, some libraries have discovered a variety of ways to help adults with DD give back.

Volunteering in the library is one way, and we discuss that at some length in the next chapter. Other programs build in community service in a more creative way. One example is the annual Trunk or Treat program of the suburban Germantown (TN) Community Library. During this Halloween program for people with disabilities, created in partnership with the town's recreation department, costumed trick-or-treaters go from car to car soliciting candy. Originally, adults made the candy-seeking rounds along with the kids. Lisa Hagen had a better idea: have the adults distribute candy to the children before getting candy for themselves, allowing them to be leaders and givers and not just recipients! This model worked well, and the program is considered a big success, attracting more than 100 participants each year.

Librarian Kayla Kuni used her arts-related programs for adults with disabilities at New Port Richey library to foster community engagement and offer participants the opportunity to learn about other issues and people. She arranged for City Hall, located right next to the library, to display art created at the library by adults with DD. One May, she developed a series of initiatives for the Red Apple school groups she worked with that she called May It Forward. They made and donated art to community organizations, including a domestic abuse shelter and the Lighthouse for the Blind and Visually Impaired.[18]

In Johnson County, Kansas, librarian Helen Hokanson partnered with Sharon Holley, who works with older adults with DD at Johnson County Developmental Supports, to address an ongoing problem at the library. Barrels used to collect food donations were often mistaken for trash receptacles. The retirees in Holley's program transformed those unsightly barrels, and the resulting attractive barrels clearly indicate their purpose. Photos show these adults posing around one of their painted barrels, and it is clear that they are proud of what they have created for their community.[19]

There are so many ways that libraries can help adults with DD work on life skills and have fun through programming. Hopefully, we have introduced some here that you can't wait to try at your library.

NOTES

1. Laguna Shores Recovery, "Adulting 101: Millennial Life Skills" (web page), https://lagunashoresrecovery.com/adulting-101-millennial-life-skills/.
2. Kate Niehoff, personal communication, November 4, 2019.
3. Janice Goldschmidt, *Teaching Authentic Cooking Skills to Adults with Intellectual and Developmental Disabilities: Active Engagement* (Silver Spring, MD: AAIDD, 2018), 25.
4. Jamie Bowers, Liz Fitzgerald, and Suzanna Urminska, *Culinary Literacy: A Toolkit for Public Libraries* (Philadelphia: Culinary Literacy Center, 2017), https://libwww.freelibrary.org/assets/pdf/programs/culinary/free-library-culinary-literacy-toolkit.pdf.

5. Cathy Rietzen, personal communication, October 11, 2019.
6. Theresa Rice, personal communication, November 24, 2019.
7. *How Money Works for Kids: A Parent's Guide* (Duluth, GA: Primerica, 2014–2015), https://wedcbiz.org/wp-content/uploads/How-Money-Works-for-Kids.pdf.
8. Pennsylvania Assistive Technology Foundation (PATF), *Cents and Sensibility: A Guide to Money Management,* 6th ed. (King of Prussia, PA: PATF, 2020), https://patf.us/what-we-do/financial-education/.
9. Kayla Kuni, personal communication, December 30, 2019.
10. Vicki Karlovsky, "Sharing Our Stories—National Library Week 2017," YouTube, posted April 13, 2017, www.youtube.com/watch?v=enB3pKPTDpl.
11. Marti Goddard, e-mail correspondence, September 17, 2020.
12. The New Jersey Self-Advocacy Project, "Internet Safety for Students and Adults with I/DD" (webinar), April 7, 2020, slide 8, www.arcnj.org/programs/njsap/webinars.html/title/4-7-20-internet-safety-for-students-and-adults-with-i-dd.
13. Dashka Devnani, "Couple with Down Syndrome Told Not to Marry, Proves Critics Wrong 25 Years Later," *The Epoch Times,* March 22, 2019, www.theepochtimes.com.
14. National Council on Independent Living (NCIL), "Introduction," *Sex Ed for People with I/DD* (10-video series), YouTube, last updated September 30, 2019, www.youtube.com/playlist?list=PLuEvYNNQ-dHeVhbyeJHx9s8oqsvBk621v.
15. Elevatus Training, "Listening to Self-Advocates' Voices: How Shameful, Negative Messages, and Fear-Based Sexuality Education Puts People at Risk," www.elevatustraining.com/listening-to-self-advocates-voices/.
16. Marc Lazar, "Online Dating (for Humans)," PowerPoint presentation, provided via e-mail, February 13, 2020.
17. American Library Association, *Libraries and Voter Engagement* (Chicago: ALA, 2020), www.ala.org/advocacy/sites/ala.org.advocacy/files/content/advleg/statelocalefforts/voterengagement/Libraries%20and%20Voter%20Engagement%20-%20PRINT%20120219.pdf.
18. Kayla Kuni and Linda Hotslander, presenters, and Sarah Osman, facilitator, "You Belong @ Your Library: Programming for Adults with Intellectual Disabilities," *Programming Librarian* (webinar series, ALA Public Programs Office), originally recorded September 15, 2015, posted to YouTube March 10, 2016, 54:41. www.youtube.com/watch?v=fuSRAuX_FEc&feature=youtu.be.
19. Helen Hokanson, personal communication, July 9, 2019.

CHAPTER 17

Programs That Support Postsecondary Education and Employment

In our society, having a job is often about more than earning money: "Having a job is a valued social role. Employment is a pathway to independence, economic self-sufficiency, respect, purpose, dignity, and full community participation."[1] With full participation comes increased visibility that in turn can lessen the stigma and isolation of people with developmental disabilities, helping to create "a sense of the value of all people, which then leads to the development of more opportunities for people with IDD to be a meaningful part of their communities."[2]

The ultimate goal for many people with DD is a competitive job and economic independence. Because of societal barriers, this is largely aspirational. National advocacy organization the Arc reminds us:

> Currently, people [with DD] often leave school with little to no com-
> munity-based vocational experience or planning for transitioning from
> school to work. Many have been placed in "prevocational" programs
> and "disability-only" workshops where they are paid below minimum
> wage and have little expectation of moving into competitive jobs where
> they can work alongside people without disabilities. These low expec-
> tations foster job discrimination.[3]

HOW LIBRARIES AND OTHERS CAN HELP

To reach their employment goals, adults with DD need opportunities to build experience and gain confidence. They also need support from schools, parents, community members, and institutions, including libraries. High expectations and persistent efforts over time are essential, as Robert's story shows.[4] His route to competitive employment was long and arduous, but with lots of support, Robert finally found success in the world of work. His path included coordination between his mother and the school to identify needed skills; six years in high school learning job skills, practicing completing job applications, developing a work ethic, and learning how to dress and groom himself for job success; and visits to more than fifty-two work sites. All of these efforts ultimately led him at twenty-one to a part-time job he liked and where he did well.

For some people with DD, like Robert, the goal is a part-time job. For others it is an apprenticeship or a full-time job in retail, food service, or an office. Some want to work in careers that require postsecondary education ranging from certificate programs to graduate degrees. Still others want to develop their own businesses or work from home. Whatever the ultimate employment goal, libraries can offer adults with DD support through programming and experience through volunteer and work opportunities.

Soft Skills Workshops

Natural opportunities to learn soft skills like being on time and communicating effectively can be few and far between for people with DD. As Robert's story illustrates, adults with DD often need job training that goes above and beyond learning the tasks of a position, the so-called hard skills. Their exclusion from many experiences like summer jobs and internships often leave them ill prepared to fit into a work environment. Autistic adults in particular may find it difficult, or even impossible, to learn the hidden social and behavioral rules that must be followed while on the job, yet they will be expected to adhere to the norms of the workplace. They need to be specifically taught how to present themselves and act in the world of work. Libraries, which have experience doing this for teens, can contribute to that effort for adults.

In many communities, there are presenters with expertise and experience working with adults with DD who would be happy to come to your library to run a workshop, either as a stand-alone session or as part of an existing program. For example, Schaumburg Township District Library in Illinois brought in Marc Lazar, who worked for Aspiritech supporting the company's autistic employees, to present to the library's monthly group for autistic young adults.

Lazar's workshop, What Not to Do at Work: Or . . . When Not to Pass Gas, handled the topic with a light touch. The session began with cartoons and photographs from popular culture illustrating hygiene behaviors to avoid. This was followed by what to do and what not to do in relation to a number of job-related topics:

- types of annoying people at work (and how to avoid being one)
- appropriate body language
- interacting with supervisors
- how to take feedback
- #1 rule: be respectful
- e-mail and text etiquette[5]

A program like this does not need to be restricted to people with DD. Other workers could also benefit from a clear explication of the behavior expected on the job. After all, who couldn't use some guidance on how to get along better with coworkers or earn promotions.

Identifying Interests

The first step in a job search is often deciding what type of job you want. Inclusive Services at Brooklyn Public Library held two workshops to assist people with this decision. The first, led by an autistic musician and the director of an inclusive music program at a local conservatory, allowed adults with DD to explore careers in music. After the initial event, attendees worked with the musician and learned how to use the library's recording studio. Several participants had not considered making a career out of their passion for music before attending this program! The second helped young adult students. A presenter from the local Parent Training Center, INCLUDEnyc, outlined the Board of Education's transition to adult services process and worked with the students to identify interests, the jobs they wanted, and the skills and training they would need for those jobs. One aim was to incorporate the needed skill development into the students' individualized education programs. Educators, caregivers, and family members also attended, making this an inclusive program.

Volunteer placements and internships, discussed later in this chapter, are other ways for people with DD to identify their interests and explore their passions through hands-on work. Sometimes volunteering is a way to rule out possible jobs. One autistic volunteer at IS/BPL discovered he did not like working in a library, so he used library resources to find an apprenticeship that he liked much better—as a carpenter in a union program. In the end, he became a glass blower. Each exploration led him closer to his final goal: a paying job and independence.

Résumé and Career Workshops

BPL's Business and Career Center (BCC) regularly offers résumé writing workshops, individualized help, interview practice, and support for entrepreneurship. To include people with disabilities, they reach out to IS/BPL for help working with specific patrons. For example, when an autistic entrepreneur with a learning disability was looking for funding for a film project, IS/BPL was able to recommend resources outside BCC's accustomed scope, such as ACCES-VR, part of the federal rehabilitation employment program for people with disabilities. IS/BPL also suggested technology to help the entrepreneur read text. Over time, BCC has become familiar with these types of resources. BCC has brought agencies that support people with disabilities in employment and education to the library and actively promotes the center's services at outreach events for people with disabilities, such as the city-wide College and Career Fair put on by the NYC Department of Education's Transition Center.

Individualized support like that offered by BCC can be given virtually as well as in person. Résumés can be shared and worked on together and mock interviews can be conducted via virtual meeting platforms. There are even some advantages to the virtual approach, such the ability to edit as you go and the opportunity to build comfort with platforms through experience using them. Working remotely with support personnel from the library can also give patrons with DD the opportunity to practice employment-related soft skills. If computer and internet access is not available, these types of consultations are also possible by phone.

College, Career, and Transition Fairs

College, career, and transition fairs can help adults with DD identify interests and plan for the future. For example, in partnership with Center for People with Disabilities, Anythink Wright Farms Library in Thornton, Colorado, hosted a job fair in September 2019 called Own It: Career Fair for All Abilities. Speaking about the value of employment for the people the library planned to serve with this event, Anythink Wright Farms adult guide Maria Mayo said, "It's not only important for empowerment and that sense of 'I earned a paycheck' but it's also important for them to meet and interact with everyone to end stigma [and] build community and friendships."[6] The fair offered three services for the teens and adults who came: résumé editing by representatives of the Adams County Workforce Center, a head shot photo, and a chance to learn about various fields by interacting with employers.

Fairs can have a specific focus, like the Anythink employment fair or the post-secondary education College for Students with Disabilities Fair at BPL. They can also be more general, addressing both education and employment. To make these events easier to plan, consider working with umbrella groups like DD councils or local advocacy groups. The Brooklyn Family Support Service Advisory Council (BFSSAC) organizes an annual fair and smaller resource events at BPL that feature representatives from vocational services, work skills training programs, colleges, service providers, and self-advocates. BFSSAC invites the exhibitors, checks them in, makes signs for the tables, and does the publicity. IS/BPL provides the space, acts as a liaison with branch staff, and sets up its own table. IS/BPL also organizes its own resource fair each year, and it is much easier when BFSSAC does the work. An outside partner can also often bring new exhibitors to the fair, enriching the event for attendees.

SUPPORT IN POSTSECONDARY INSTITUTIONS

The Higher Education Opportunity Act made postsecondary education, once unheard of for people with DD, a viable option, and some institutions, including Adelphi University in New York, provide expanded services for these students through their Disability Services offices. Others have certificate programs, many of which are affiliated with Think College, discussed further in the following section. Still others allow students with ID to audit classes. At least one institution, the College for the Adaptive Arts in San José, California, was created specifically for students with DD. These models all tend to "focus on three broad areas: independent living, academic access, and employment."[7]

Ensuring Library Access

Library access is a critical element in all of these models. Think College, a clearinghouse for certificate programs for students with ID, views libraries as an integral part of the college experience for students with DD and thus includes access to libraries as part of the college's guidelines. For the most part, Think College libraries have been welcoming to these students, and the students have responded. Of the programs that Think College supports, 98 percent report that their students use the library, whereas only 69 percent report student use of campus disability or career services.[8]

For Clare Papay, Think College senior research associate, library access is more "than just about physical accessibility. I think feeling welcomed by the staff would be important." It is critical, Papay continues, to have staff "trained to help explain things to students with ID in a way that is clear."[9] Staff should also understand that these students are part of the larger student body, with the same rights and privileges as other students.

Think College institutions tend to offer library orientations. The University of Delaware does orientations on a one-to-one basis. A librarian takes each student around the library, introduces them to services and materials, and answers questions. According to Jay Sellers, programming manager for the Career and Life Studies Certificate program, library staff have been very supportive of the program: "We've had librarians reach out to us to ask how students can use the library. . . . They just opened up their library to our students just like any other student."[10] An early sign of success was when, unbeknownst to either the certificate program or library staff, a student with DD used the studio room to record an album.

Other schools use a group model. At the College of Adaptive Arts, the initial orientation is brief because the library is very small. The students all get library cards automatically, the first one for some of these students. Head librarian Suzanne Williams notes that "they are head over heels for that."[11] The orientation is done in a group, but because the college is so small, the librarian knows all of the students and offers one-on-one assistance at all times.

BEST PRACTICES FOR ACADEMIC LIBRARY ORIENTATIONS
- Focus on the students' needs.
- Use hands-on exercises.
- Use a UDL approach.
- Teach through example.*
- Involve the students in developing the programs.

---

*The preceding four practices are from Gerard Shae and Sebastian Derry, "How Do We Help? Academic Libraries and Students with Autism Spectrum Disorder," in *Recasting the Narrative: Proceedings of the Association of College and Research Libraries*, Cleveland, OH, April 10–13, 2019, 348–355, www.ala.org/acrl/conferences/acrl2019/papers.

Involving Students

The Library of Trinity College Dublin wanted to make itself easier for students with DD to use, so the library reached out to the students themselves and to the Trinity Centre for People with Intellectual Disabilities. The library held focus groups, created brochures, and produced a video, made by students with DD, "so . . . [the students] wouldn't feel nervous about asking for the help they need in the library."[12] Following the success of this video, they made a second one, this time on how to renew books. As they had hoped, involving the students helped make the library more accessible.

Some students with DD become more involved in campus life over time, and academic libraries offer them programs that go beyond library how-tos. For example, the library at the College of Adaptive Arts has a full programming schedule for these students, including hosting a book club and a twice-quarterly lecture series that brings artists, musicians, and the odd NASA scientist to the library. Head librarian Williams says that one of the keys to success is to develop focused lectures that teach concrete skills. The surprising part is that the lectures are as beneficial to the presenters as they are to the students. They "go away with a different idea about what it is to be an adult with . . . [disabilities]. They go away with a whole new picture [when] they see people with disabilities doing the same things as them."[13]

VOLUNTEERING AS A PROGRAM

Volunteers with DD can assist during programs and with other tasks, and you can consider their work a program in your repertoire. If done correctly, a volunteer program can be a fun, social, and life-enhancing experience for adults with DD, while also making the library a better place for all patrons. Volunteers with DD will often be accompanied by a job coach, at least in the beginning. Job coaches are professionals who help individuals learn the requirements of a job, assess the environment for needed accommodations, and act as a liaison between the individuals and the agency that supports them. Their role is to empower the volunteer or new hire in an unfamiliar role and to act as a bridge to independence. As the individual learns the job, the coach's involvement decreases. Library staff, the coach, and the volunteer should function as a team to anticipate issues, troubleshoot them if they arise, and pave the way for success.

Volunteer Success Stories

In a book chapter called "Volunteers with Disabilities: How to Make It Work," Carrie introduced readers to a number of volunteer success stories and pointed out how volunteers with DD can improve the library experience for others, often in unexpected ways.[14] In one example, Carrie introduced Melinda, a volunteer with an intellectual disability who put her artistic talent at the disposal of the library, helping staff develop craft ideas that continued to be used long after she left. In another, readers met Jan, a volunteer with cerebral palsy who had trouble navigating the library's aisles because of end-of-row displays and books that stuck out from the shelves. Eliminating these barriers for Jan also made the library more accessible for parents with strollers and for seniors with walkers.

Carrie's chapter also discusses how to recruit volunteers, and some of Carrie's ideas are encapsulated in the following best practices. Josh O'Shea, who manages a successful volunteer program for adults with DD at the Glen Ellyn Public Library in Illinois, also contributed several ideas.[15]

Volunteer Program Best Practices

As you plan your volunteer program, be clear about your goals. Will the emphasis be on getting library tasks done or on the volunteers' skill development, enhanced independence, and possibilities for accomplishment? If you are developing the program from scratch, think about how many volunteers you want and can effectively supervise, and limit recruits to that number. Prepare the staff and get input and buy-in from coworkers. Create a staff orientation and training plan that includes information on accommodations for any disabilities the volunteers may have. Work with staff to identify specific tasks for the volunteers, and create precise job descriptions that the volunteers can understand.

Sample Volunteer Jobs

Volunteers with ID at Oakland Public Library's César E. Chávez branch tend that library's garden. The volunteers reflect the diverse community; they are English and Spanish speaking, and they include two African Americans and two Asian Americans. Branch manager Pete Villaseñor comments: "One thing that really touches me is the care that our volunteers with disabilities take and the pride with watering. It is so beautiful to see them working with nature and helping the library in that way."[16]

POSSIBLE TASKS FOR VOLUNTEERS

- assisting in programs
- shelving books
- cleaning toys and books
- entering data
- writing a newsletter
- preparing mailings
- making displays
- creating spreadsheets
- creating personalized book lists
- craft preparation
- working in library gardens

Volunteers also lead programs. A BPL autistic volunteer loved the decommissioned battleship *Intrepid*, now a museum on New York City's Hudson River. He knew as much about the *Intrepid* as anyone could, including all of its deployments and battles and the number of nuts and bolts in the structure. While volunteering, he developed a program about this NYC museum that was presented at the library. Another BPL volunteer with a developmental disability whose family came from China translated children's inclusive gardening programs from English into Mandarin and occasionally Cantonese. His expertise made these programs accessible throughout the Chinese-speaking community, and his connections helped expand BPL's reach in that community.

Don't rule out the idea of offering virtual volunteer opportunities. Virtual volunteers with DD can leverage their social media accounts to get the word out about programs. Tech-savvy volunteers can provide support for online programs and can help edit captions. You can also recruit volunteers to develop book lists and activities based on their personal interests that can be shared online.

Recruiting, Training, and Integrating Volunteers

Look to your patrons and existing partnerships to recruit volunteers. Villaseñor recruited his from a day habilitation program that uses the library. Reach out to your school's transition programs. Work with your library's volunteer recruiters.

The next step after recruiting volunteers is to develop orientation and training for them. Use plain language in any written training materials and communicate with the volunteers in ways they are comfortable with. Demonstrate tasks as you want them performed, one step at a time. Start with simple tasks and introduce more complex ones as warranted. Don't move on until each step is understood and mastered. This will be an ongoing process.

During recruitment and orientation, begin to develop the relationships that are the key to success. Getting to know your volunteers before making assignments allows you to tailor jobs to individuals' strengths and interests. If there are communication barriers, reach out to job coaches or others who know the individuals well. Figure out what, if any, accommodations will be needed and put them in place.

Once your volunteers are trained, have a set of regular jobs that they can do when they come in for work shifts. Make sure volunteers and staff know what these are and where supplies are kept so they can start work independently on arrival.

As much as possible, treat regular volunteers like staff. Get emergency contact information. Include them when you can in break room conversations, and invite them to staff events, including staff meetings, when appropriate. Remember, as with staff, volunteers' disabilities are theirs to reveal. It is fine to tell others about needed accommodations, but not the reasons why they are needed.

Be sure to recognize and thank volunteers for their contributions, both verbally and with more tangible expressions. Common acknowledgments include coupons for coffee at the library café, books from the book sale, and the occasional lunch treat. Consider an annual thank-you event for all volunteers, including those with disabilities. And don't forget to nominate them for volunteer recognition programs.

INTERNING AS A STEP TO COMPETITIVE EMPLOYMENT

Through volunteer programs and other initiatives, libraries can play a role in helping adults with DD make the crucial move to competitive paid employment and avoid the sheltered workshop model. Programs can teach needed skills, information and referral services can point to community resources, and libraries can actively recruit and hire adults with disabilities. For example, San Francisco Public Library has a paid library internship program for young adults with DD. Students over age eighteen come to the library weekly for one and a half hours of work. They are paid through library partner Access San Francisco, part of the local school district. The program has been operating for years in a number of library branches, and it began at the main library in January 2020. The goal of the teachers and school staff is to have these internships lead to employment opportunities.

The Ferguson Library in Stamford, Connecticut, guarantees paid employment at the library to the interns in their program. Working in partnership with two community agencies, Ferguson offers six-week-long work trials to a few adults with disabilities. The partner agencies select the interns and provide a job coach who helps them learn and master the tasks associated with the job. At the end of the trial period, those who succeed in the program are offered paid part-time jobs. Though small scale, the program has led to meaningful paid work for several adults with disabilities. One woman who got a job in this way had always wanted to work in a library. She started out shelving books, and over time her responsibilities have expanded to include displays in the library's new book room.

LIBRARY CAFÉ PROGRAMS

In addition to enlisting volunteer help with administrative tasks and running programs, libraries have used volunteers with DD in a number of creative ways. For example, a couple of libraries in Illinois found a way to have a café while also providing meaningful volunteer opportunities for older high school students with disabilities. Both the St. Charles Public Library and Addison Public Library café projects are partnerships between the local school district and the library. The St. Charles model is simple. The library provides a room, utilities, water for coffeemaking, and a handwashing station. The local high school's independent living and transition program provides student volunteer staff, a job coach, and the coffee. Prepackaged snacks, such as muffins and brownies, and small craft items like bookmarks, made by students off-site, are also for sale. Students learn to make coffee, operate the cash register, and interact with customers during their assigned shifts. Without this partnership, the availability of coffee and snacks for staff and patrons at this library would be an unfulfilled dream.

The Addison café operates on a slightly larger scale. When a failed partnership with a commercial vendor left the library looking for a way to run its existing café, director Mary Medjo approached the nearby high school. The transition team loved the café idea, the Knights of Columbus donated start-up funds, and the Perks and Possibilities Café Training Program was born. Prices are low, and the choices are limited to beverages and a few snack items. The point-of-sale system has been adapted for some of the students by using visuals for the number keys. Modifications like this and the involvement of the school's job coach ensure a positive customer experience and a successful job experience for the student workers. The café and its volunteer workers are such an integral part of the library that in 2013 the staff selected them as the Team of the Year! On their nominations, staff had wonderful things to say about these workers: "I am proud to work in the same building as them and to have them as part of our library team," said one. Another said enthusiastically, "They do a ton of work for us, cheerfully. Some Mondays I don't think we'd survive without them!" The library director said, "I know how much it meant to everyone involved in the Transitions Program and I hope it will reiterate to them how much they mean to us. We are thrilled to have them as part of our Addison Public Library team!"[17] In addition to this recognition of their place in the library, at least two former café volunteers were able to move into paid employment at the library after aging out of school.

Everyone wins when our libraries offer programs like the ones in this chapter. The library gets trained volunteers or employees, the individuals learn both soft and hard job skills, and the community benefits from the contributions of these workers as well as the opportunity to observe or get to know some of these hard-working adults on the job.

NOTES

1. Amy Gunty, Joe Timmons, and Kelly M. Nye-Lengerman, "Work and Careers: It's More Than Just a Job," in *Community Living and Participation for People with Intellectual and Developmental Disabilities,* ed. Amy S. Hewitt and Kelly M. Nye-Lengerman (Silver Spring, MD: AAIDD, 2019), 90.
2. Gunty, Timmons, and Nye, "Work and Careers," 90.
3. The Arc, "Employment, Training, and Wages," https://thearc.org/policy-advocacy/ employment-training-and-wages/.
4. John J. Heldrich Center for Workforce Development at Rutgers University, *Great Expectations: Preparing Your Child with Developmental Disabilities for Employment Success* (Trenton, NJ: New Jersey Council on Developmental Disabilities, December 2008), www.heldrich .rutgers.edu/sites/default/files/products/uploads/Heldrich%20Center_Great _Expectations.pdf.
5. Marc Lazar, PowerPoint slide deck, shared via e-mail, February 13, 2020.
6. Michael Abeyta, "Anythink Wright Farms Hosts Job Fair for Adults with Disabilities," Adams County News, *CBS Denver*, September 26, 2019, https://denver.cbslocal.com/2019/ 09/26/anythink-wright-farms-job-fair-adams-county/.
7. Hayley Glatter, "The Path to Higher Education with an Intellectual Disability," *The Atlantic,* May 1, 2017, www.theatlantic.com/education/archive/2017/05/the-path-to-higher -education-with-an-intellectual-disability/524748/.
8. Clare Papay, personal communication, October 9, 2019.
9. Papay, pers. comm.
10. Jay Sellers, personal communication, October 9, 2019.
11. Suzanne Williams, personal communication, October 14, 2019.
12. Trinity College Dublin, Trinity Centre for People with Intellectual Disabilities, "Reflections of Getting to Know Trinity Library: A Guide for Students with Intellectual Disabilities," YouTube, June 6, 2018, www.youtube.com/watch?v=kr5Wkq2-aOU).
13. Suzanne Williams, personal communication, October 14, 2019.
14. Carrie S. Banks, "Volunteers with Disabilities: How to Make It Work," in *Library Volunteers Welcome! Strategies for Attracting, Retaining and Making the Most of Willing Helpers,* ed. Carol Smallwood and Lara Sanborn (Jefferson, NC: McFarland, 2016), 204–12.
15. Josh O'Shea, personal communication, October 31, 2019.
16. Pete Villaseñor, personal communication, June 15, 2018.
17. "Perks and Possibilities Café Training Program Awarded 'Team of the Year' by the Addison Public Library," Parents Alliance Employment Project (website; log-in required), www.parents -alliance.org/news/PAEP-Perks-Award-2013.pdf.

Conclusion
Next Steps and Best Practices

Since you've picked up this book, we assume that you have more than a passing interest in programming for the adults with developmental disabilities in your community. If you've read the program chapters in part III, you've probably gotten a pretty good idea of what other libraries have done and what you can begin to do at your library. If you've read the entire book, in addition to knowing about lots of programs you can try, you have a basic understanding of the issues surrounding programming for adults with DD and an idea of how programming fits into an overall institutional culture of inclusion. Hopefully, reading this volume has inspired you to start programming or to build on what you are already doing. You're enthusiastic and ready to go. Now what?

NEXT STEPS

Keep Up Momentum

Start where you are. You know what your library currently does and what resources it has to offer. If people with DD are not using your library, reach out to them. Bring self-advocates to the table to evaluate existing programs and plan new ones. If day habilitation and residential agencies bring groups to the library, develop relationships with the agencies and enhance their visits. If you already have those relationships, explore offering tours or developing one or more programs to serve those groups. Go beyond caregivers and families and start to cultivate relationships directly with your patrons with DD. Find out what they are interested in. Reach out to leaders in self-advocacy communities. This is essential. Offer them space to meet and opportunities to present. Examine your own ableism and that of your institution. Challenge the myths that underly the interactions between society and people with DD. If you currently offer one program, you can try a second program—and on and on. No matter what else you do, you can begin to acquire some of the tools and use some of the strategies that will make the programs you already offer more inclusive.

Make sure that your focused program planning coincides with your library's programming calendar or your fiscal year, and that regularly planned events are inclusive. Do you normally plan programs three months out? Longer? Do you create a calendar of all library programs monthly? Quarterly? What is the lead time for production of promotional materials? Do your focused programs go on hiatus during the summer or for the winter holiday season? What will you do for adults with DD during these periods? Are your usual summer programs and reading clubs accessible for adults with DD? If not, what will you have to do during your regular annual planning to make these programs more inclusive? When should you begin to promote summer programs to community residents with DD and how? Taking questions like these into account as you go through your programming year will help you move closer to a full culture of inclusion.

In this book we are intentionally aspirational. We know that even libraries that aim for the best practices we present may not be able to implement them right away given real-world constraints. Becoming a fully inclusive library does not happen overnight. It is a process, especially because moving toward equitable programming and full inclusion will involve a shift in the paradigm of your institution. We offer some guidance on how to do this here and in earlier chapters, introducing ways to change perceptions, develop a culture of inclusion, and involve multiple staff members and the administration. Adopting these strategies will help, but they may take time. Be patient and persistent.

Continue to Assess Needs

In this book, we say repeatedly that cultivating relationships with the adults with DD in your community, their caregivers, and the agencies that serve them is critical to programming success. This is not a one-time action to take as you begin programming but an ongoing process. Agencies that serve adults with DD experience frequent staff turnover, and this might mean that you have to approach someone new from time to time in order to continue the relationship. Teens and young adults with DD who have participated in your library's youth programs will grow up and become adults, newly eligible for your adult programs and services and ready to be introduced to your offerings. The needs of those adults who already attend your programs will change as they get older. Ongoing communication with all of these stakeholders will ensure that your programming continues to align with the interests, abilities, and needs of the adults with DD whom you serve.

Share with and Learn from Others

During the process of conducting research for this book, we discovered that it was difficult to ascertain which libraries offered programs for adults with DD. As we interviewed library staff, we found that they were also interested in learning what others were doing and some were constantly on the lookout for new ideas to add to their repertoire. So, it is important to not only feature what you do on your library's website but also share it with colleagues from other institutions. If you want to share your successes in programming for adults with DD or develop a network for learning and support, there are a number of ways to do that:

- Write or present for Programming Librarian (www.programminglibrarian .org), a website from ALA's Public Programs Office. Programming Librarian is always open to new contributors and program ideas.
- Write an article for a library periodical, such as *American Libraries* or *Public Libraries Magazine,* or for your state or provincial library association's newsletter.
- Write or contribute to a blog.
- Present at a library conference, either in your own state or province or in one that serves a national audience, such as the annual conference of the Public Library Association (PLA) or the American Library Association (ALA). Slides from these presentations often remain online, and we discovered a number of programs featured in this book by that means. Also, attendees at these sessions often compare notes and exchange contact information after the presentation, so you'll meet people to add to your network.
- Join or create a geographically based networking group. There is one called NEO Adaptive Librarians that operates in Northeast Ohio. NEO serves primarily youth services librarians but also welcomes adult services staff. Adult services librarians from a variety of libraries in any metropolitan area could easily create a group to educate, encourage, and support one another.
- If you are an ALA member, participate in an ALA-sponsored group, like the Association of College and Research Libraries' (ACRL) Universal Accessibility Interest Group (www.ala.org/acrl/aboutacrl/directoryofleadership/ interestgroups/acr-igua), the Reference and User Services Association's (RUSA) Accessibility Assembly, (www.ala.org/rusa/members/accessibility -assembly), or the Office for Diversity, Literacy, and Outreach Services' (ODLOS) Universal Access Interest Group (www.ala.org/aboutala/diversity/ interest-groups).

- Connect with networking groups that focus on disability-related topics, even if they are not necessarily for librarians. One example is the Michigan Alliance for Cultural Accessibility (MACA; www.miculturalaccess.org), whose members come from a variety of institutions.

Sharing your programming successes not only supports other libraries and helps you build a network; it can also be affirming and energizing. Your institution may be very committed to inclusion for adults with DD, and you may get a lot of encouragement and support from your library's administration and board. Or your library may give only lukewarm support to your efforts or may think that they divert from other priorities. If you aren't getting support at home, reaching out to librarians from other institutions who share your commitment to adults with DD can give you a much-needed boost as you work with your own board and administration to move them closer to full inclusion.

Stay Informed

Engaging in the aforementioned activities will allow you to keep learning from others and can help you stay focused and motivated. But there are sources beyond your community and the library world that you should look to as well. Researchers and practitioners continue to discover new information, and the ways in which issues are discussed and symbolized changes frequently, so continued reading and outreach are also needed to ensure that your programs and services reflect current understanding and practices. With this in mind, we offer you an assortment of sources in the appendix that you can access to stay up-to-date.

FINAL THOUGHTS

To sum up, a library that programs for and serves adults with DD in a comprehensive and equitable way will follow the practices and use the strategies that we introduce throughout this book. As the many programs we cite demonstrate, libraries of different types from around the United States and Canada apply these principles in numerous ways, offering patrons with DD rich and diverse opportunities for community engagement and fun at the library.

This book and the best practices in the text box are your road map. Feel free to print the best practices and use them as a checklist so you can monitor your progress in creating a culture of inclusion in your library. Don't get discouraged if

TWENTY BEST PRACTICES

1. Give adults with DD a seat at the table and listen to their experiences and ideas.
2. Build relationships with all stakeholders: adult patrons with DD, caregivers, agencies, and self-advocates and allies in the community.
3. Take into account the multiple identities that adults with DD may have and the varied cultures in the community.
4. Partner with community organizations and advocacy groups for program planning, promotion, and implementation.
5. Acknowledge, confront, and work to overcome staff members' and institutional ableism.
6. Obtain buy-in from department managers and the library's administration and board.
7. Use Universal Design, Universal Design for Learning, and multiple intelligences theory to guide program planning.
8. Offer sensory tools and spaces, visual supports, and communication options.
9. Conduct an internal and a community assessment before planning programming.
10. Train all staff more than once and in more than one way.
11. Work across departments and branches to create programming and support inclusion.
12. Network with other libraries to share resources, replicable program ideas, and support.
13. Make existing programs for children, teens, and adults inclusive, and teach presenters and volunteers about inclusive programming.
14. Build accessibility into the design of all virtual programs.
15. In focused programs, use chronological age to guide content and developmental age to determine presentation style and materials.
16. Be person centered, offering choices to ensure that individual needs, abilities, and interests are accounted for.
17. Evaluate programs and build on successes.
18. Recruit and train adults with DD to work as volunteers and employees.
19. Develop a comprehensive marketing plan that includes community outreach, an accessible website, and an easy-to-find accessibility or inclusion web page.
20. Most important, never underestimate the capabilities of adult patrons with DD.

you encounter setbacks. Instead, look to colleagues, your community partners, and your patrons with DD for support and encouragement and keep trying. We will be cheering you on as you continue on this journey with your community.

Appendix

Resources for Programming, Outreach, and Training

The following resources are well-established and likely to remain stable over time. You can use them to develop trainings and to help you find local self-advocates and program presenters. These resources are organized into categories to make it easier to find what you need. Many others can be found throughout the book.

ADAPTIVE TECHNOLOGY TRAINING

"Explore AT": This page on the AT3 Center's website provides numerous examples of both high- and low-tech assistive technology; see https://exploreat.net/.

Reference and User Services Association: RUSA provides links to Library Accessibility Toolkits, including a guide to assistive technology, at www.ala.org/rusa/guidelines-resources/resources-by-topic.

"Speech Disorders: Common Assistive Technologies": This LibGuide on augmentative and alternative communication is from the University of Illinois; see https://guides.library.illinois.edu/c.php?g=613892&p=4265891.

ADVOCACY AND SELF-ADVOCACY ORGANIZATIONS

The Arc: Through hundreds of local chapters, this organization supports people with DD throughout the United States and works to ensure their human rights and full inclusion in society; visit https://thearc.org.

Autistic Self Advocacy Network: ASAN seeks to organize the autistic community and advocates on a national level. The network can also provide speakers and consultants. For more information visit https://autisticadvocacy.org/about-asan/.

Autistic Women and Nonbinary Network: AWN Network is a support community for autistic women, nonbinary people, and people of all marginalized genders. They share information, including health care resources, to dispel myths and to increase understanding about autism and the needs of intersectional people. Check out the website at https://awnnetwork.org.

Centers for Independent Living: These centers provide information and referral, advocacy, counseling, transition planning, skill building, and other services for people with all types of disabilities. They are located in every U.S. state and territory. Find a center near you at www.ilru.org/projects/cil-net/cil-center-and-association-directory.

National Down Syndrome Congress: This organization provides support and information for people with Down syndrome through the national organization and local affiliates; see www.ndsccenter.org.

Self Advocates Becoming Empowered: SABE is comprised of local organizations that support self-advocacy for people with disabilities. Find more information and resources at www.sabeusa.org.

Self-Advocacy Online: This website for and by self-advocates includes lots of information in plain language as well as videos, resources, and a list of local self-advocacy organizations; visit www.selfadvocacyonline.org/learning/.

BLOGS, NEWS, AND SOCIAL MEDIA SITES

Actually Autistic Blogs List: This website is a source for finding numerous blogs written by autistic people; see https://anautismobserver.wordpress.com/?wref=bif.

***Adaptive Umbrella*:** This is librarian Jen Taggart's blog about "accessible and inclusive library programming, collections, and services"; visit https://adaptiveumbrella.blogspot.com.

Disability Scoop: This national news site focuses on all types of disabilities; see www.disabilityscoop.com. After three free articles there is a paywall.

The Mighty: This national blog features authentic voices that address a wide range of disability and LGBTQ+ topics. Separate newsletters for individual topics like parenting, Down syndrome, and autism provide support and advocacy. The Mighty also hosts events. Check out this online community at https://themighty.com.

CONFERENCES

Library conferences: Consider attending or presenting at conferences held by ALA and its divisions or state library associations.

Partner agency conferences: Some local agencies with which libraries partner for programming sponsor conferences or meetings that you can attend or at which you can speak about the library.

Subject-related conferences: Also consider presenting at or attending the regional or national conferences of organizations like the Autism Society, the Arc, the Down Syndrome Association, or other agencies discussed in this book.

DISABILITY ETIQUETTE

Disability Etiquette: Tips on Interacting with People with Disabilities: This useful, illustrated guide from the United Spinal Association is available online as a PDF at http://unitedspinal.org/pdf/DisabilityEtiquette.pdf.

"It's Time for a Reimagining of Disability Etiquette": This article by Andrew Pulrang, published in *Forbes* on January 17, 2020, can be accessed online at www.forbes.com/sites/andrewpulrang/2020/01/17/its-time -for-a-reimagining-of-disability-etiquette/#49f75128d6d8.

EMPLOYMENT

Association of People Supporting Employment First: APSE offers resources, best practices, and advocacy for advancing competitive employment for people with disabilities; much of it is free but some is available to members only. Check out the website at www.apse.org.

Job Accommodation Network: JAN offers free, expert, and confidential guidance on workplace accommodations and disability employment issues and is Banks's go-to resource on these issues. Specific sections address employers, employees, and job seekers; see https://askjan.org.

National Organization on Disability: The NOD website is a source for resources for employers; visit www.nod.org.

ThinkWork: Part of the Institute for Community Inclusion at the University of Massachusetts Boston, ThinkWork is a clearinghouse for programs related to employment for people with IDD; see www.thinkwork.org.

GOVERNMENT AGENCIES

ADA National Network: This government network of regional centers provides information and training about the ADA. Find resources and a link to regional centers at https://adata.org.

Administration on Disabilities: AoD encourages relationships between government, private, and not-for-profit entities to facilitate independence and community inclusion for people with disabilities. Find links to programs on the Administration for Community Living website at https://acl.gov/about-acl/administration-disabilities.

"State Agencies—NASDDS": This web page from the National Association of State Directors of Developmental Disabilities Services links to the state agencies that oversee services for people with IDD; see www.nasddds.org/state-agencies/.

"State Councils on Developmental Disabilities": This Administration for Community Living web page provides information about the DD councils and a link to state contacts; go to https://acl.gov/programs/aging-and-disability-networks/state-councils-developmental-disabilities.

"State Libraries": Some state libraries have disability advocacy committees and other resources of interest. Check your state library to see what it offers; see https://dpi.wi.gov/pld/directories/state-agency/websites.

U.S. Department of Labor, Office of Disability Employment Policy: This government clearinghouse for employers of people with disabilities offers an array of disability resources at www.dol.gov/odep/topics/disability.htm.

LIBRARY STAFF NETWORKING GROUPS

Special Needs and Inclusive Library Services (SNAILS): This networking group in the Chicago area focuses on services and programming for young people with disabilities. It is a good model for starting your own, similar group. Check out the group's blog at https://snailsgroup.blogspot.com.

Universal Access Interest Group: This ODLOS interest group was previously part of ASGCLA. Members address accessibility in all types of libraries. The interest group provides networking, collaboration opportunities, and information for library staff. ALA members can find information about the group at www.ala.org/aboutala/diversity/interest-groups.

Universal Accessibility Interest Group: For academic librarians, this group is part of ACRL, a division of ALA. To find out more and access resources, visit www .ala.org/acrl/aboutacrl/directoryofleadership/interestgroups/acr-igua.

NATIONAL ORGANIZATIONS

American Association of People with Disabilities: AAPD, a policy and advocacy group, has some projects of interest to libraries, including a disability mentoring day and disability storytelling fellowship. To find out more, visit www .aapd.com.

University Centers for Excellence in Developmental Disabilities Education, Research, and Service (UCEDD): These centers are a link between communities and universities, providing stakeholders with services, research, and training with the aim of increasing the capacity of communities to support residents with disabilities. They are funded through the DD Act. To access UCEDD programs by state, go to www.aucd.org/directory/directory .cfm?program=UCEDD.

VOR (A Voice of Reason): This national advocacy group deals with legislation and focuses on resources for families and some medical and health care support; visit www.vor.net.

WEBINARS AND SELF-PACED TRAINING

Infopeople: Part of a nonprofit library consortium, Infopeople offers fee-based services that include webinars and courses to libraries for ongoing professional development. Barbara and Carrie taught a webinar for Infopeople that covered some of the material in this book. For a list of archived webinars, go to https://infopeople.org/training/view/webinar/archived.

Project ENABLE (Expanding Non-discriminatory Access by Librarians Everywhere): These training modules and resources, created by Syracuse University for school librarians, are useful for staff in other library settings as well; see https://projectenable.syr.edu.

WebJunction: A project of OCLC Research, WebJunction webinars are free and available on a range of topics, including disability; visit https://learn.web junction.org/course/index.php?categoryid=56.

WEBSITES TO FIND LOCAL RESOURCES

New Horizons Un-Limited: This company offers direct services to people with disabilities and links to many local organizations and programs, including a state-by-state listing of adaptive arts programs; see www.new-horizons .org/adparp.html.

Self-Advocacy Online: This website, organized by state, links to many self-advocacy groups. Search for self-advocacy groups in your state at /www .selfadvocacyonline.org/find/.

Index

Index

Index

Index

Index

Index

Index

Index

Index